SNOW ANGELS ™

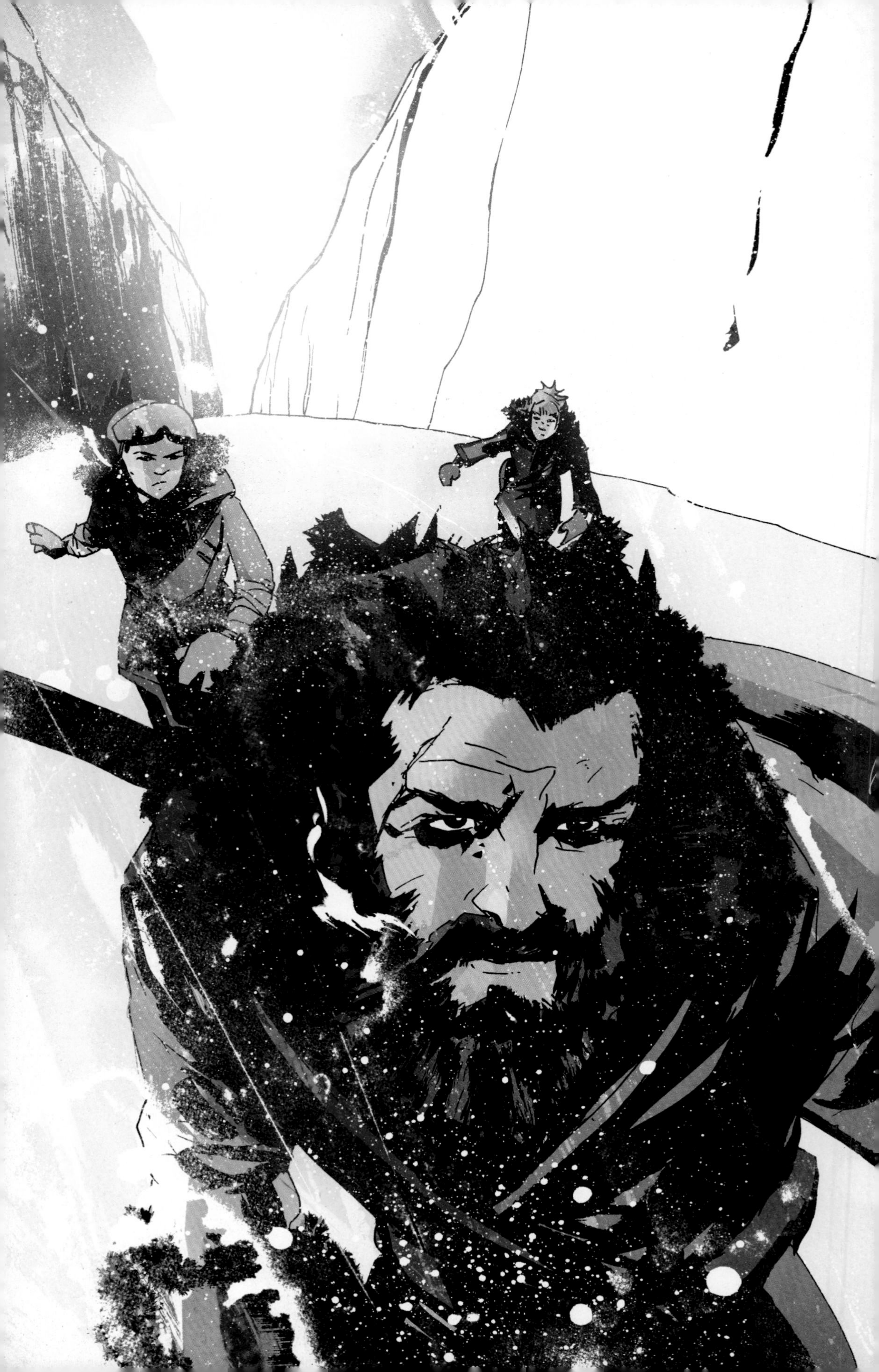

SNOW ANGELS

VOLUME 1

SCRIPT
JEFF LEMIRE

ART AND COVER
JOCK

LETTERING
STEVE WANDS

ORIGINAL PUBLICATION TEAM

EDITOR
WILL DENNIS

ASSISTANT EDITOR
TYLER JENNES

SNOW ANGELS CREATED BY JEFF LEMIRE AND JOCK

DARK HORSE BOOKS

DARK HORSE TEAM

PRESIDENT & PUBLISHER
MIKE RICHARDSON

EDITOR
DANIEL CHABON

ASSISTANT EDITORS
CHUCK HOWITT & KONNER KNUDSEN

DESIGNER
MAY HIJIKURO

DIGITAL ART TECHNICIAN
JASON RICKERD

SPECIAL THANKS

DAVID STEINBERGER
CHIP MOSHER
BRYCE GOLD

NEIL HANKERSON Executive Vice President TOM WEDDLE Chief Financial Officer DALE LAFOUNTAIN Chief Information Officer TIM WIESCH Vice President of Licensing MATT PARKINSON Vice President of Marketing VANESSA TODD-HOLMES Vice President of Production and Scheduling MARK BERNARDI Vice President of Book Trade and Digital Sales RANDY LAHRMAN Vice President of Product Development KEN LIZZI General Counsel DAVE MARSHALL Editor in Chief DAVEY ESTRADA Editorial Director CHRIS WARNER Senior Books Editor CARY GRAZZINI Director of Specialty Projects LIA RIBACCHI Art Director MATT DRYER Director of Digital Art and Prepress MICHAEL GOMBOS Senior Director of Licensed Publications KARI YADRO Director of Custom Programs KARI TORSON Director of International Licensing

---

PUBLISHED BY DARK HORSE BOOKS
A DIVISION OF DARK HORSE COMICS LLC
10956 SE MAIN STREET, MILWAUKIE, OR 97222

FIRST EDITION: FEBRUARY 2022
TRADE PAPERBACK ISBN: 978-1-50672-648-9

10 9 8 7 6 5 4 3 2 1
PRINTED IN CHINA

COMIC SHOP LOCATOR SERVICE: COMICSHOPLOCATOR.COM

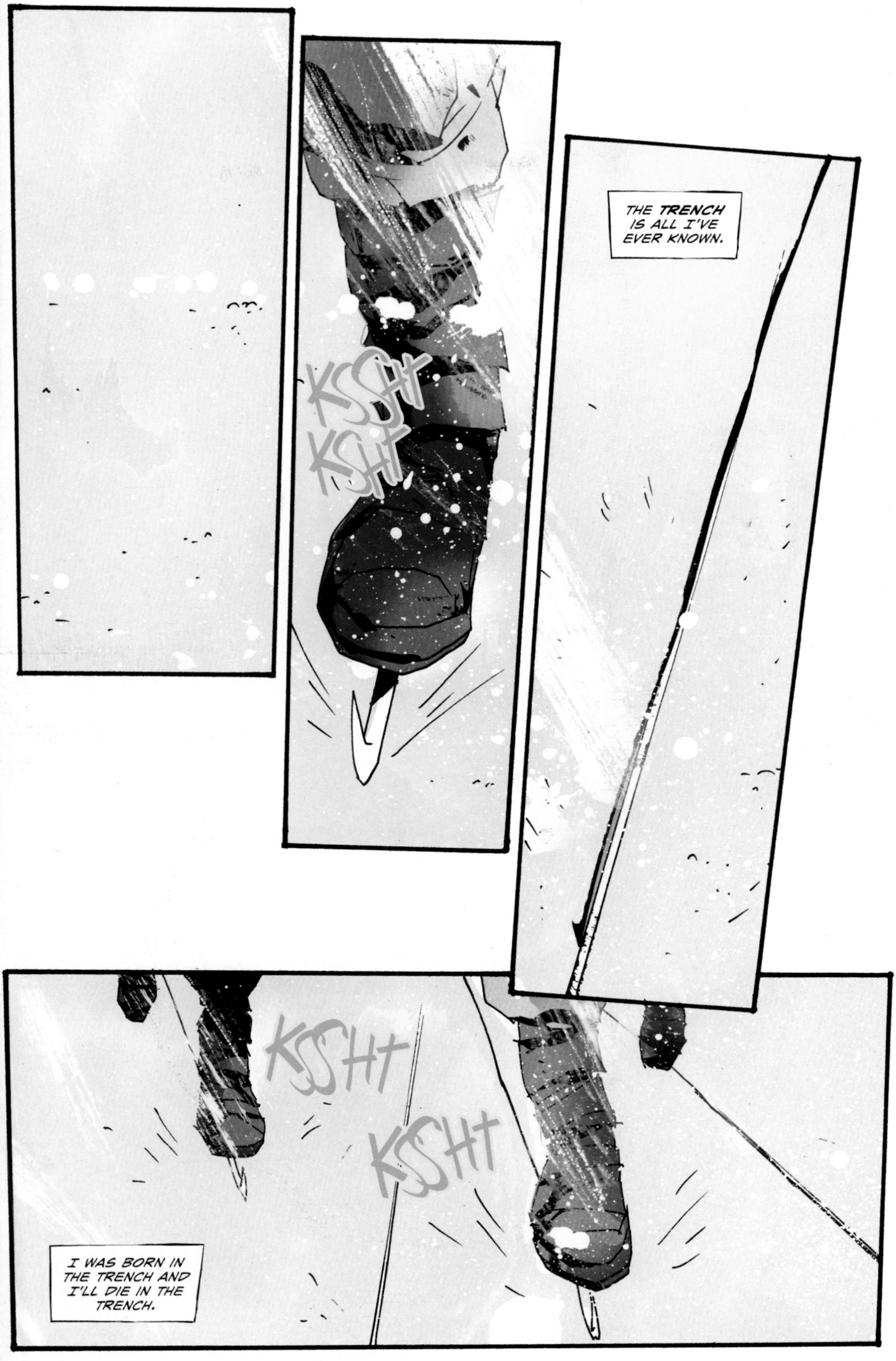

KSSHT
KSHT
THE TRENCH IS ALL I'VE EVER KNOWN.
KSSHT
KSSHT
I WAS BORN IN THE TRENCH AND I'LL DIE IN THE TRENCH.

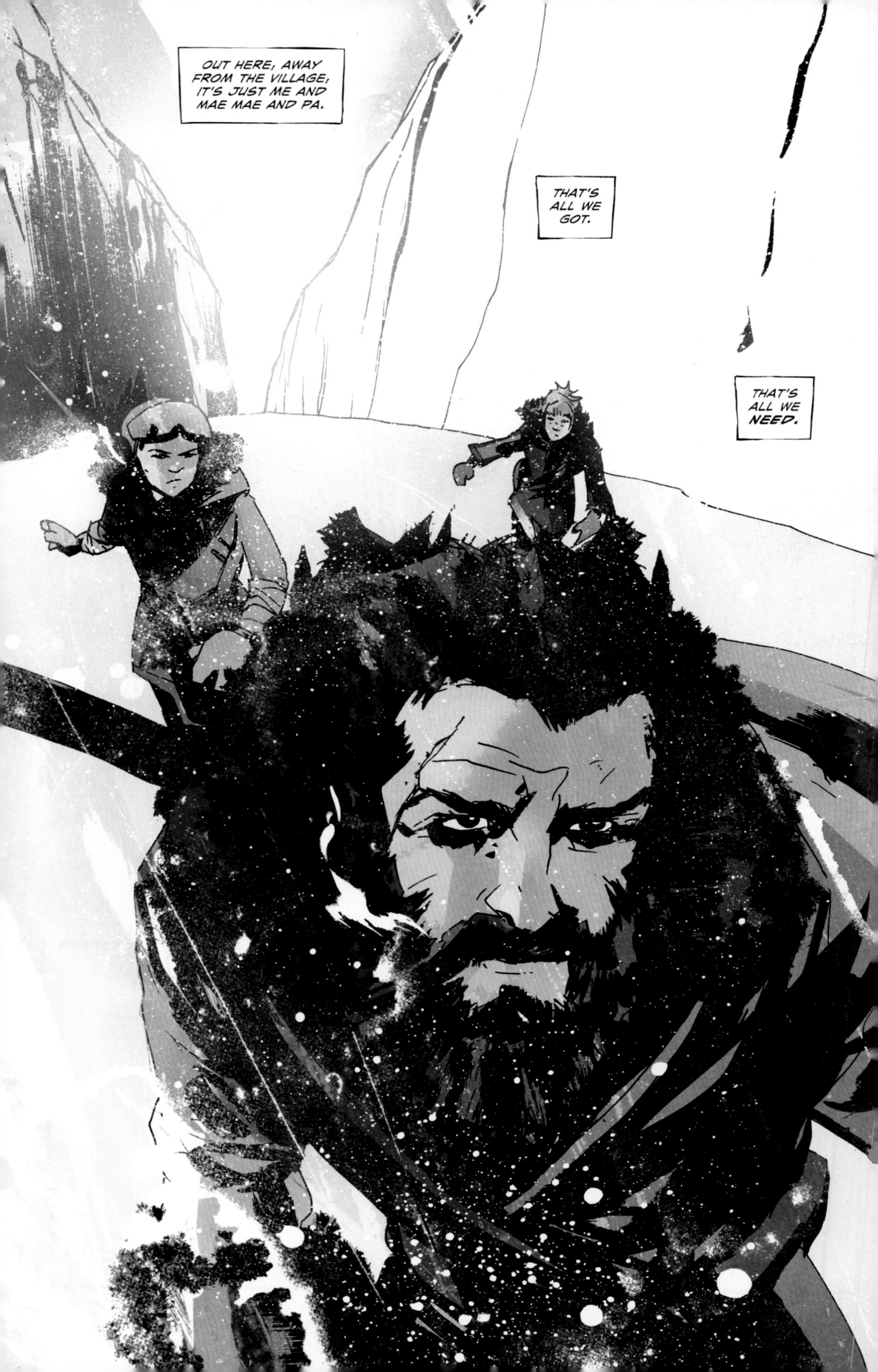
OUT HERE, AWAY FROM THE VILLAGE, IT'S JUST ME AND MAE MAE AND PA.
THAT'S ALL WE GOT.
THAT'S ALL WE **NEED**.

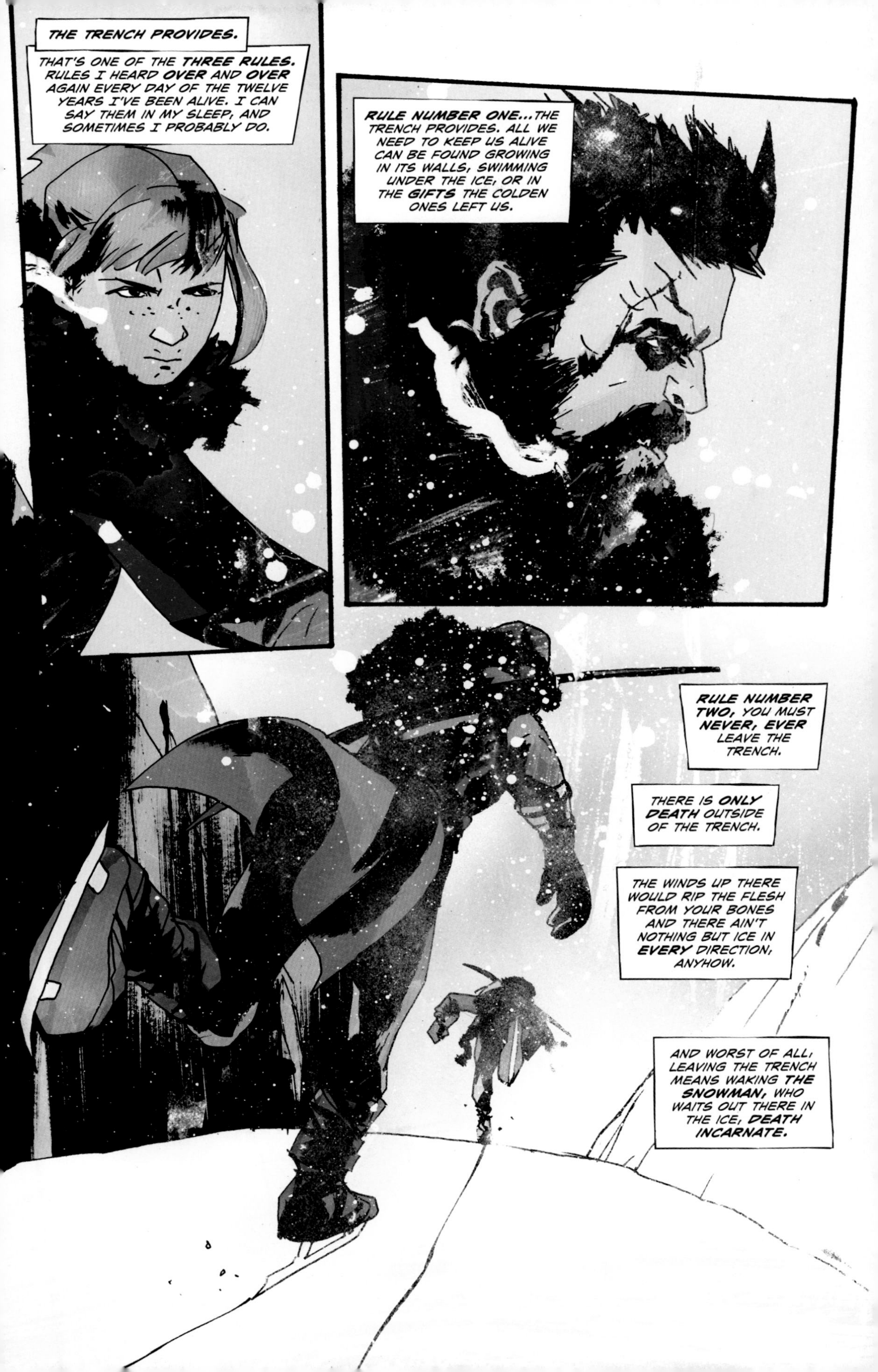
THE TRENCH PROVIDES.
THAT'S ONE OF THE THREE RULES. RULES I HEARD OVER AND OVER AGAIN EVERY DAY OF THE TWELVE YEARS I'VE BEEN ALIVE. I CAN SAY THEM IN MY SLEEP, AND SOMETIMES I PROBABLY DO.
RULE NUMBER ONE... THE TRENCH PROVIDES. ALL WE NEED TO KEEP US ALIVE CAN BE FOUND GROWING IN ITS WALLS, SWIMMING UNDER THE ICE, OR IN THE GIFTS THE COLDEN ONES LEFT US.
RULE NUMBER TWO, YOU MUST NEVER, EVER LEAVE THE TRENCH.
THERE IS ONLY DEATH OUTSIDE OF THE TRENCH.
THE WINDS UP THERE WOULD RIP THE FLESH FROM YOUR BONES AND THERE AIN'T NOTHING BUT ICE IN EVERY DIRECTION, ANYHOW.
AND WORST OF ALL, LEAVING THE TRENCH MEANS WAKING THE SNOWMAN, WHO WAITS OUT THERE IN THE ICE, DEATH INCARNATE.

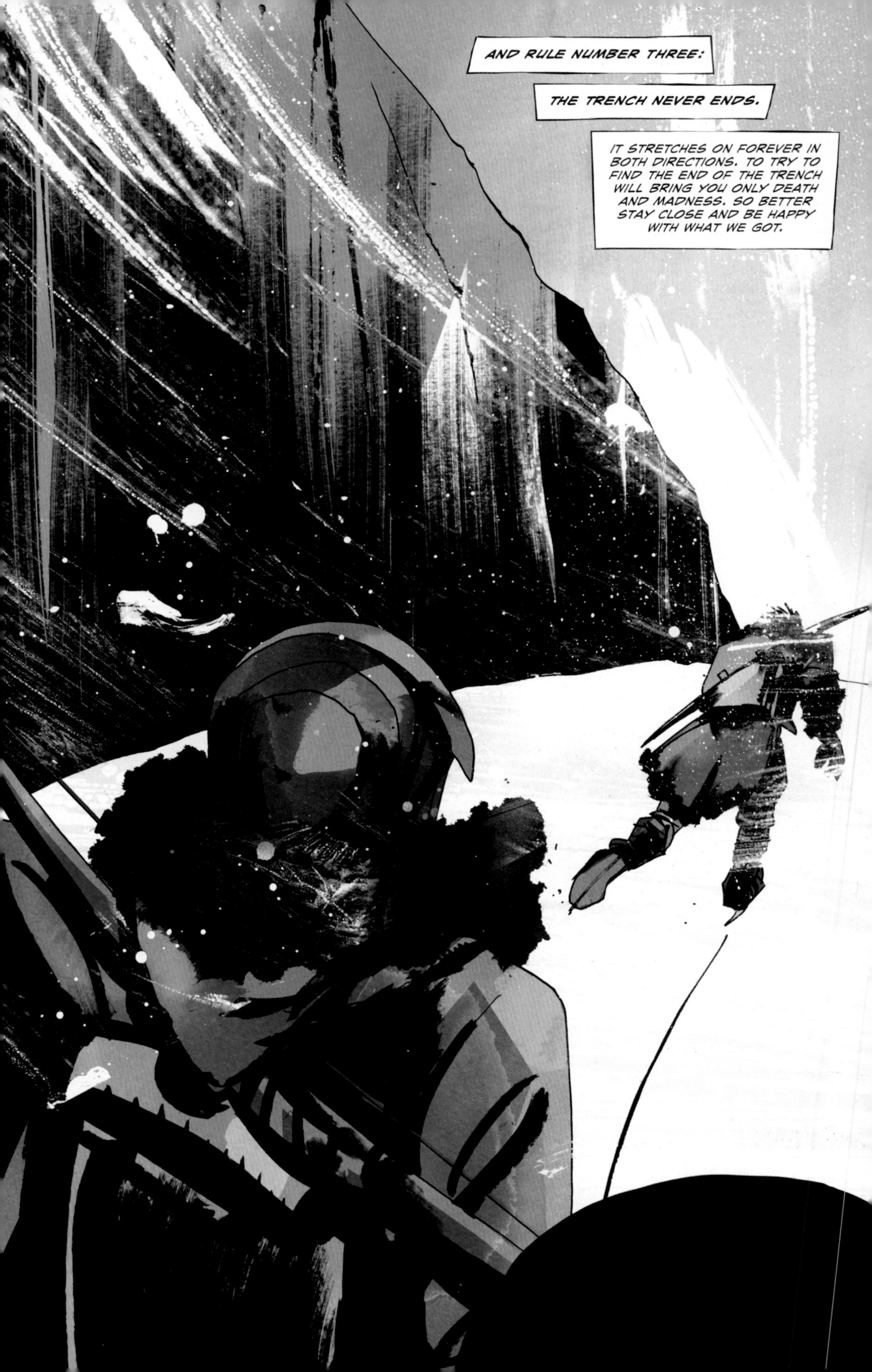
AND RULE NUMBER THREE:
THE TRENCH NEVER ENDS.
IT STRETCHES ON FOREVER IN BOTH DIRECTIONS. TO TRY TO FIND THE END OF THE TRENCH WILL BRING YOU ONLY DEATH AND MADNESS. SO BETTER STAY CLOSE AND BE HAPPY WITH WHAT WE GOT.

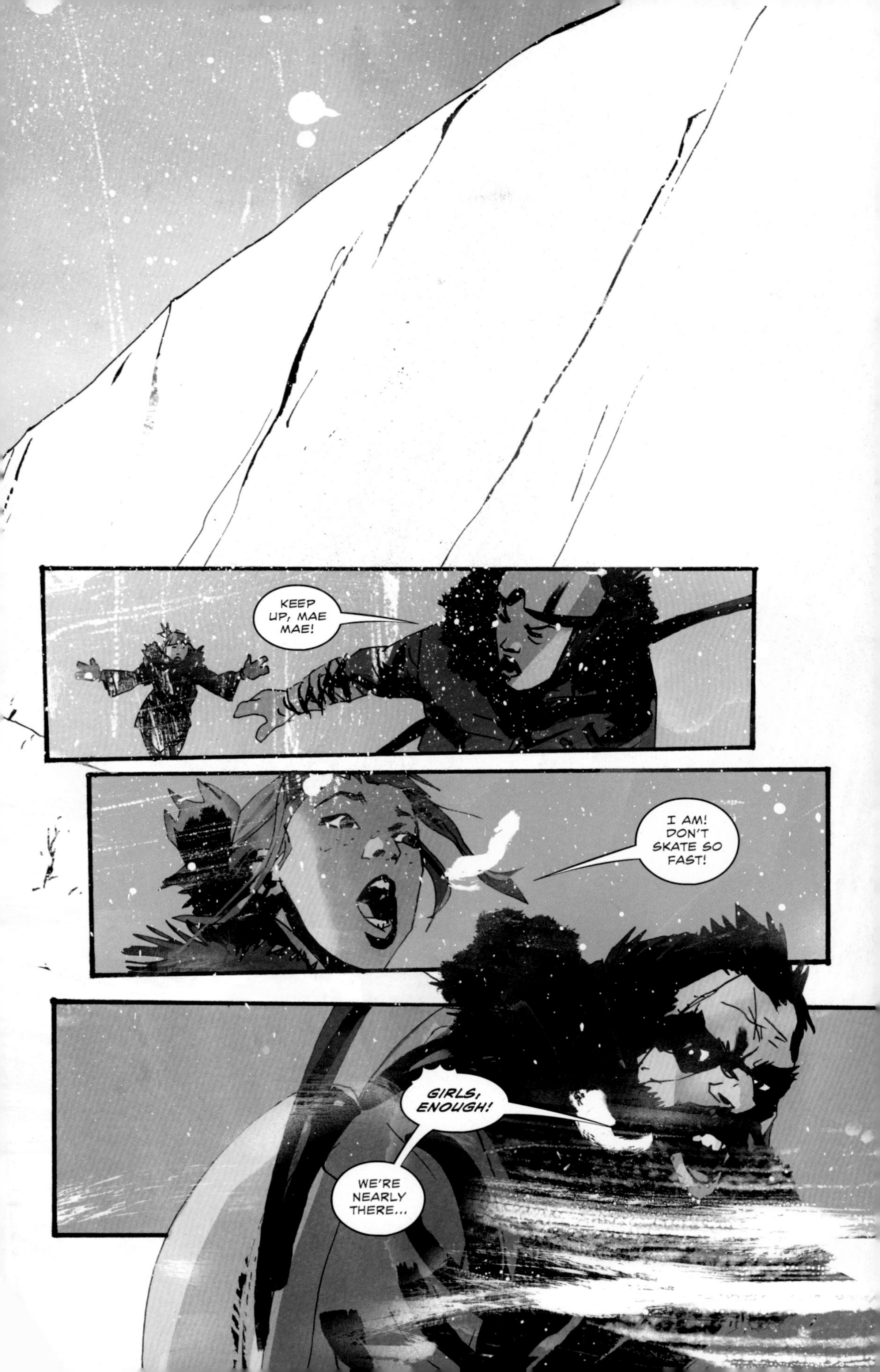
KEEP UP, MAE MAE!
I AM! DON'T SKATE SO FAST!
GIRLS, ENOUGH!
WE'RE NEARLY THERE...

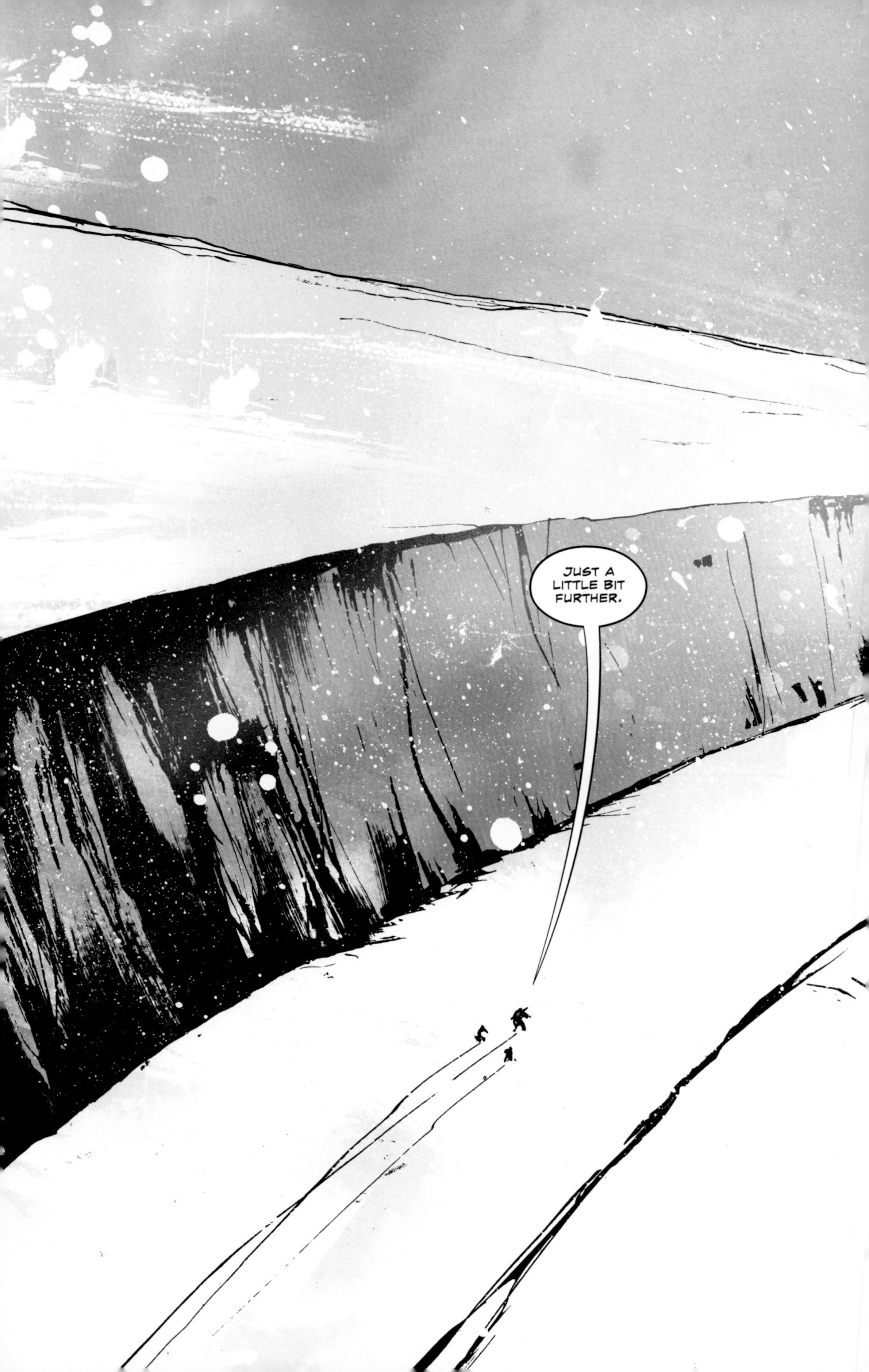
JUST A LITTLE BIT FURTHER.

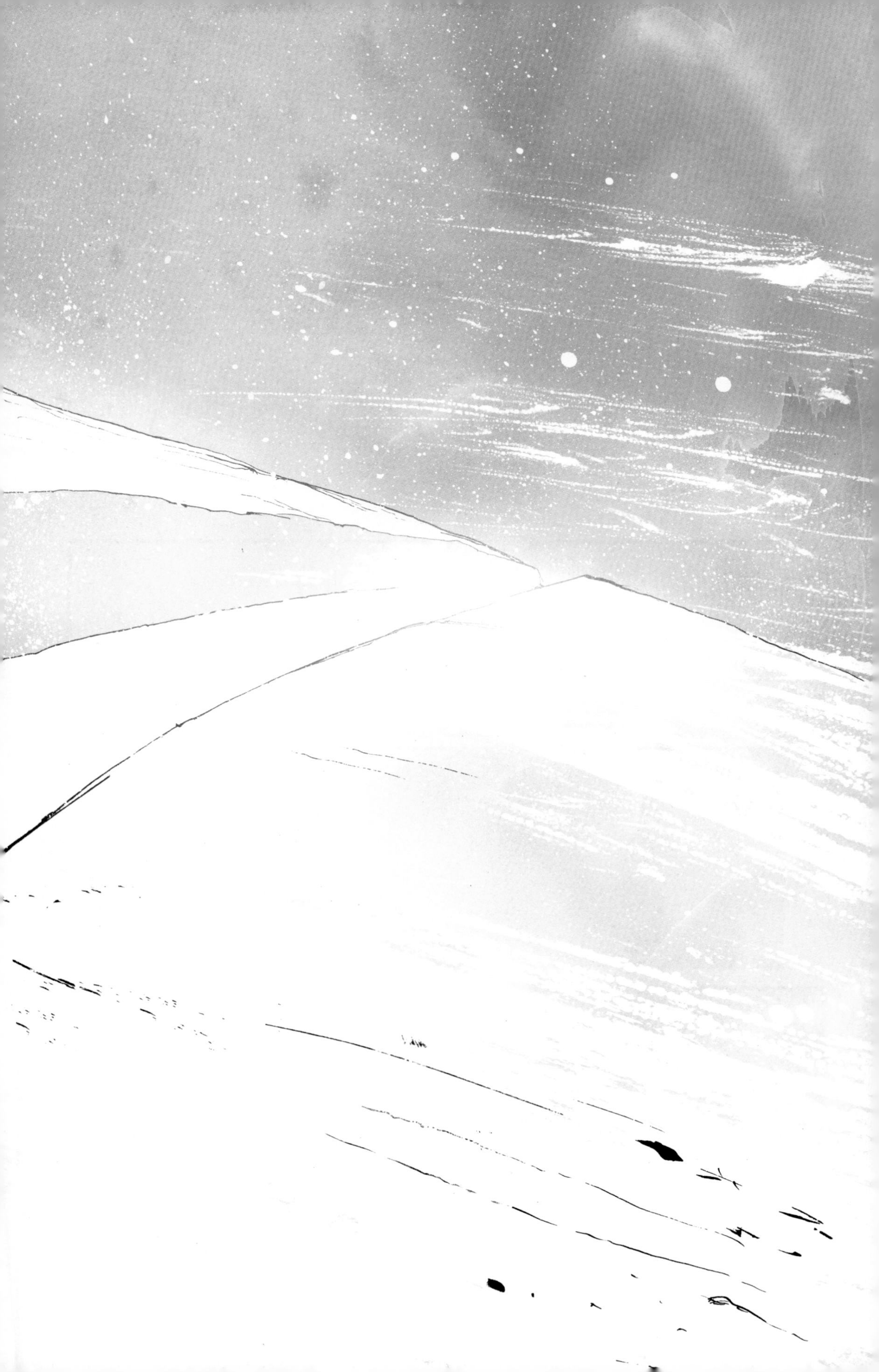

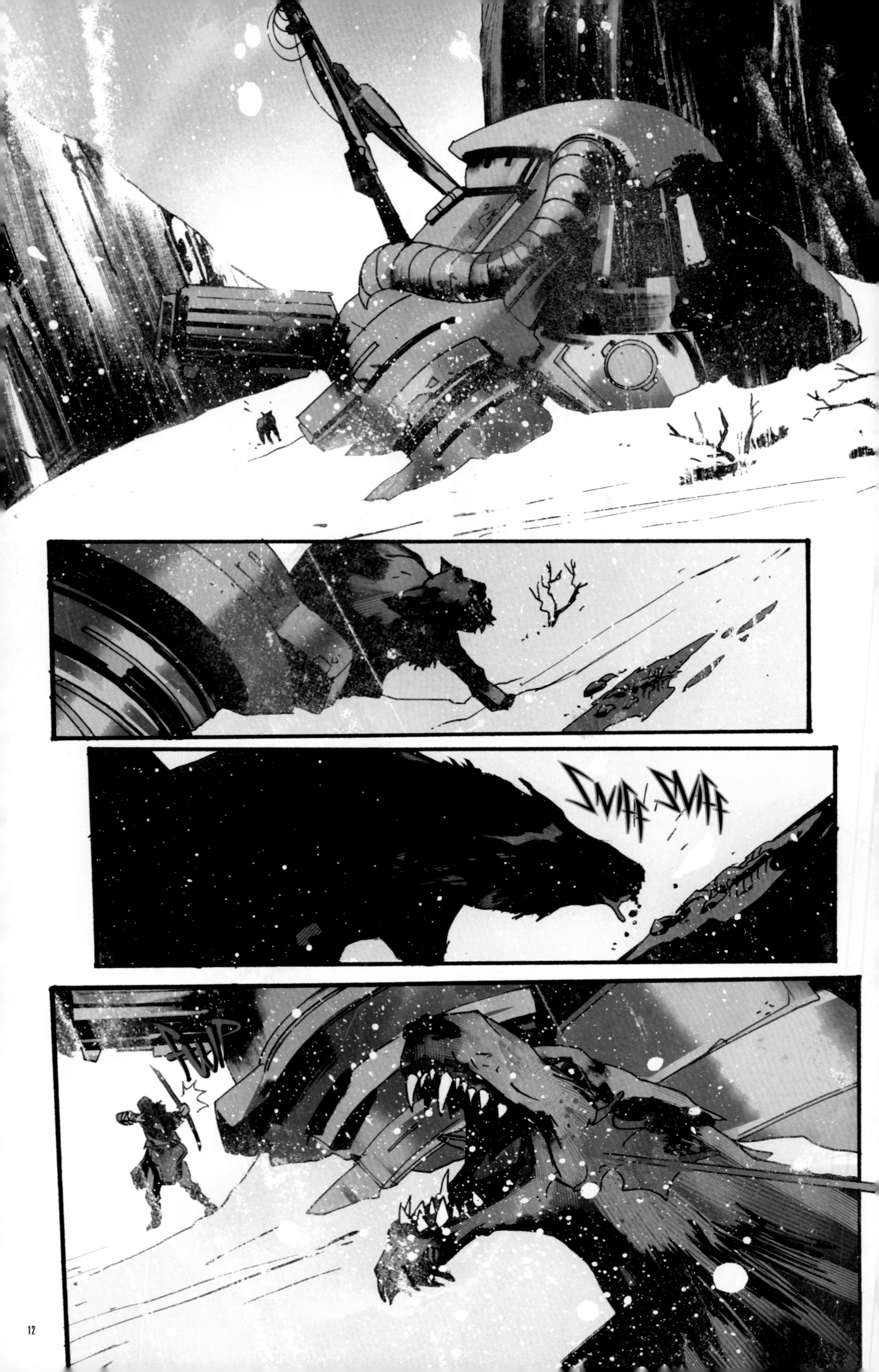
SNIFF SNIFF
FWIP

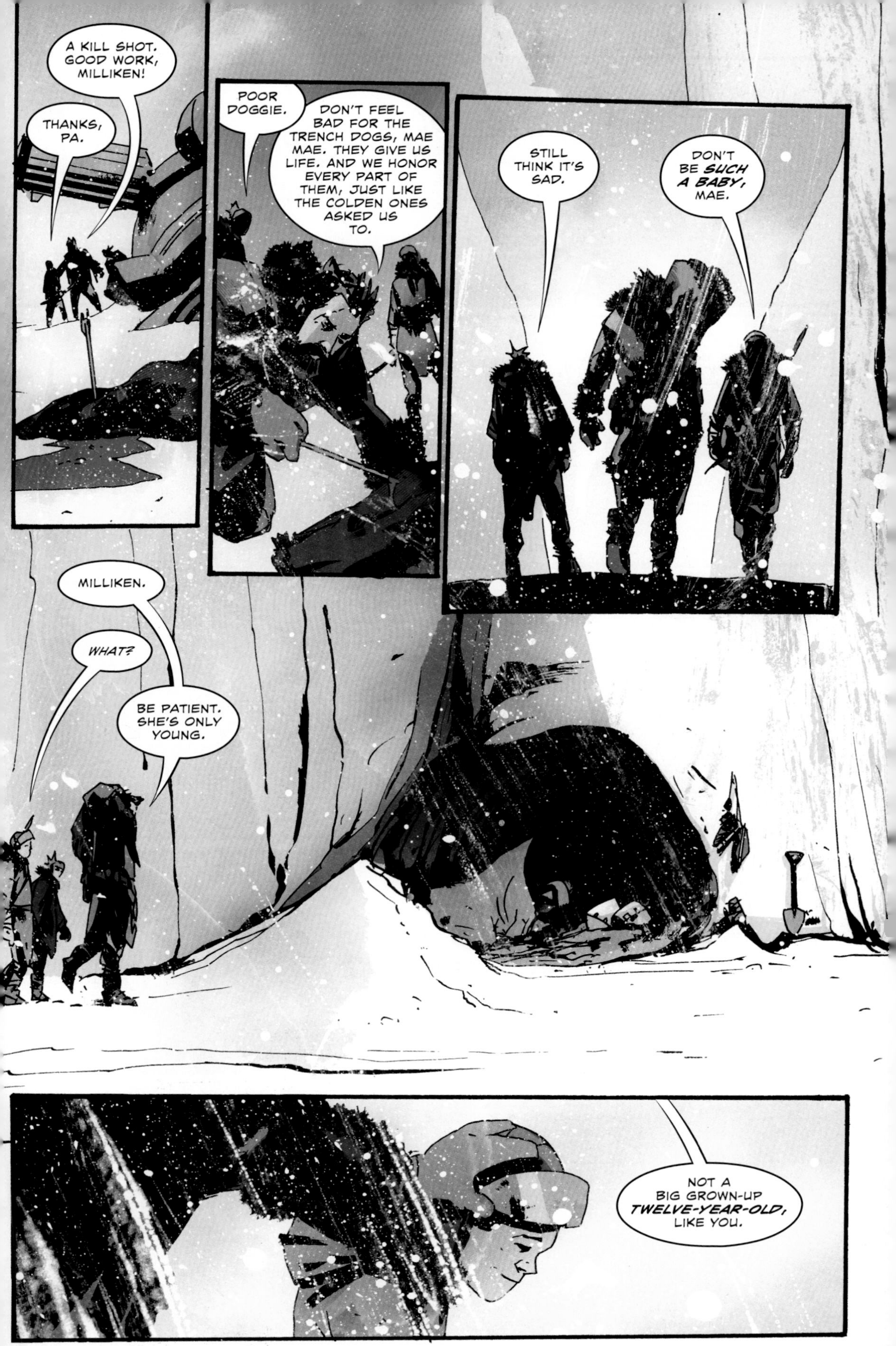
A KILL SHOT. GOOD WORK, MILLIKEN!
THANKS, PA.
POOR DOGGIE.
DON'T FEEL BAD FOR THE TRENCH DOGS, MAE MAE. THEY GIVE US LIFE. AND WE HONOR EVERY PART OF THEM, JUST LIKE THE COLDEN ONES ASKED US TO.
STILL THINK IT'S SAD.
DON'T BE *SUCH A BABY,* MAE.
MILLIKEN.
WHAT?
BE PATIENT. SHE'S ONLY YOUNG.
NOT A BIG GROWN-UP *TWELVE-YEAR-OLD,* LIKE YOU.

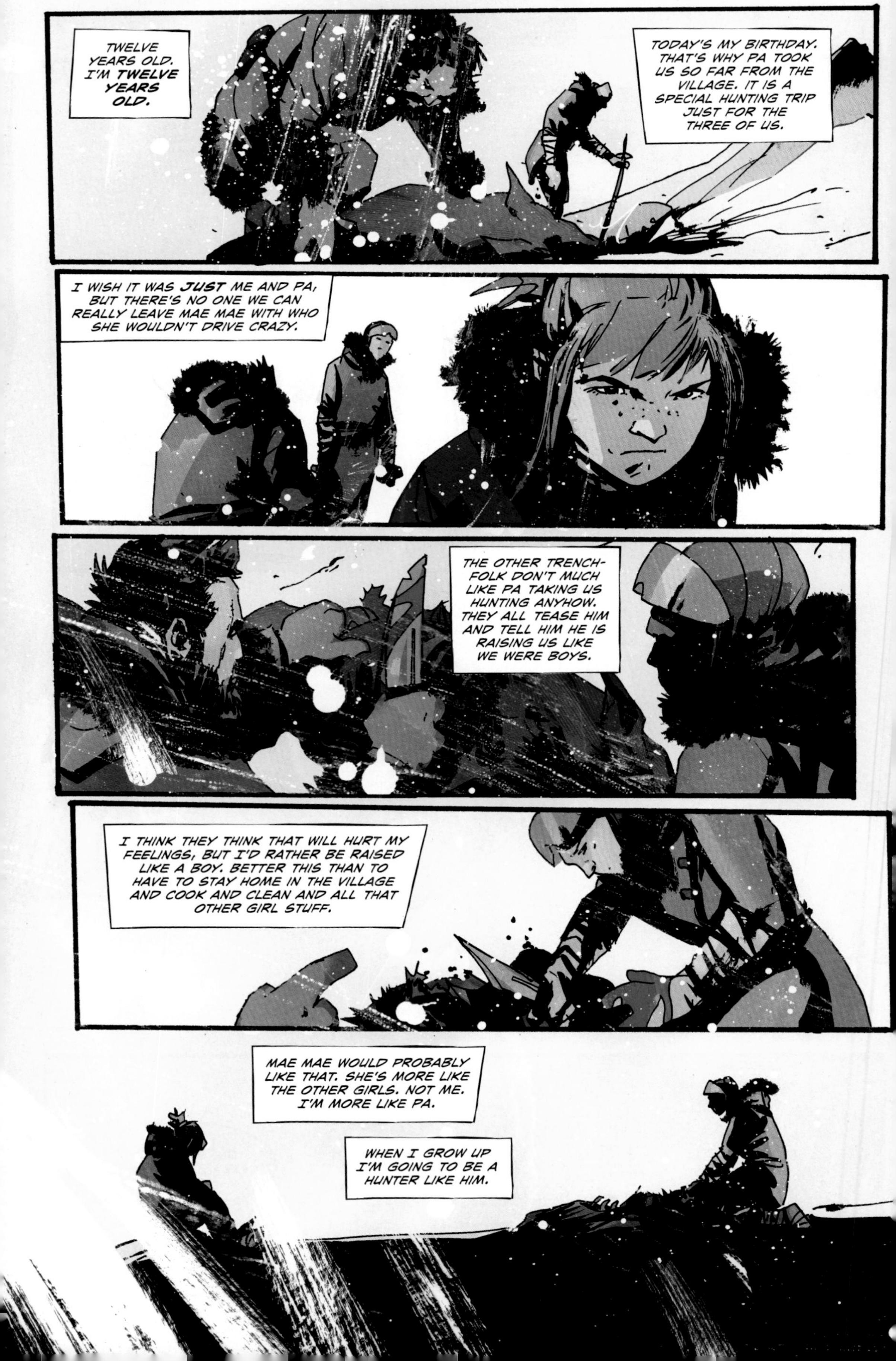
TWELVE YEARS OLD. I'M TWELVE YEARS OLD.
TODAY'S MY BIRTHDAY. THAT'S WHY PA TOOK US SO FAR FROM THE VILLAGE. IT IS A SPECIAL HUNTING TRIP JUST FOR THE THREE OF US.
I WISH IT WAS JUST ME AND PA, BUT THERE'S NO ONE WE CAN REALLY LEAVE MAE MAE WITH WHO SHE WOULDN'T DRIVE CRAZY.
THE OTHER TRENCH-FOLK DON'T MUCH LIKE PA TAKING US HUNTING ANYHOW. THEY ALL TEASE HIM AND TELL HIM HE IS RAISING US LIKE WE WERE BOYS.
I THINK THEY THINK THAT WILL HURT MY FEELINGS, BUT I'D RATHER BE RAISED LIKE A BOY. BETTER THIS THAN TO HAVE TO STAY HOME IN THE VILLAGE AND COOK AND CLEAN AND ALL THAT OTHER GIRL STUFF.
MAE MAE WOULD PROBABLY LIKE THAT. SHE'S MORE LIKE THE OTHER GIRLS. NOT ME. I'M MORE LIKE PA.
WHEN I GROW UP I'M GOING TO BE A HUNTER LIKE HIM.

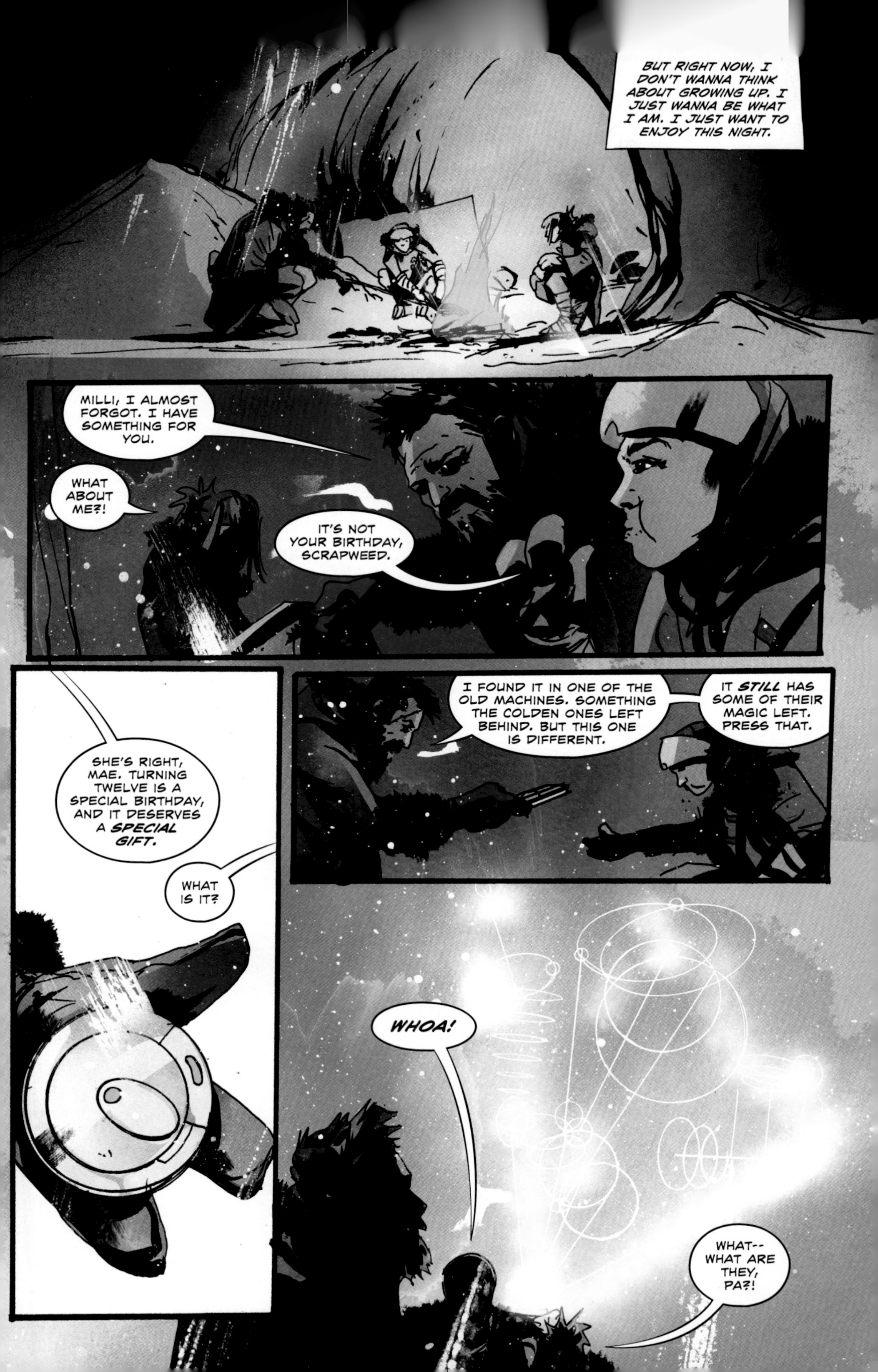

BUT RIGHT NOW, I DON'T WANNA THINK ABOUT GROWING UP. I JUST WANNA BE WHAT I AM. I JUST WANT TO ENJOY THIS NIGHT.
MILLI, I ALMOST FORGOT. I HAVE SOMETHING FOR YOU.
WHAT ABOUT ME?!
IT'S NOT YOUR BIRTHDAY, SCRAPWEED.
SHE'S RIGHT, MAE. TURNING TWELVE IS A SPECIAL BIRTHDAY, AND IT DESERVES A SPECIAL GIFT.
WHAT IS IT?
I FOUND IT IN ONE OF THE OLD MACHINES. SOMETHING THE COLDEN ONES LEFT BEHIND. BUT THIS ONE IS DIFFERENT.
IT STILL HAS SOME OF THEIR MAGIC LEFT. PRESS THAT.
WHOA!
WHAT-- WHAT ARE THEY, PA?!

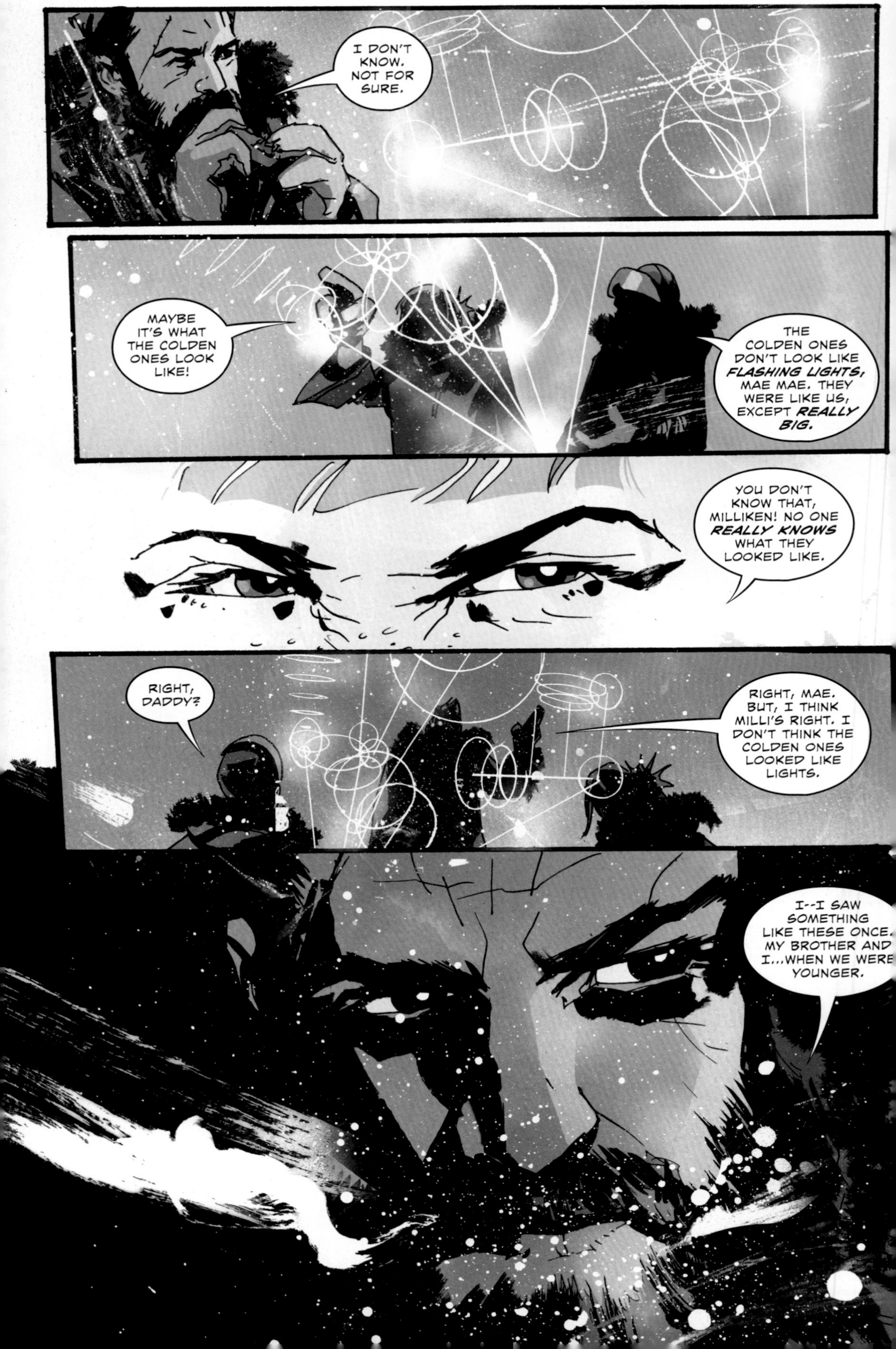
I DON'T KNOW. NOT FOR SURE.
MAYBE IT'S WHAT THE COLDEN ONES LOOK LIKE!
THE COLDEN ONES DON'T LOOK LIKE FLASHING LIGHTS, MAE MAE. THEY WERE LIKE US, EXCEPT REALLY BIG.
YOU DON'T KNOW THAT, MILLIKEN! NO ONE REALLY KNOWS WHAT THEY LOOKED LIKE.
RIGHT, DADDY?
RIGHT, MAE. BUT, I THINK MILLI'S RIGHT. I DON'T THINK THE COLDEN ONES LOOKED LIKE LIGHTS.
I--I SAW SOMETHING LIKE THESE ONCE. MY BROTHER AND I...WHEN WE WERE YOUNGER.

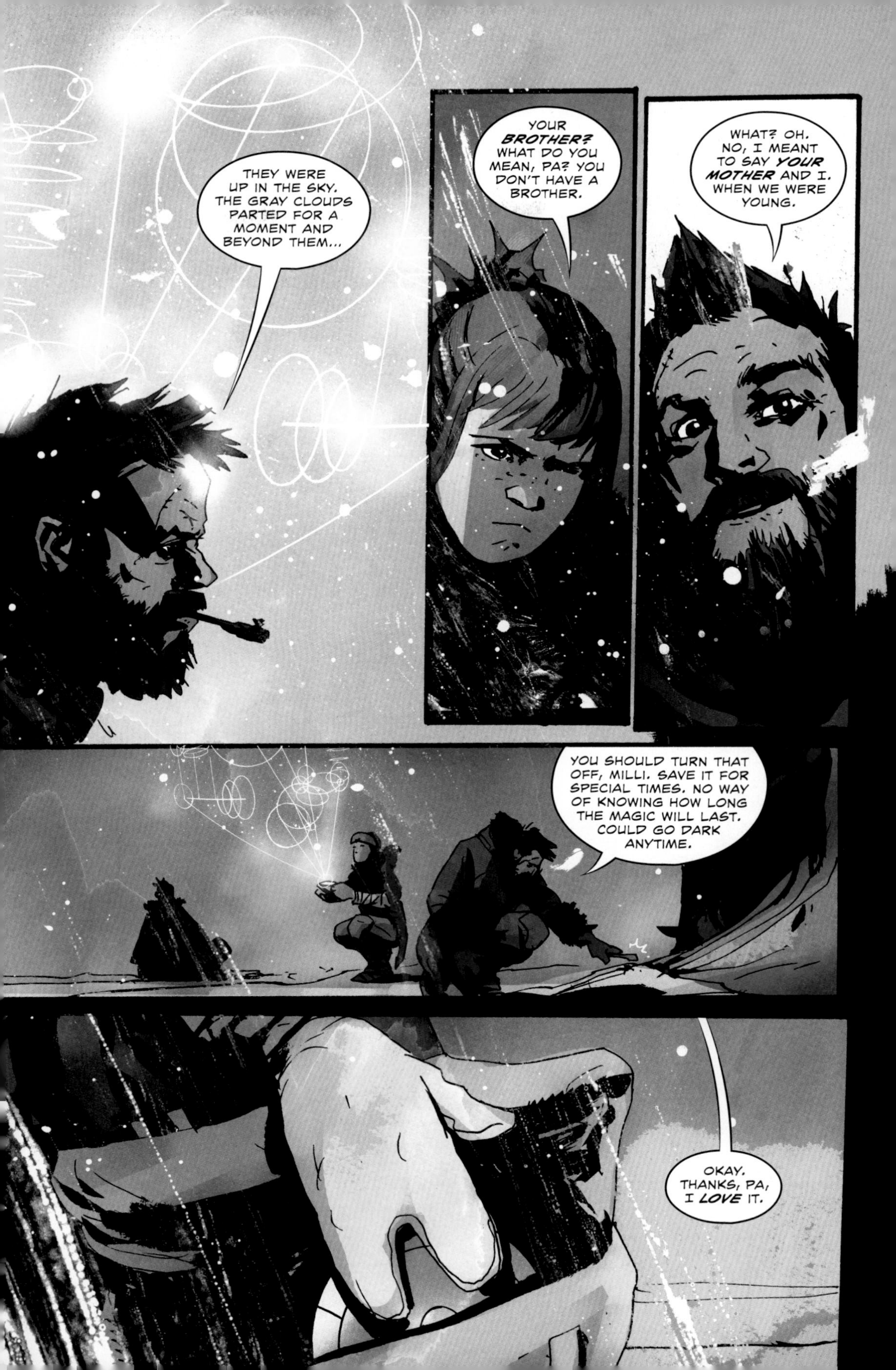
THEY WERE UP IN THE SKY. THE GRAY CLOUDS PARTED FOR A MOMENT AND BEYOND THEM...
YOUR BROTHER? WHAT DO YOU MEAN, PA? YOU DON'T HAVE A BROTHER.
WHAT? OH. NO, I MEANT TO SAY YOUR MOTHER AND I. WHEN WE WERE YOUNG.
YOU SHOULD TURN THAT OFF, MILLI. SAVE IT FOR SPECIAL TIMES. NO WAY OF KNOWING HOW LONG THE MAGIC WILL LAST. COULD GO DARK ANYTIME.
OKAY. THANKS, PA, I LOVE IT.

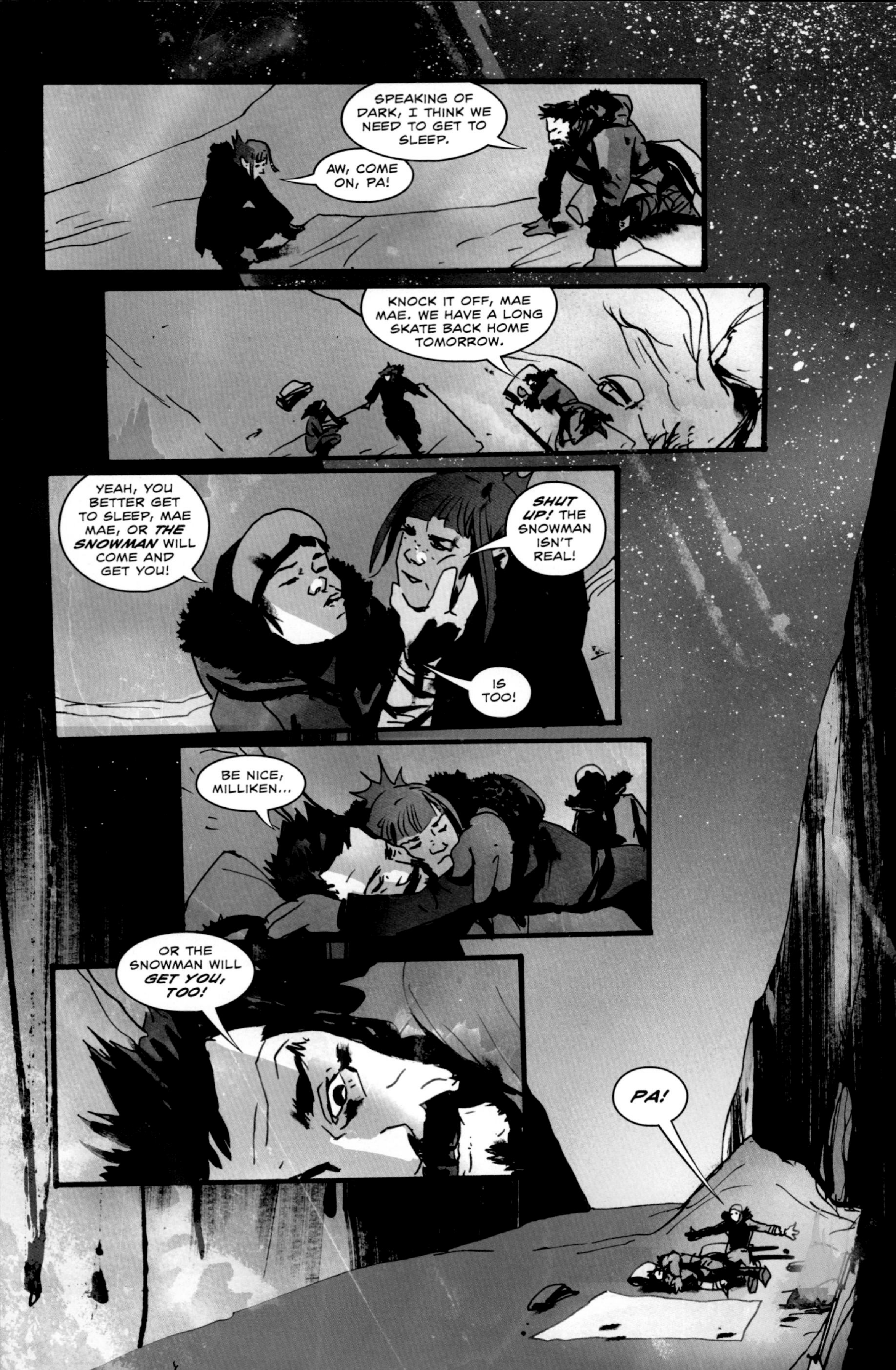
SPEAKING OF DARK, I THINK WE NEED TO GET TO SLEEP.
AW, COME ON, PA!
KNOCK IT OFF, MAE MAE. WE HAVE A LONG SKATE BACK HOME TOMORROW.
YEAH, YOU BETTER GET TO SLEEP, MAE MAE, OR *THE SNOWMAN* WILL COME AND GET YOU!
SHUT UP! THE SNOWMAN ISN'T REAL!
IS TOO!
BE NICE, MILLIKEN...
OR THE SNOWMAN WILL *GET YOU, TOO!*
PA!

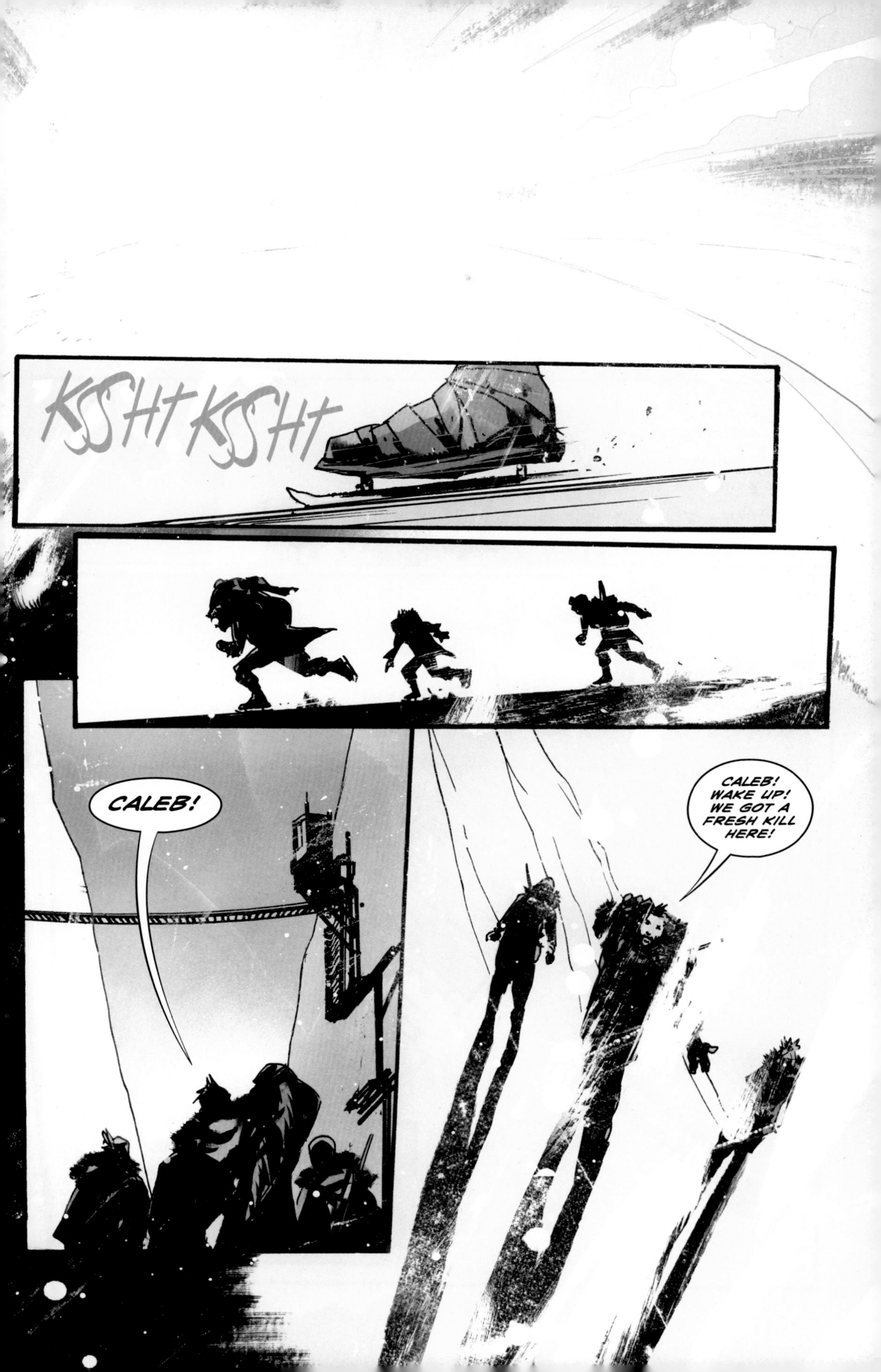
KSSHT KSSHT
CALEB!
CALEB! WAKE UP! WE GOT A FRESH KILL HERE!

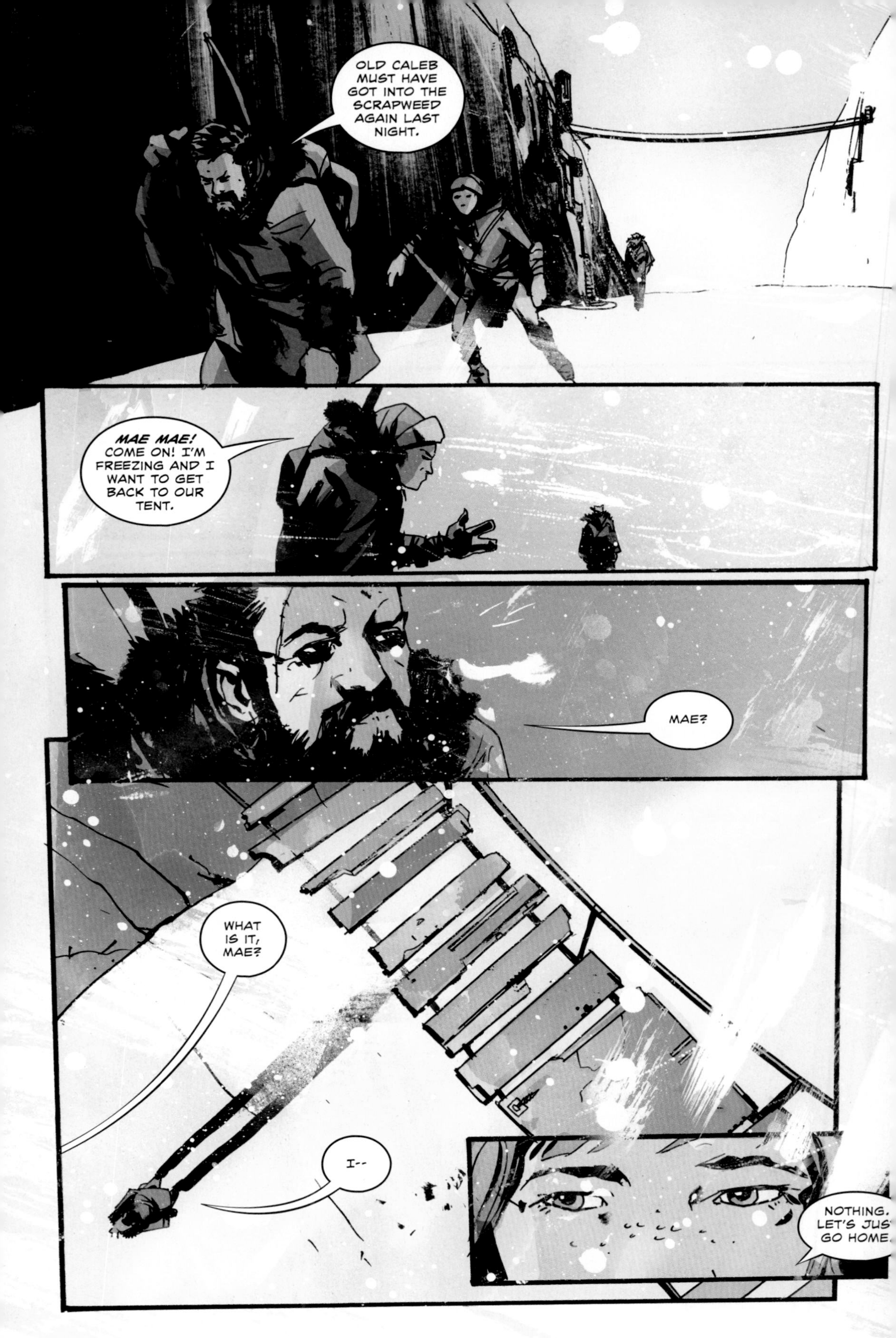
OLD CALEB MUST HAVE GOT INTO THE SCRAPWEED AGAIN LAST NIGHT.
MAE MAE! COME ON! I'M FREEZING AND I WANT TO GET BACK TO OUR TENT.
MAE?
WHAT IS IT, MAE?
I--
NOTHING. LET'S JUS GO HOME.

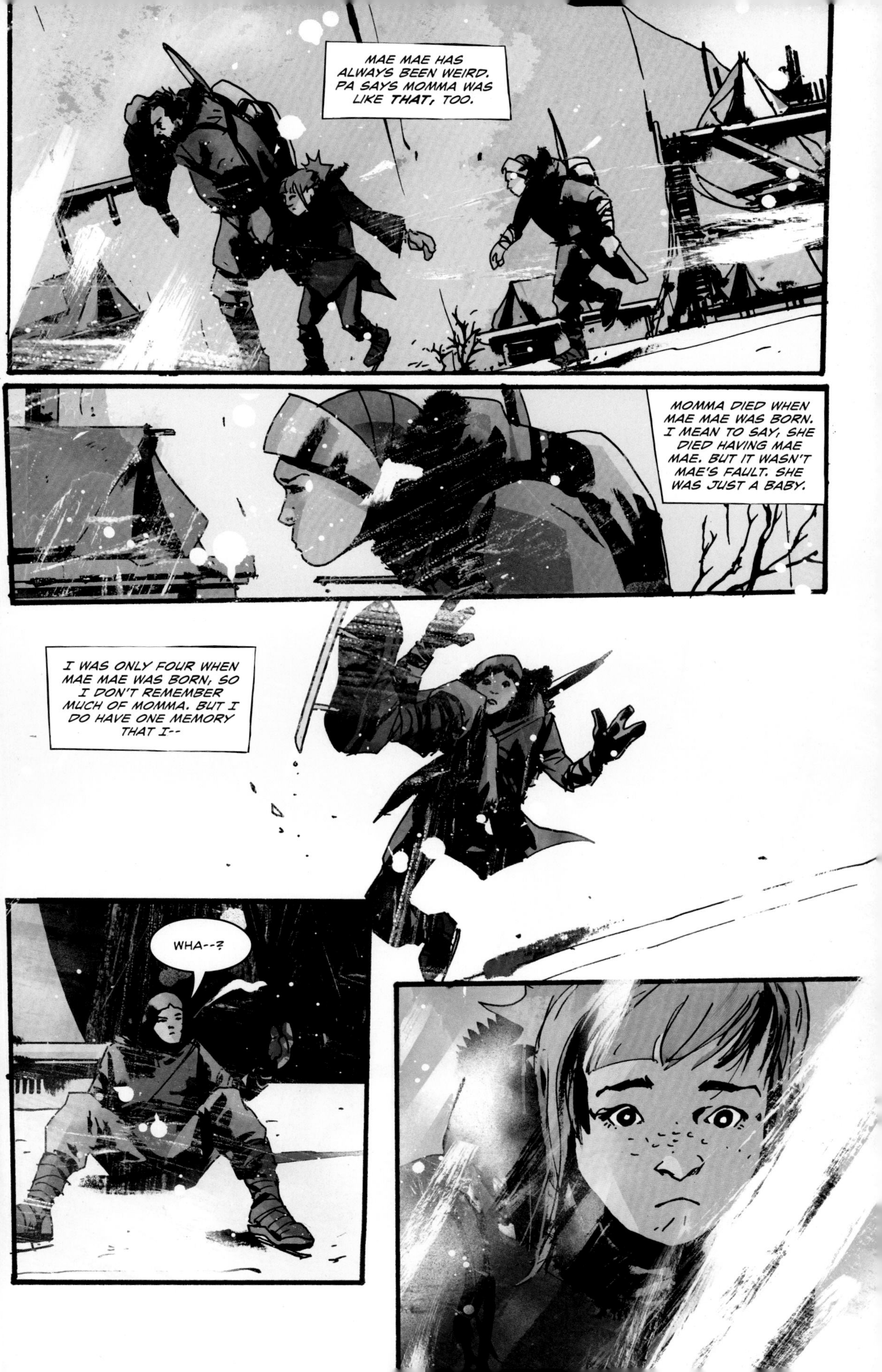
MAE MAE HAS ALWAYS BEEN WEIRD. PA SAYS MOMMA WAS LIKE *THAT*, TOO.
MOMMA DIED WHEN MAE MAE WAS BORN. I MEAN TO SAY, SHE DIED HAVING MAE MAE. BUT IT WASN'T MAE'S FAULT. SHE WAS JUST A BABY.
I WAS ONLY FOUR WHEN MAE MAE WAS BORN, SO I DON'T REMEMBER MUCH OF MOMMA. BUT I DO HAVE ONE MEMORY THAT I--
WHA--?

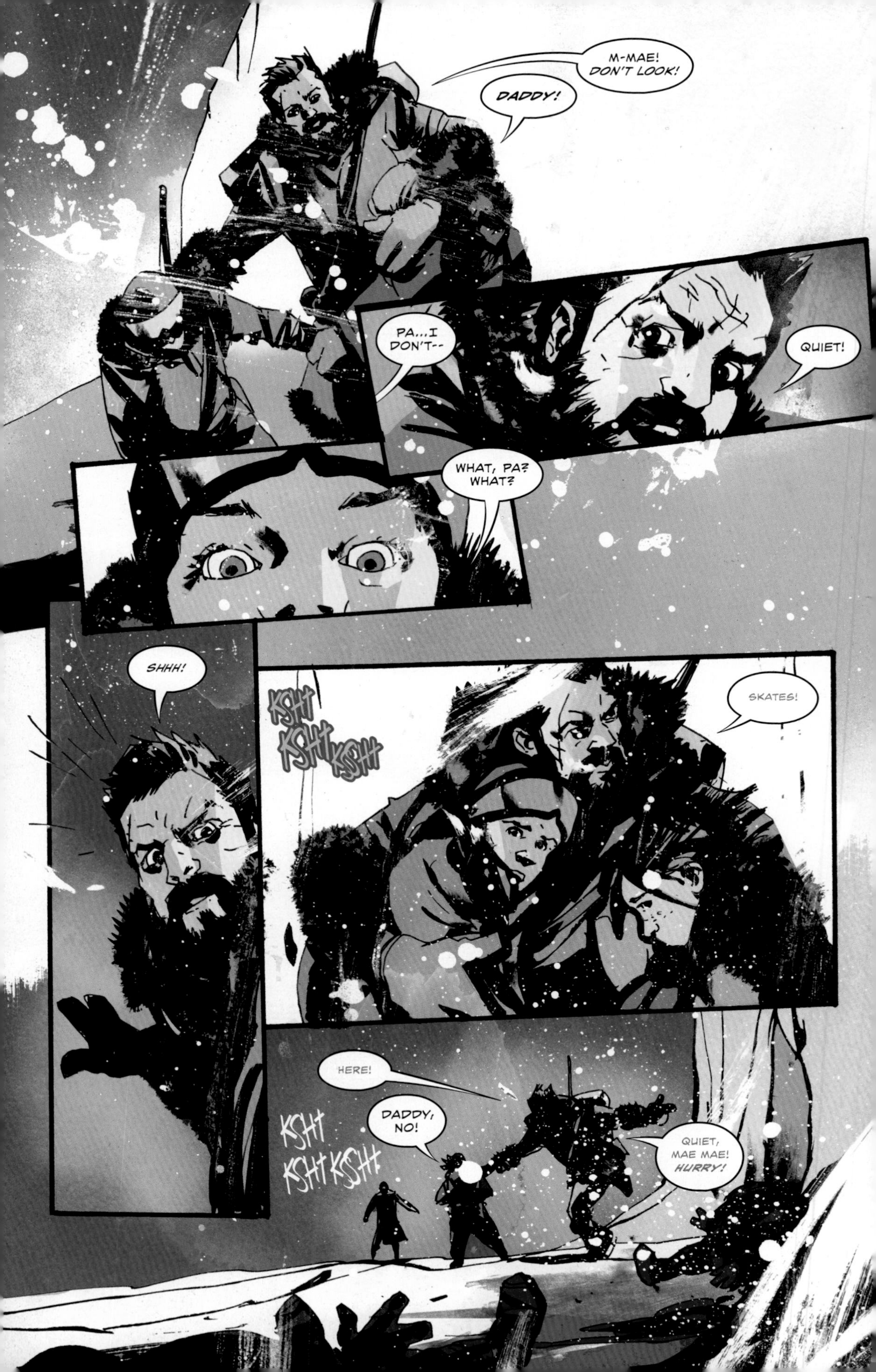
M-MAE! DON'T LOOK!
DADDY!
PA...I DON'T--
QUIET!
WHAT, PA? WHAT?
SHHH!
KSH KSH KSH
SKATES!
HERE!
DADDY, NO!
KSH KSH KSH
QUIET, MAE MAE! HURRY!

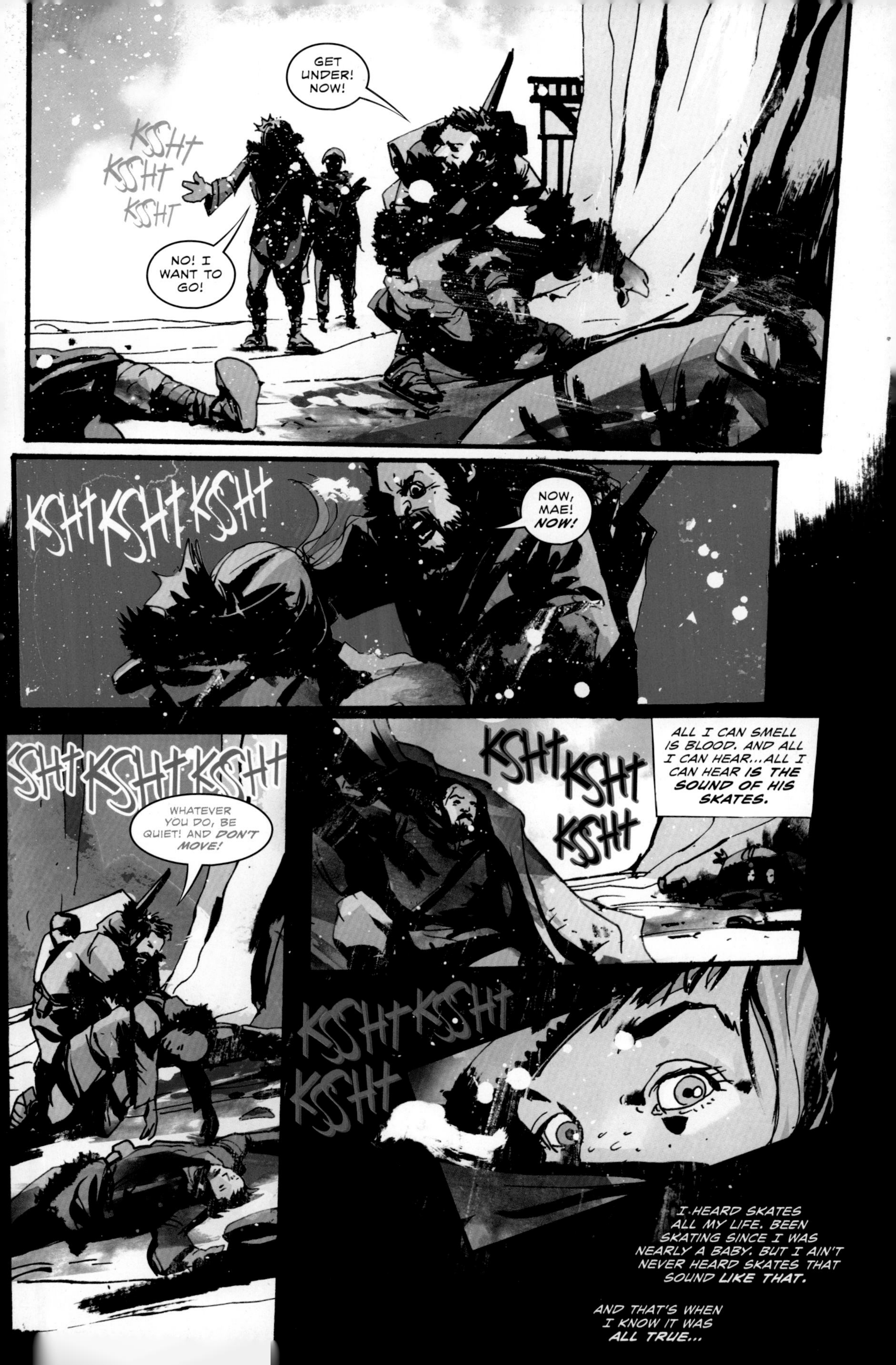
GET UNDER! NOW!
KSSHT KSSHT KSSHT
NO! I WANT TO GO!
KSHT KSHT KSSHT
NOW, MAE! NOW!
KSHT KSHT KSSHT
WHATEVER YOU DO, BE QUIET! AND DON'T MOVE!
KSHT KSHT KSHT
ALL I CAN SMELL IS BLOOD. AND ALL I CAN HEAR...ALL I CAN HEAR IS THE SOUND OF HIS SKATES.
KSSHT KSSHT KSHT
I HEARD SKATES ALL MY LIFE. BEEN SKATING SINCE I WAS NEARLY A BABY. BUT I AIN'T NEVER HEARD SKATES THAT SOUND LIKE THAT.
AND THAT'S WHEN I KNOW IT WAS ALL TRUE...

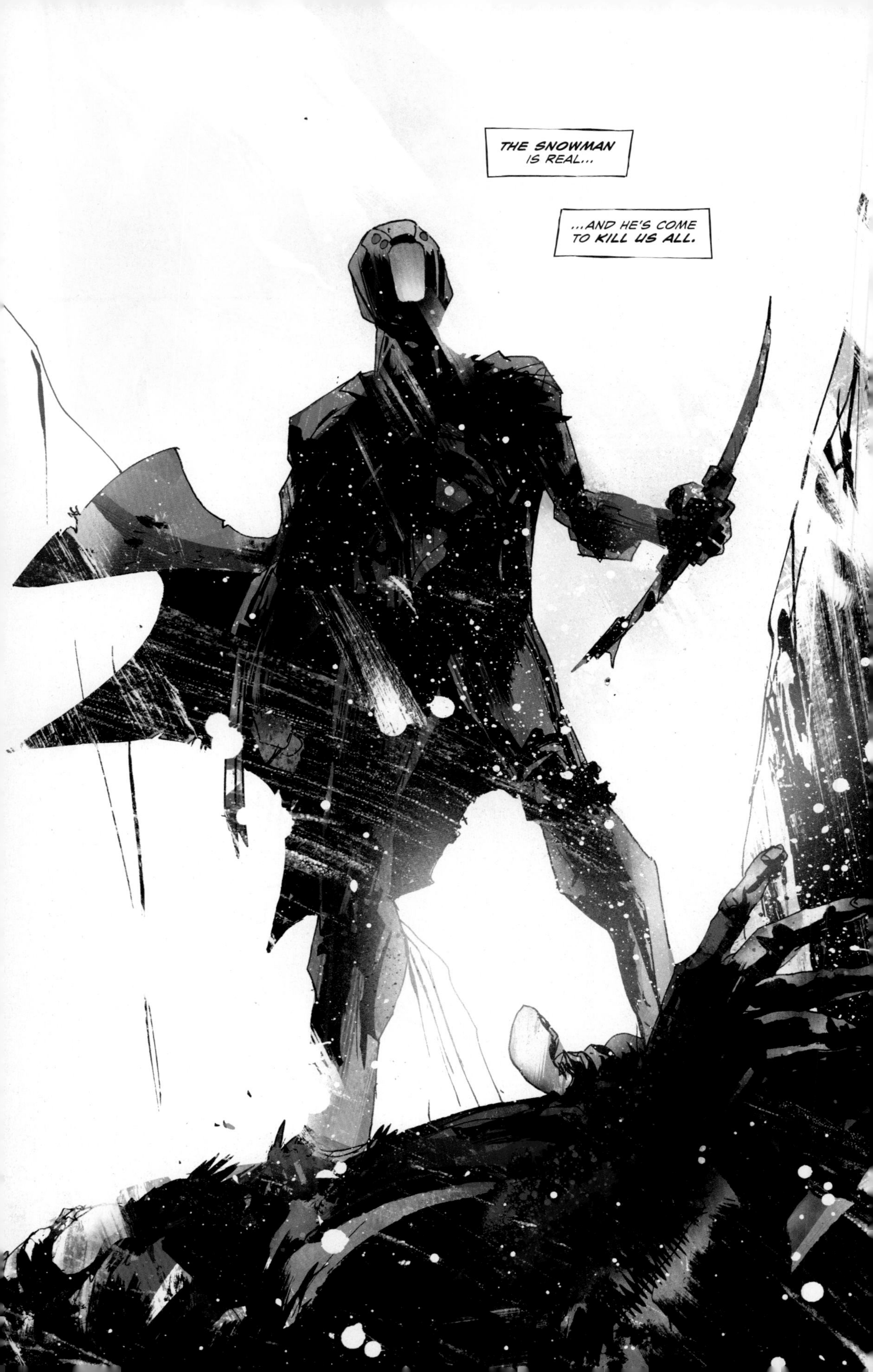
THE SNOWMAN IS REAL...
...AND HE'S COME TO KILL US ALL.

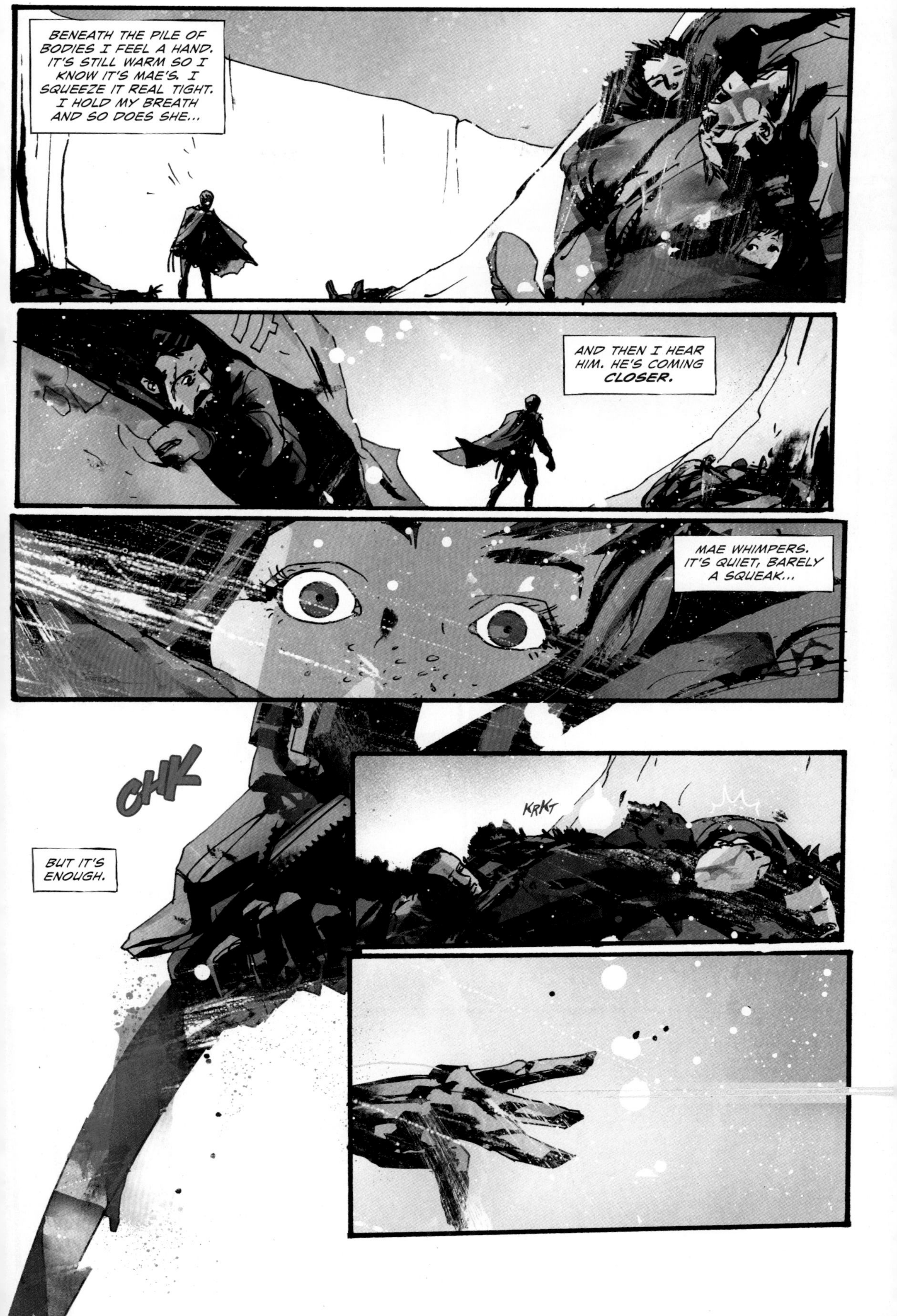
BENEATH THE PILE OF BODIES I FEEL A HAND. IT'S STILL WARM SO I KNOW IT'S MAE'S. I SQUEEZE IT REAL TIGHT. I HOLD MY BREATH AND SO DOES SHE...
AND THEN I HEAR HIM. HE'S COMING CLOSER.
MAE WHIMPERS. IT'S QUIET, BARELY A SQUEAK...
OHK
BUT IT'S ENOUGH.
KRKT

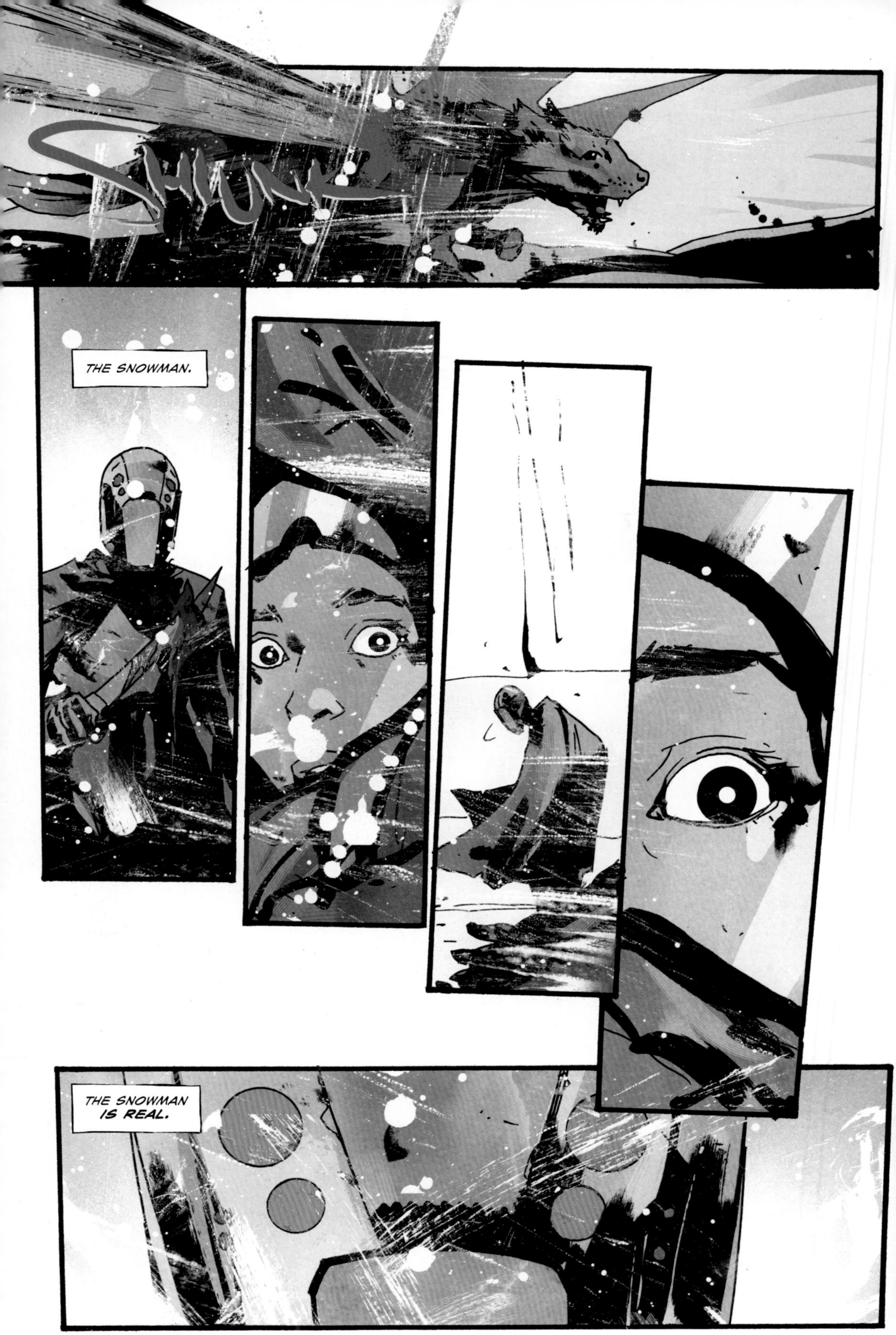
SHUNK
THE SNOWMAN.
THE SNOWMAN IS REAL.

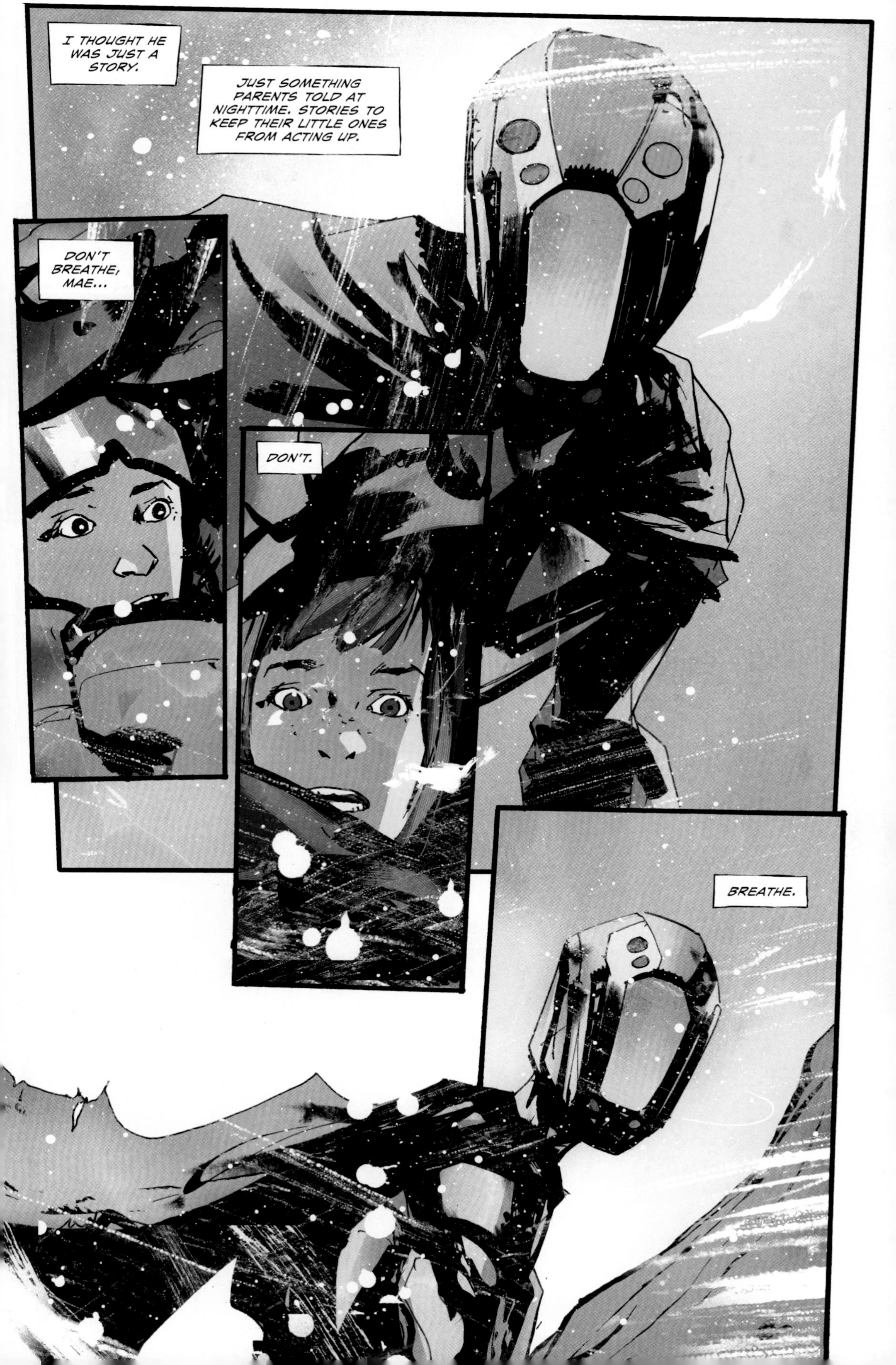
I THOUGHT HE WAS JUST A STORY.
JUST SOMETHING PARENTS TOLD AT NIGHTTIME. STORIES TO KEEP THEIR LITTLE ONES FROM ACTING UP.
DON'T BREATHE, MAE...
DON'T.
BREATHE.

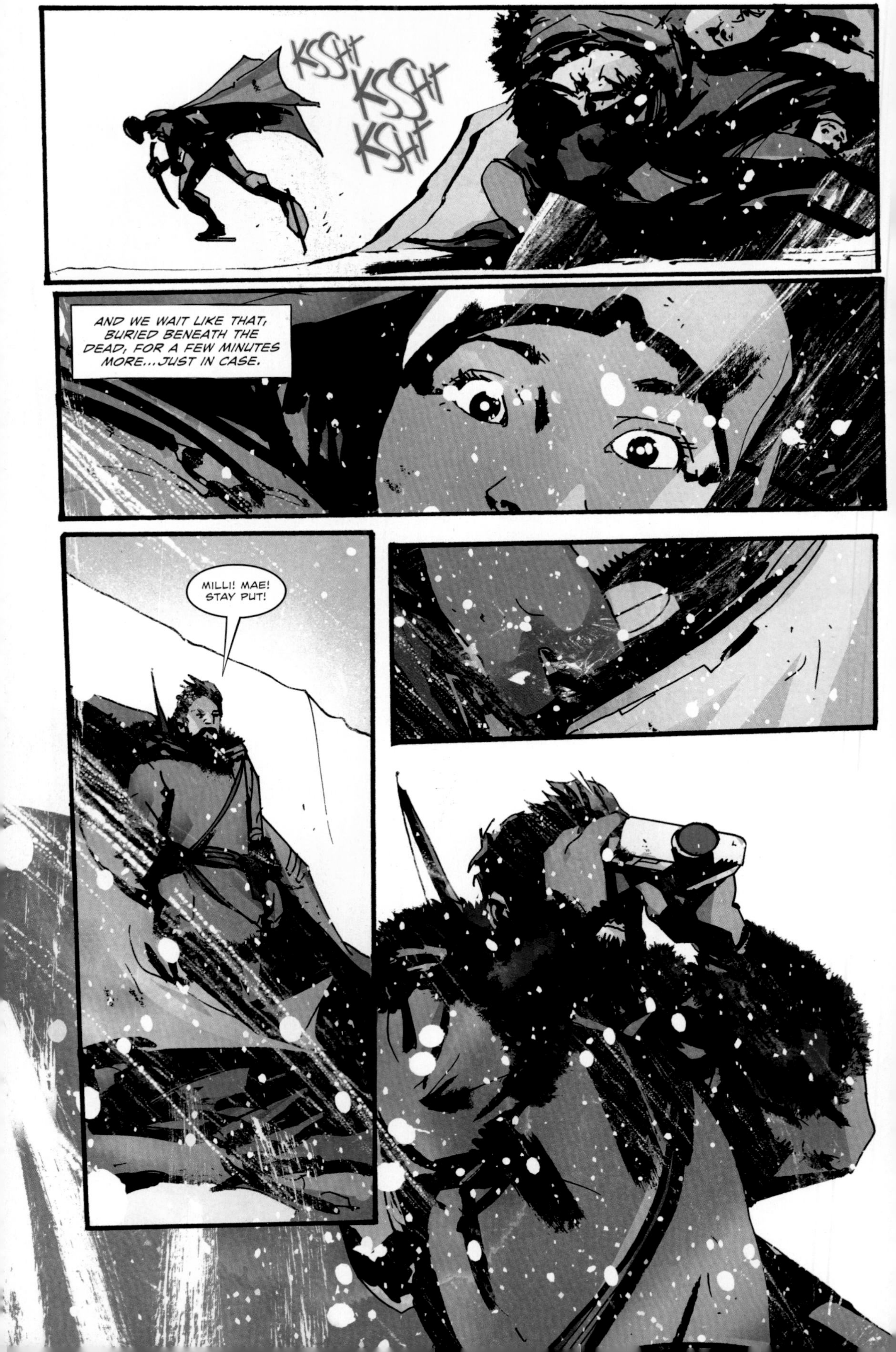
KSSHT
KSSHT
KSHT
AND WE WAIT LIKE THAT, BURIED BENEATH THE DEAD, FOR A FEW MINUTES MORE...JUST IN CASE.
MILLI! MAE! STAY PUT!

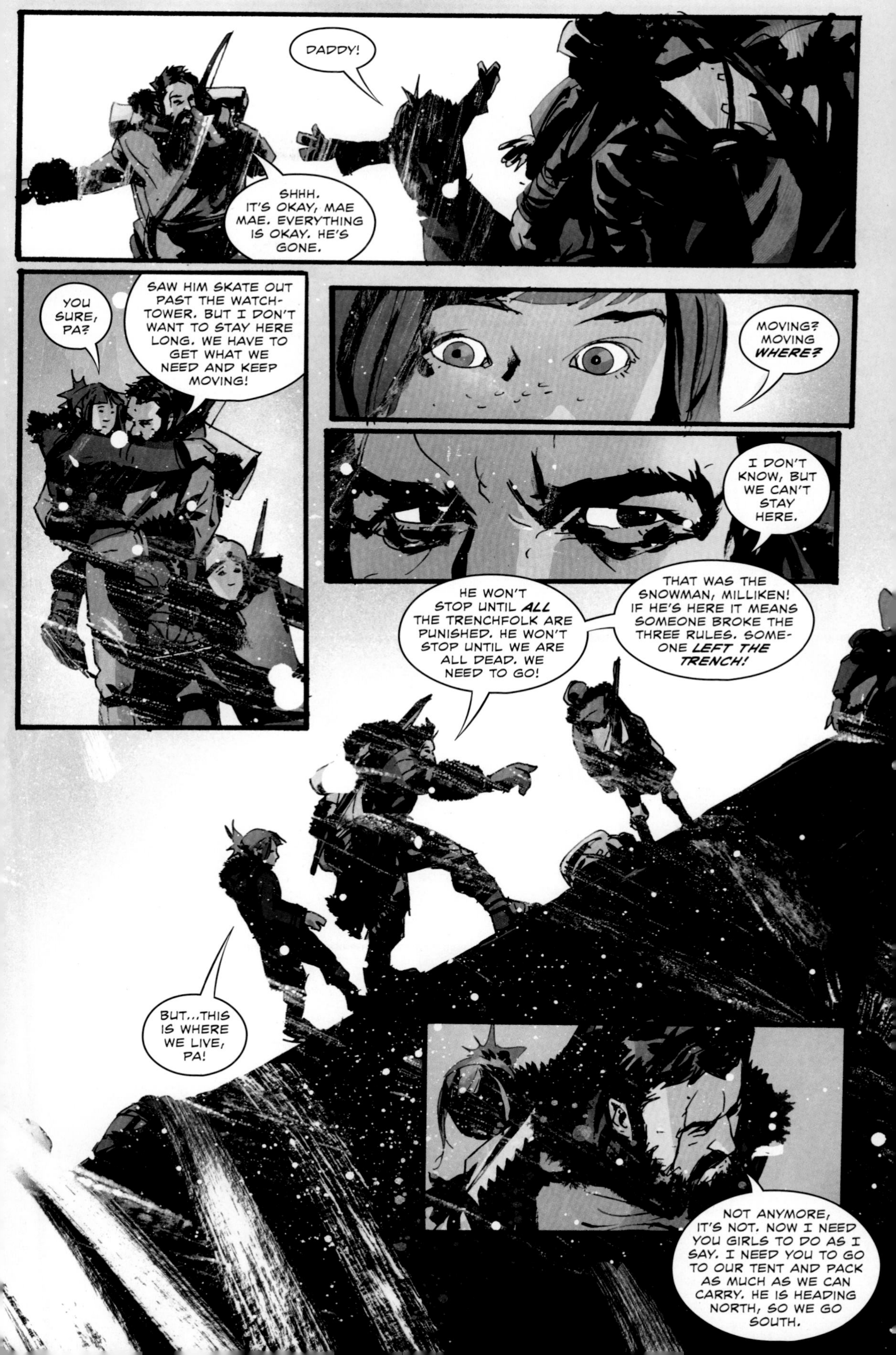
DADDY!
SHHH. IT'S OKAY, MAE MAE. EVERYTHING IS OKAY. HE'S GONE.
YOU SURE, PA?
SAW HIM SKATE OUT PAST THE WATCH-TOWER. BUT I DON'T WANT TO STAY HERE LONG. WE HAVE TO GET WHAT WE NEED AND KEEP MOVING!
MOVING? MOVING *WHERE?*
I DON'T KNOW, BUT WE CAN'T STAY HERE.
THAT WAS THE SNOWMAN, MILLIKEN! IF HE'S HERE IT MEANS SOMEONE BROKE THE THREE RULES. SOME-ONE *LEFT THE TRENCH!*
HE WON'T STOP UNTIL *ALL* THE TRENCHFOLK ARE PUNISHED. HE WON'T STOP UNTIL WE ARE ALL DEAD. WE NEED TO GO!
BUT...THIS IS WHERE WE LIVE, PA!
NOT ANYMORE, IT'S NOT. NOW I NEED YOU GIRLS TO DO AS I SAY. I NEED YOU TO GO TO OUR TENT AND PACK AS MUCH AS WE CAN CARRY. HE IS HEADING NORTH, SO WE GO SOUTH.

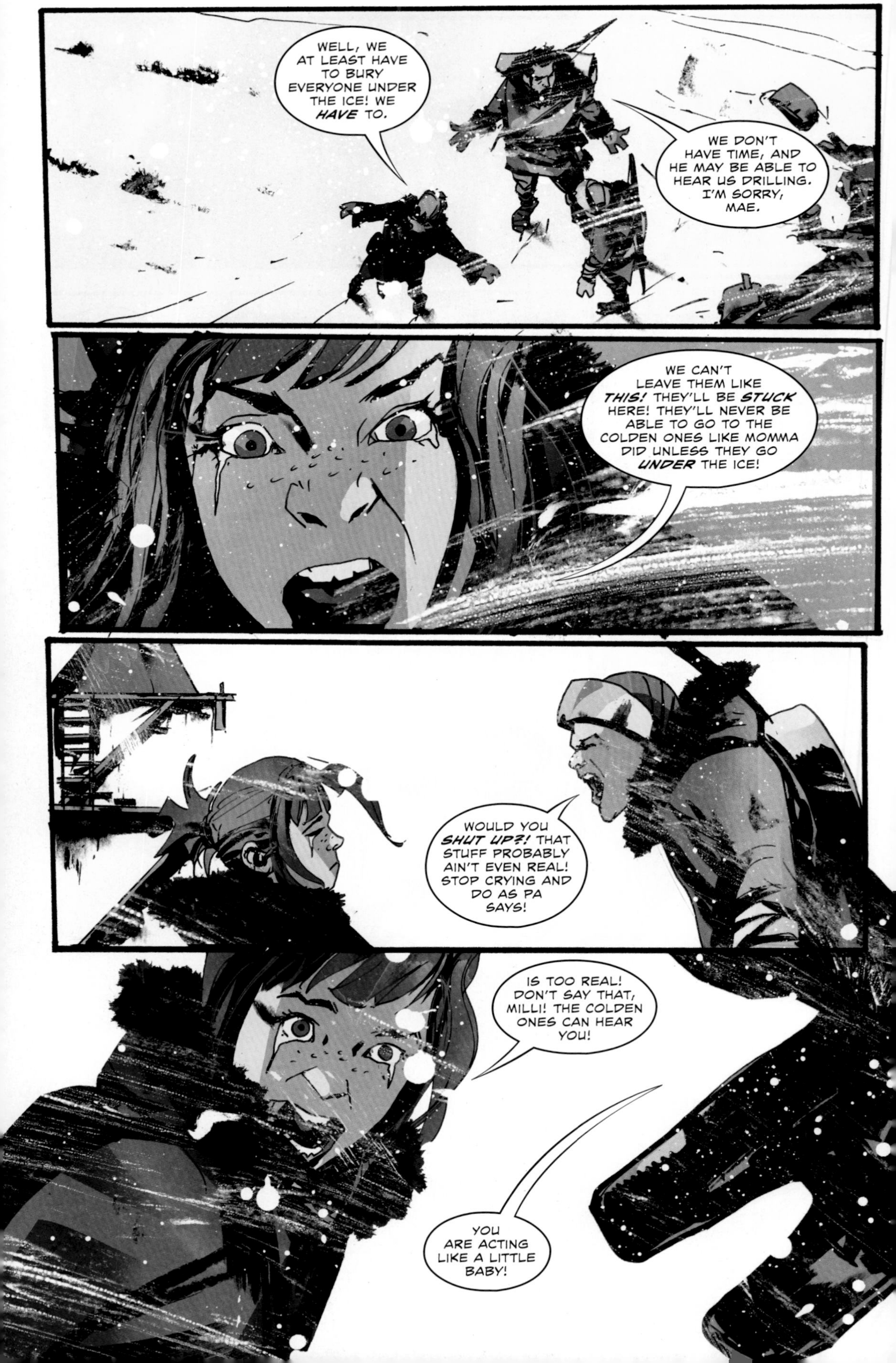
WELL, WE AT LEAST HAVE TO BURY EVERYONE UNDER THE ICE! WE *HAVE* TO.
WE DON'T HAVE TIME, AND HE MAY BE ABLE TO HEAR US DRILLING. I'M SORRY, MAE.
WE CAN'T LEAVE THEM LIKE *THIS!* THEY'LL BE *STUCK* HERE! THEY'LL NEVER BE ABLE TO GO TO THE COLDEN ONES LIKE MOMMA DID UNLESS THEY GO *UNDER* THE ICE!
WOULD YOU *SHUT UP?!* THAT STUFF PROBABLY AIN'T EVEN REAL! STOP CRYING AND DO AS PA SAYS!
IS TOO REAL! DON'T SAY THAT, MILLI! THE COLDEN ONES CAN HEAR YOU!
YOU ARE ACTING LIKE A LITTLE BABY!

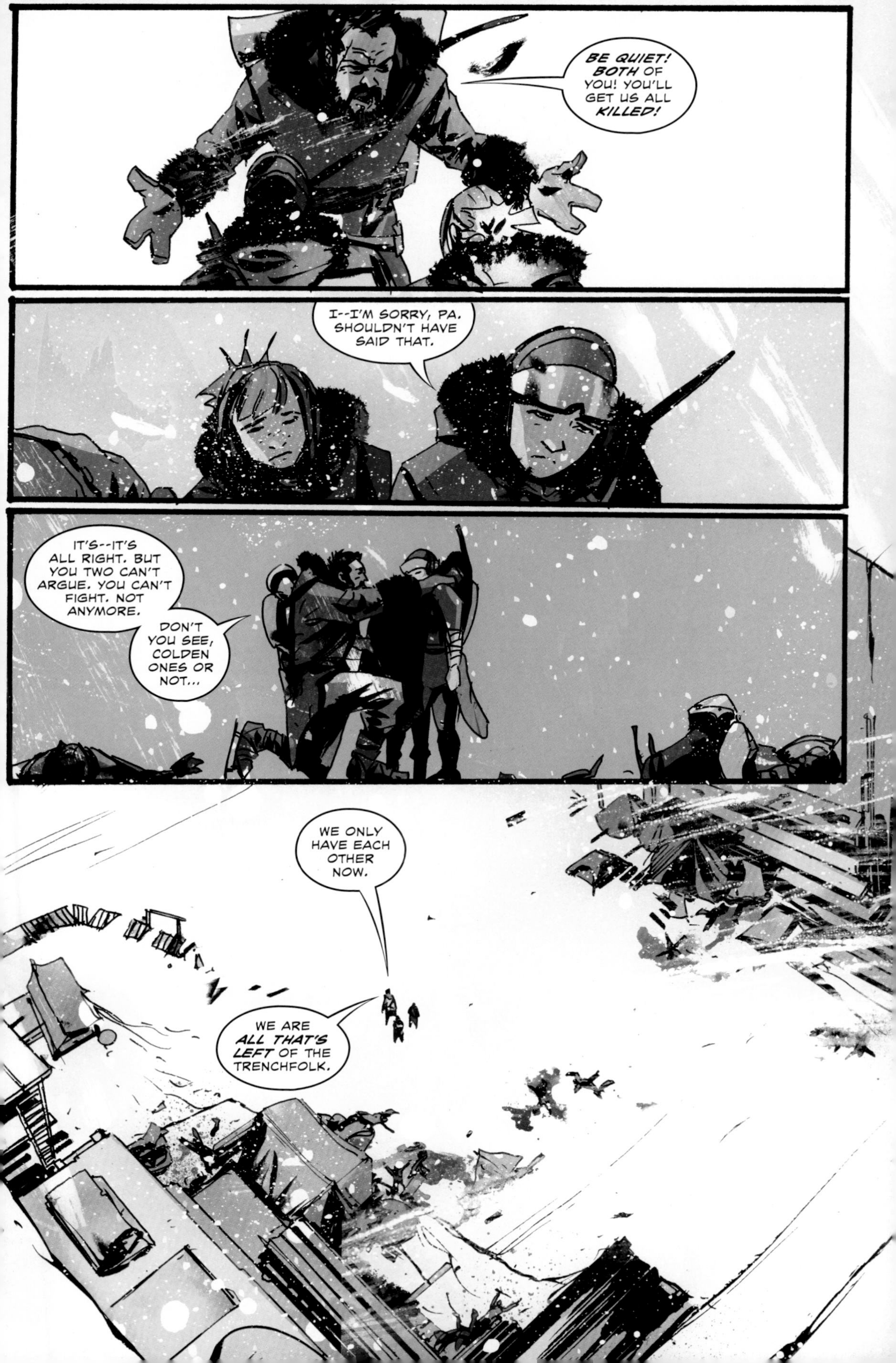

BE QUIET! BOTH OF YOU! YOU'LL GET US ALL KILLED!
I--I'M SORRY, PA. SHOULDN'T HAVE SAID THAT.
IT'S--IT'S ALL RIGHT. BUT YOU TWO CAN'T ARGUE. YOU CAN'T FIGHT. NOT ANYMORE.
DON'T YOU SEE, COLDEN ONES OR NOT...
WE ONLY HAVE EACH OTHER NOW.
WE ARE ALL THAT'S LEFT OF THE TRENCHFOLK.

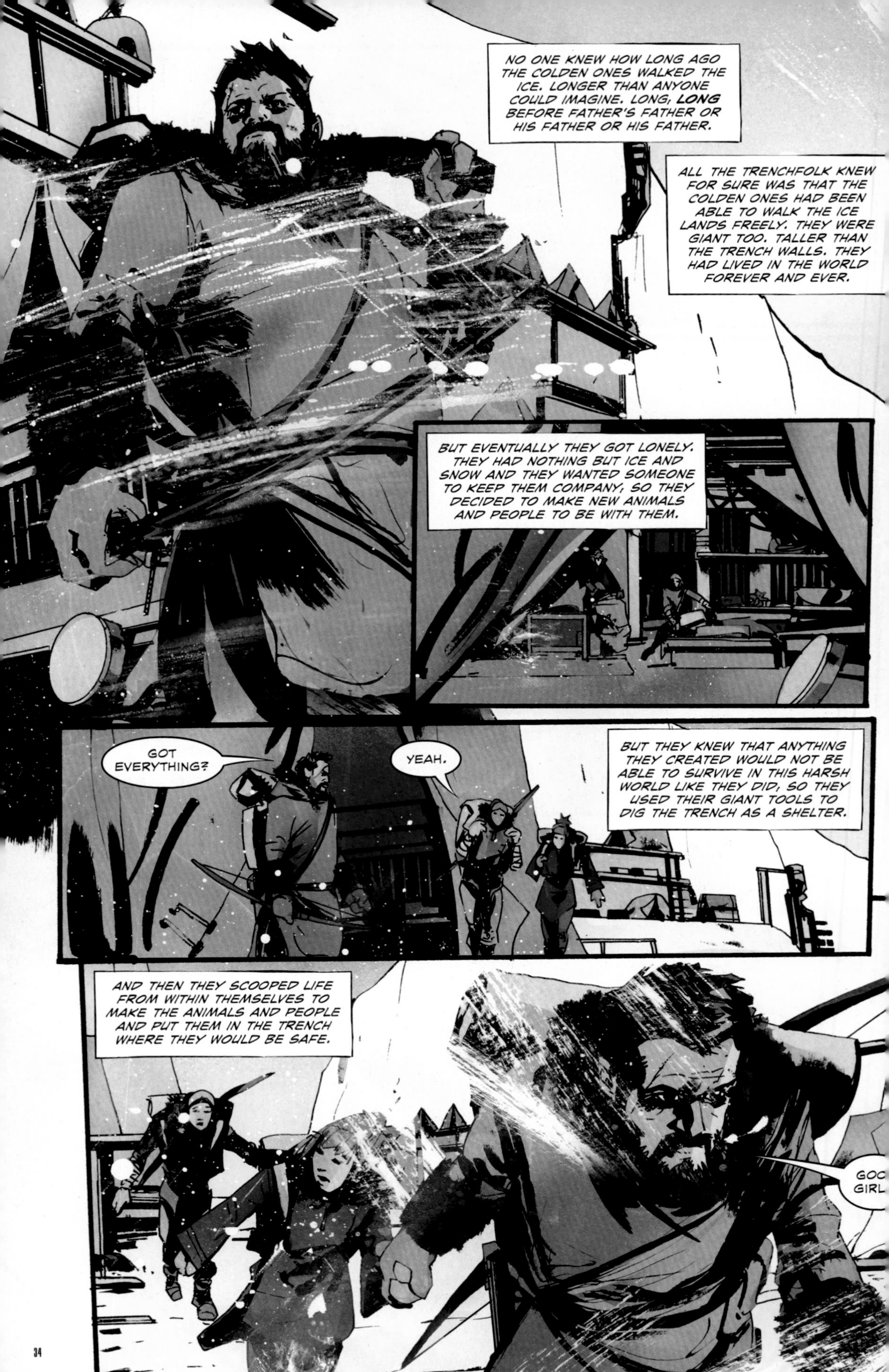
NO ONE KNEW HOW LONG AGO THE COLDEN ONES WALKED THE ICE. LONGER THAN ANYONE COULD IMAGINE. LONG, **LONG** BEFORE FATHER'S FATHER OR HIS FATHER OR HIS FATHER.
ALL THE TRENCHFOLK KNEW FOR SURE WAS THAT THE COLDEN ONES HAD BEEN ABLE TO WALK THE ICE LANDS FREELY. THEY WERE GIANT TOO. TALLER THAN THE TRENCH WALLS. THEY HAD LIVED IN THE WORLD FOREVER AND EVER.
BUT EVENTUALLY THEY GOT LONELY. THEY HAD NOTHING BUT ICE AND SNOW AND THEY WANTED SOMEONE TO KEEP THEM COMPANY, SO THEY DECIDED TO MAKE NEW ANIMALS AND PEOPLE TO BE WITH THEM.
GOT EVERYTHING?
YEAH.
BUT THEY KNEW THAT ANYTHING THEY CREATED WOULD NOT BE ABLE TO SURVIVE IN THIS HARSH WORLD LIKE THEY DID, SO THEY USED THEIR GIANT TOOLS TO DIG THE TRENCH AS A SHELTER.
AND THEN THEY SCOOPED LIFE FROM WITHIN THEMSELVES TO MAKE THE ANIMALS AND PEOPLE AND PUT THEM IN THE TRENCH WHERE THEY WOULD BE SAFE.

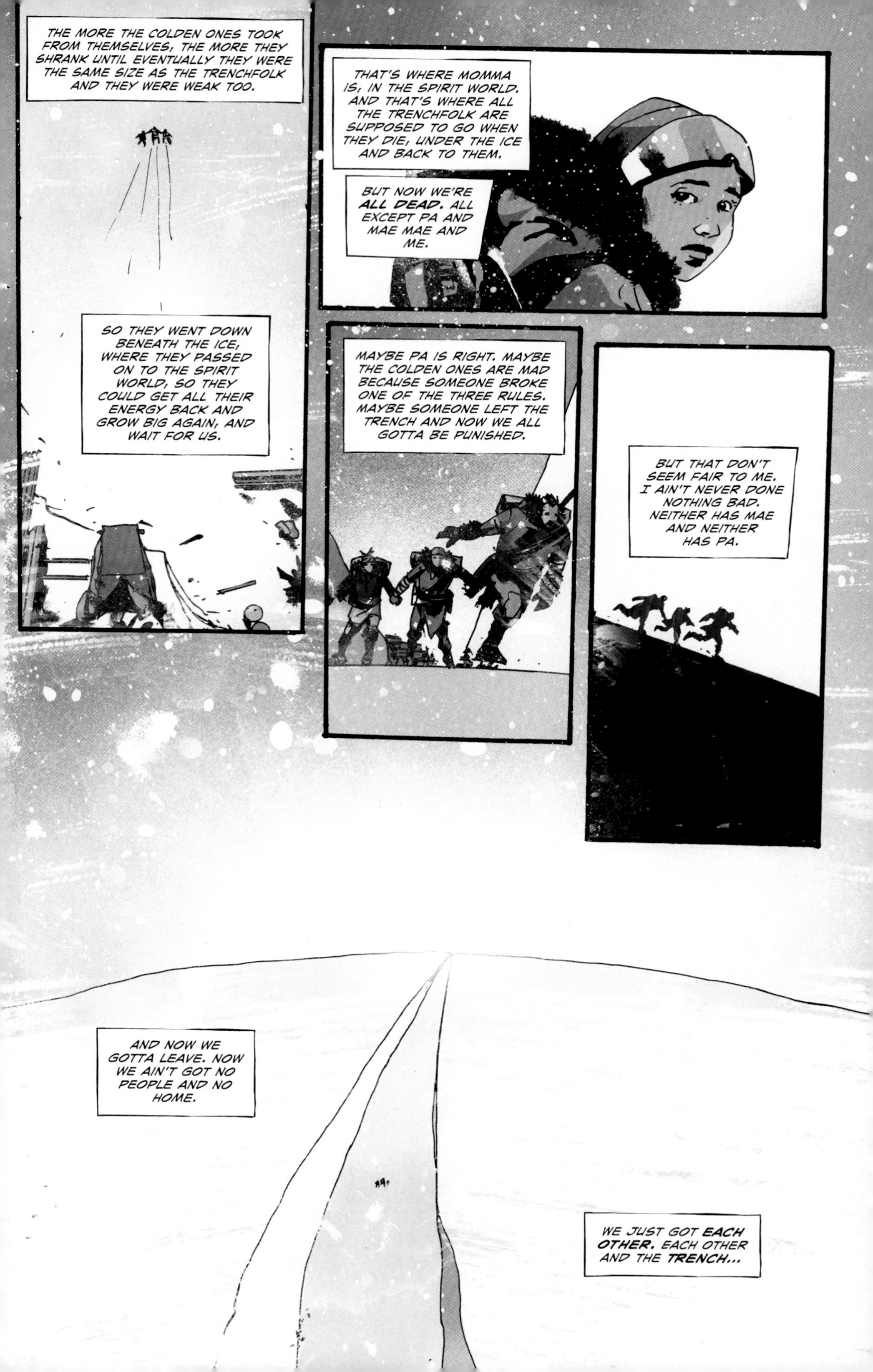
THE MORE THE COLDEN ONES TOOK FROM THEMSELVES, THE MORE THEY SHRANK UNTIL EVENTUALLY THEY WERE THE SAME SIZE AS THE TRENCHFOLK AND THEY WERE WEAK TOO.
SO THEY WENT DOWN BENEATH THE ICE, WHERE THEY PASSED ON TO THE SPIRIT WORLD, SO THEY COULD GET ALL THEIR ENERGY BACK AND GROW BIG AGAIN, AND WAIT FOR US.
THAT'S WHERE MOMMA IS, IN THE SPIRIT WORLD. AND THAT'S WHERE ALL THE TRENCHFOLK ARE SUPPOSED TO GO WHEN THEY DIE, UNDER THE ICE AND BACK TO THEM.
BUT NOW WE'RE **ALL DEAD.** ALL EXCEPT PA AND MAE MAE AND ME.
MAYBE PA IS RIGHT. MAYBE THE COLDEN ONES ARE MAD BECAUSE SOMEONE BROKE ONE OF THE THREE RULES. MAYBE SOMEONE LEFT THE TRENCH AND NOW WE ALL GOTTA BE PUNISHED.
BUT THAT DON'T SEEM FAIR TO ME. I AIN'T NEVER DONE NOTHING BAD. NEITHER HAS MAE AND NEITHER HAS PA.
AND NOW WE GOTTA LEAVE. NOW WE AIN'T GOT NO PEOPLE AND NO HOME.
WE JUST GOT **EACH OTHER.** EACH OTHER AND THE **TRENCH...**

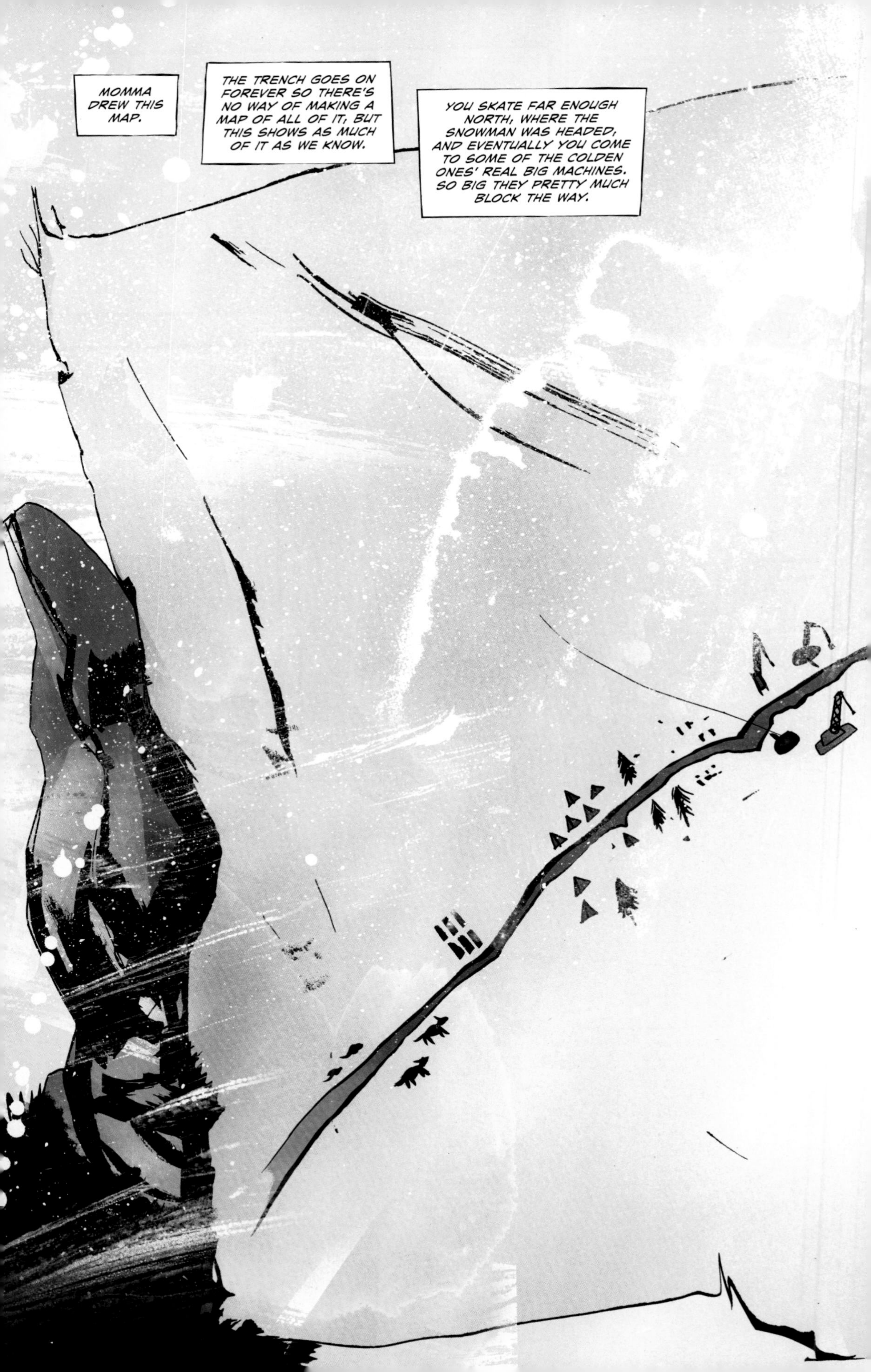
MOMMA DREW THIS MAP.
THE TRENCH GOES ON FOREVER SO THERE'S NO WAY OF MAKING A MAP OF ALL OF IT, BUT THIS SHOWS AS MUCH OF IT AS WE KNOW.
YOU SKATE FAR ENOUGH NORTH, WHERE THE SNOWMAN WAS HEADED, AND EVENTUALLY YOU COME TO SOME OF THE COLDEN ONES' REAL BIG MACHINES. SO BIG THEY PRETTY MUCH BLOCK THE WAY.

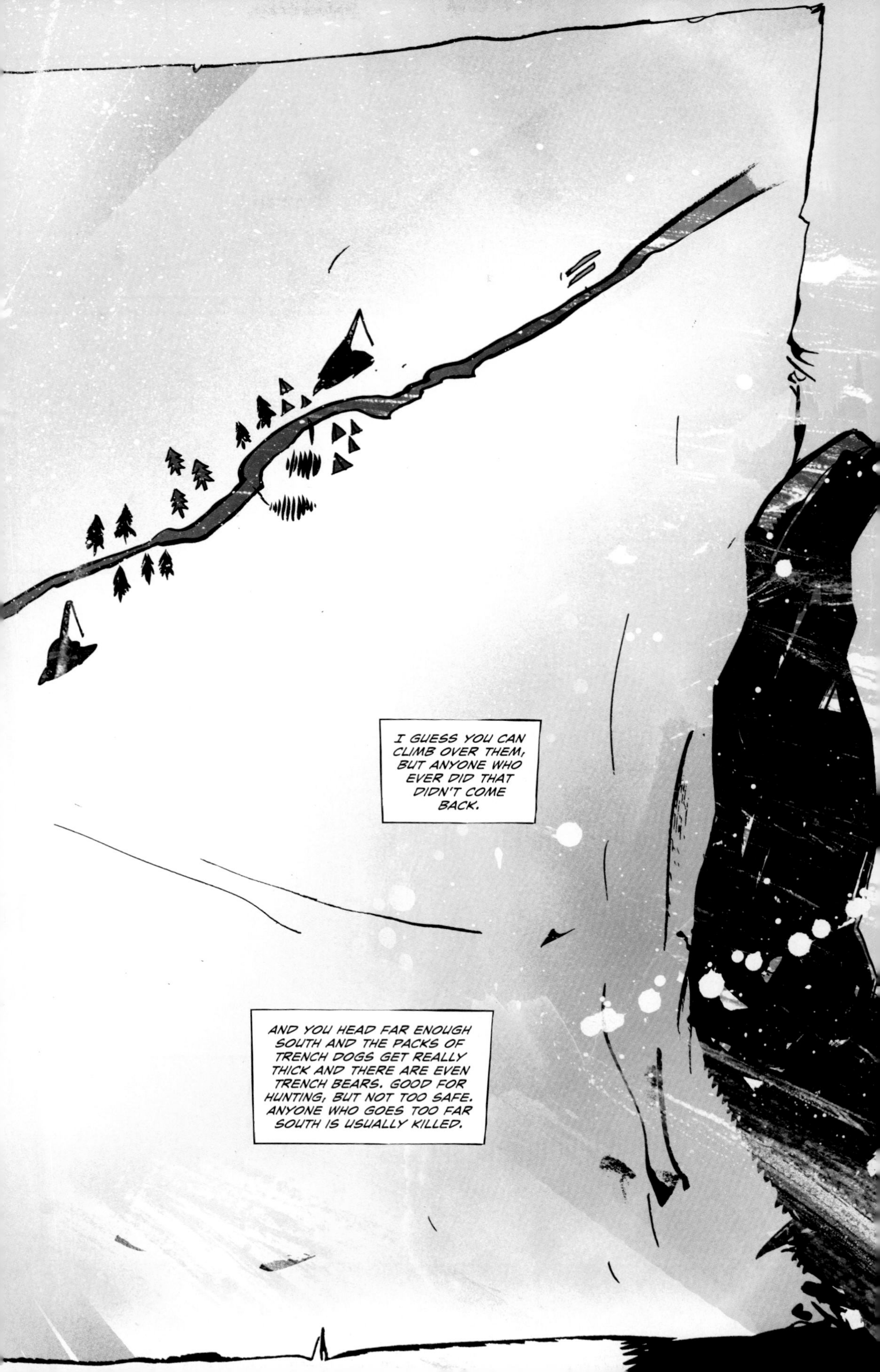
I GUESS YOU CAN CLIMB OVER THEM, BUT ANYONE WHO EVER DID THAT DIDN'T COME BACK.
AND YOU HEAD FAR ENOUGH SOUTH AND THE PACKS OF TRENCH DOGS GET REALLY THICK AND THERE ARE EVEN TRENCH BEARS. GOOD FOR HUNTING, BUT NOT TOO SAFE. ANYONE WHO GOES TOO FAR SOUTH IS USUALLY KILLED.

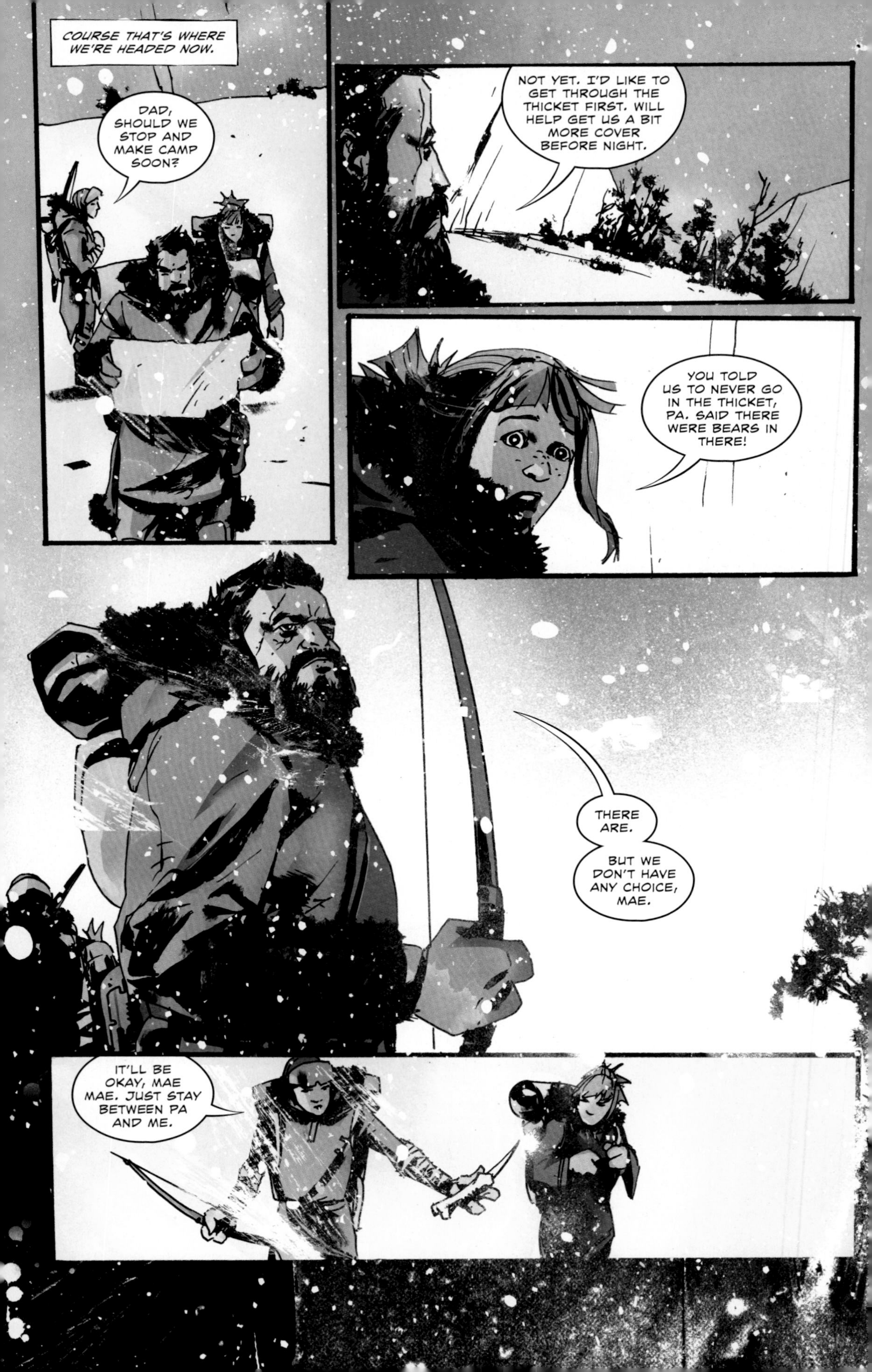
COURSE THAT'S WHERE WE'RE HEADED NOW.
DAD, SHOULD WE STOP AND MAKE CAMP SOON?
NOT YET. I'D LIKE TO GET THROUGH THE THICKET FIRST. WILL HELP GET US A BIT MORE COVER BEFORE NIGHT.
YOU TOLD US TO NEVER GO IN THE THICKET, PA. SAID THERE WERE BEARS IN THERE!
THERE ARE.
BUT WE DON'T HAVE ANY CHOICE, MAE.
IT'LL BE OKAY, MAE MAE. JUST STAY BETWEEN PA AND ME.

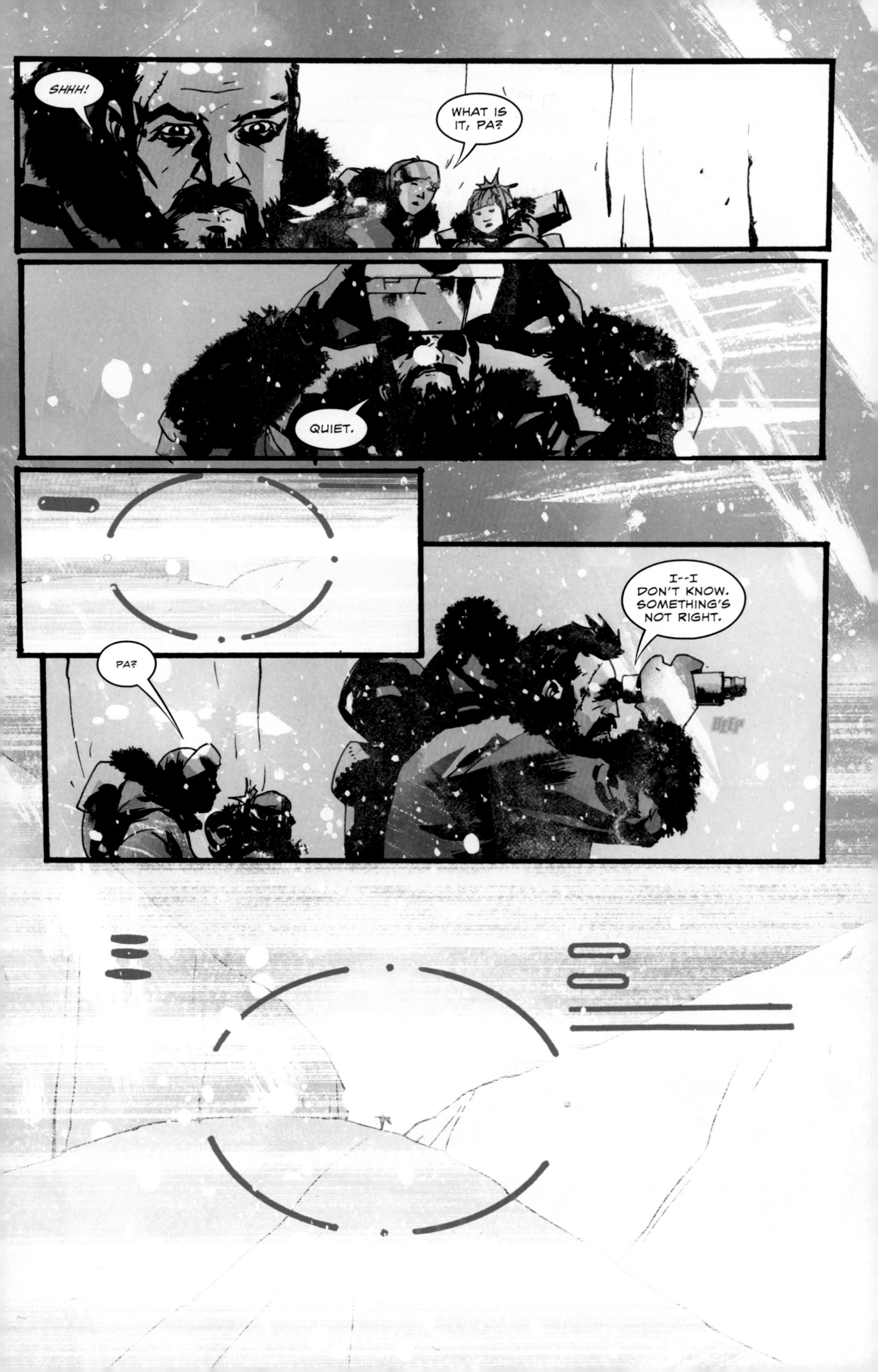
SHHH!
WHAT IS IT, PA?
QUIET.
PA?
I--I DON'T KNOW. SOMETHING'S NOT RIGHT.
BEEP

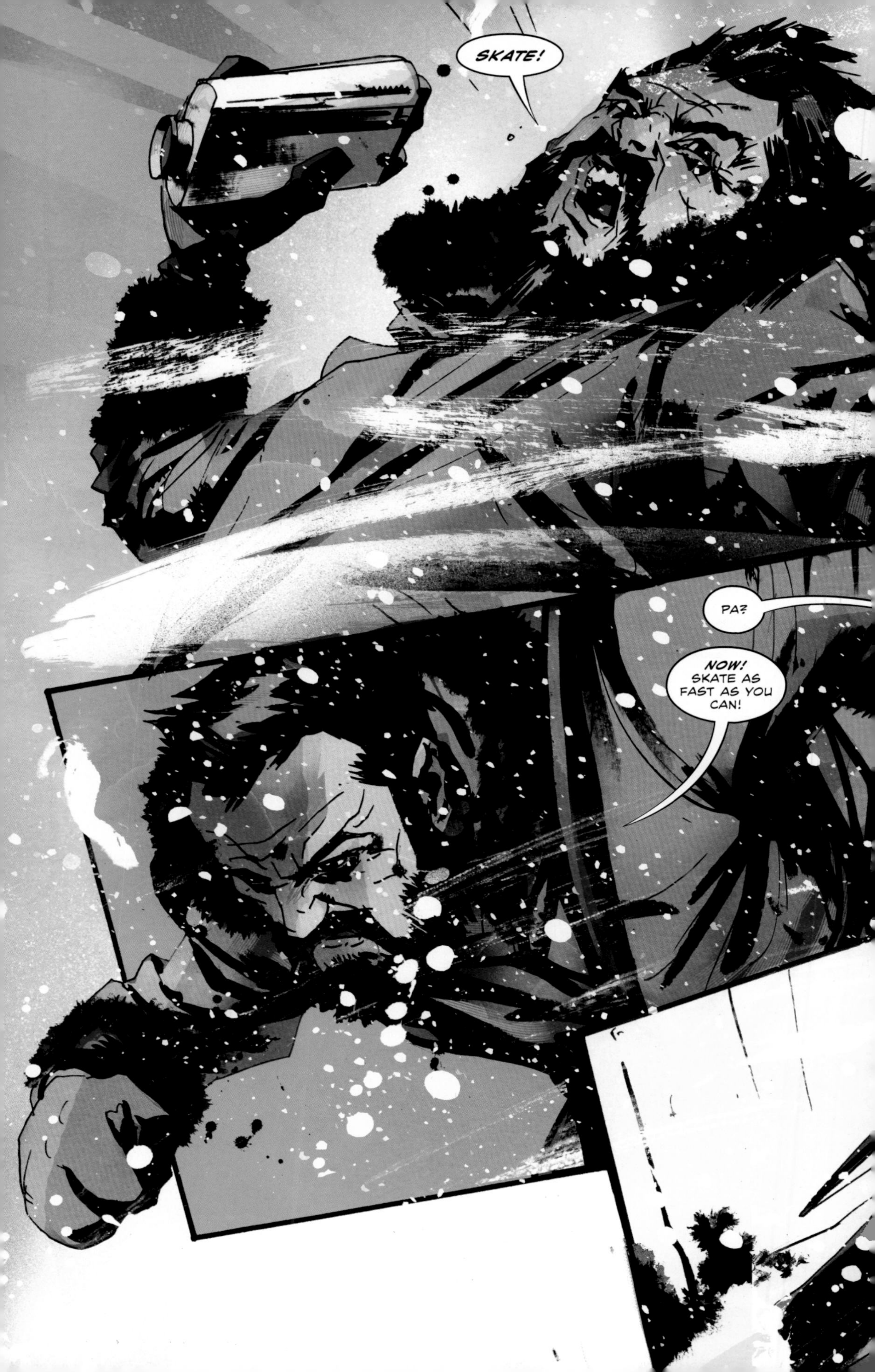
SKATE!
PA?
NOW! SKATE AS FAST AS YOU CAN!

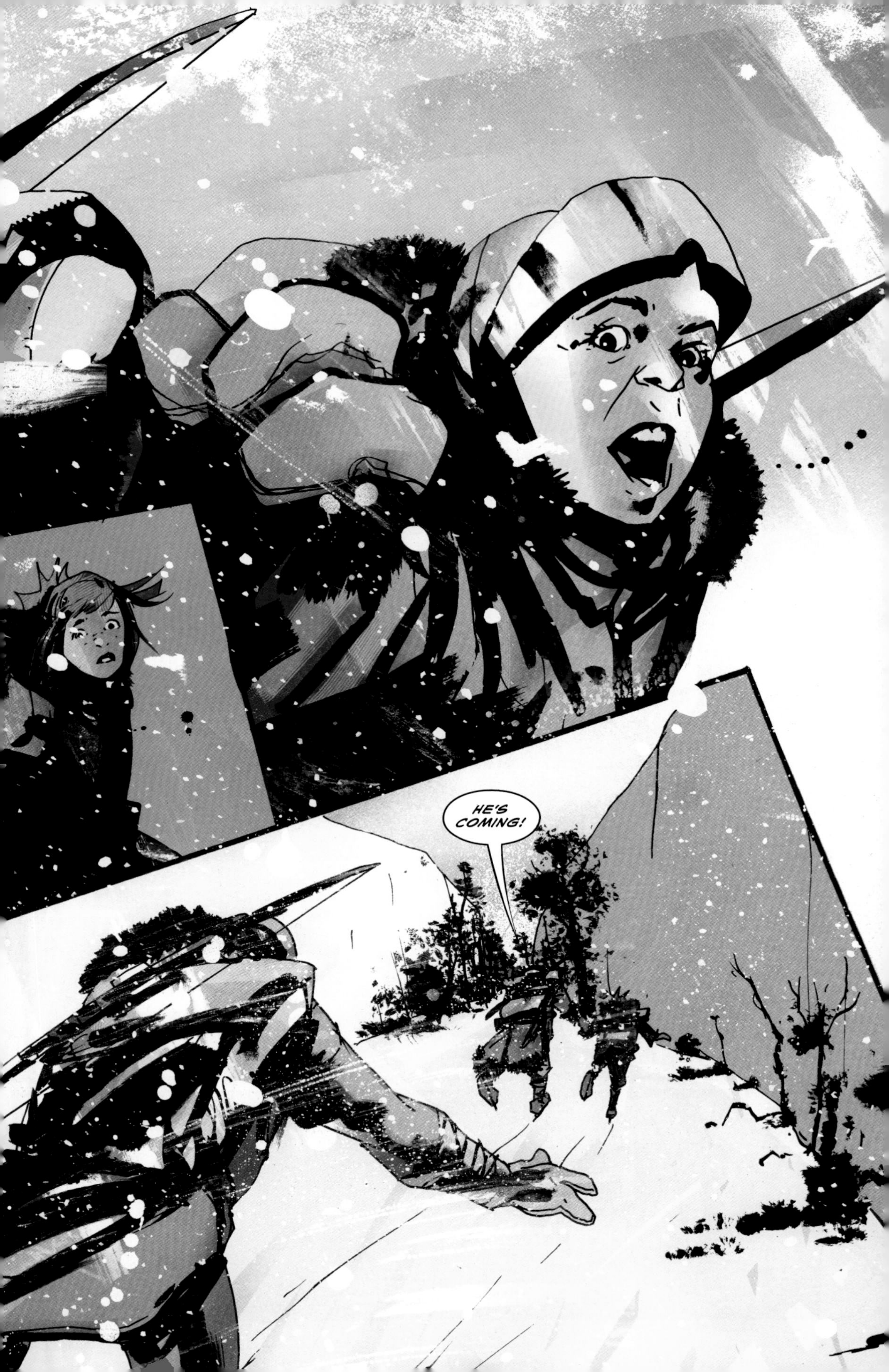
HE'S COMING!

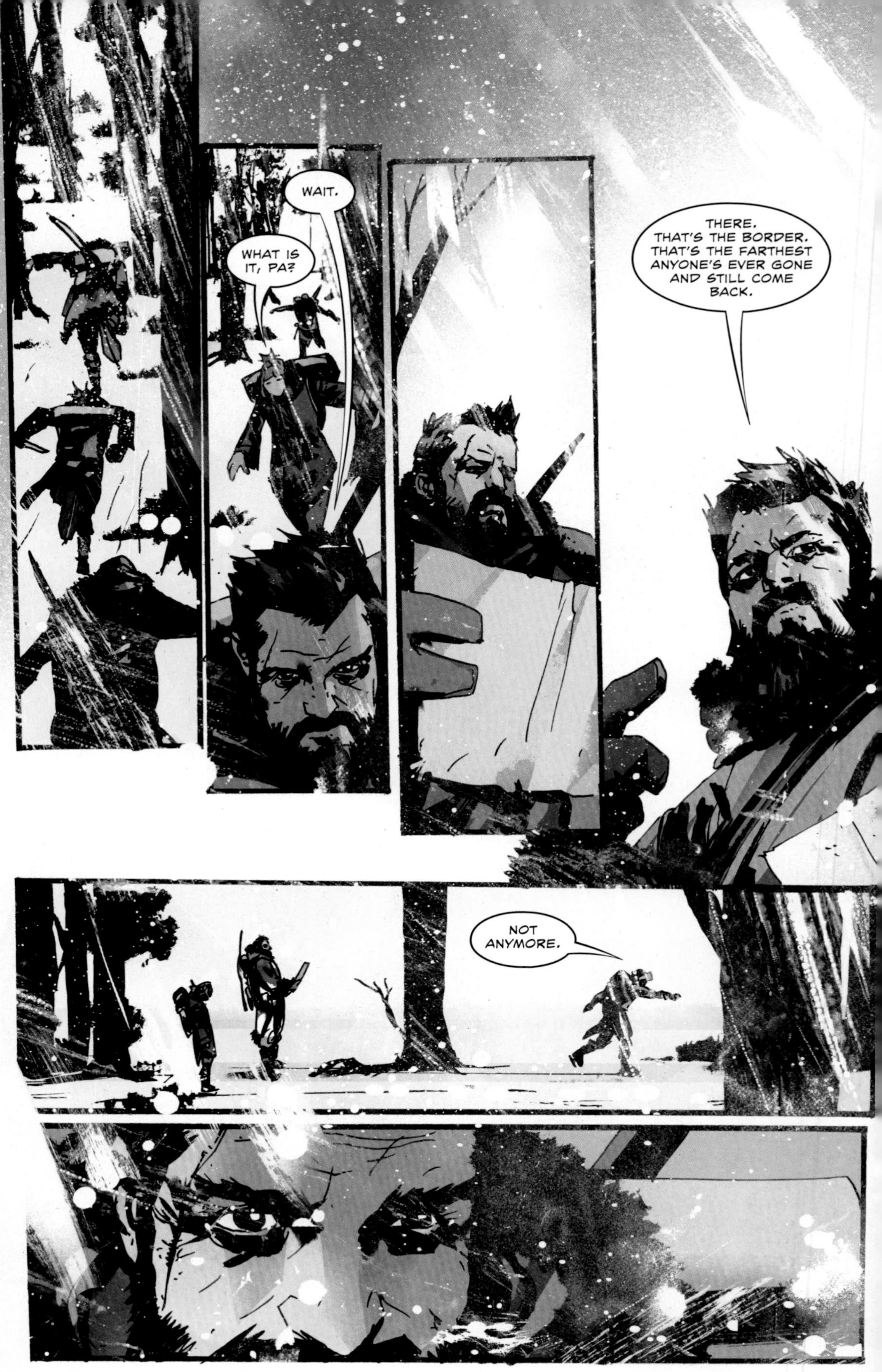
WHAT IS IT, PA?
WAIT.
THERE. THAT'S THE BORDER. THAT'S THE FARTHEST ANYONE'S EVER GONE AND STILL COME BACK.
NOT ANYMORE.

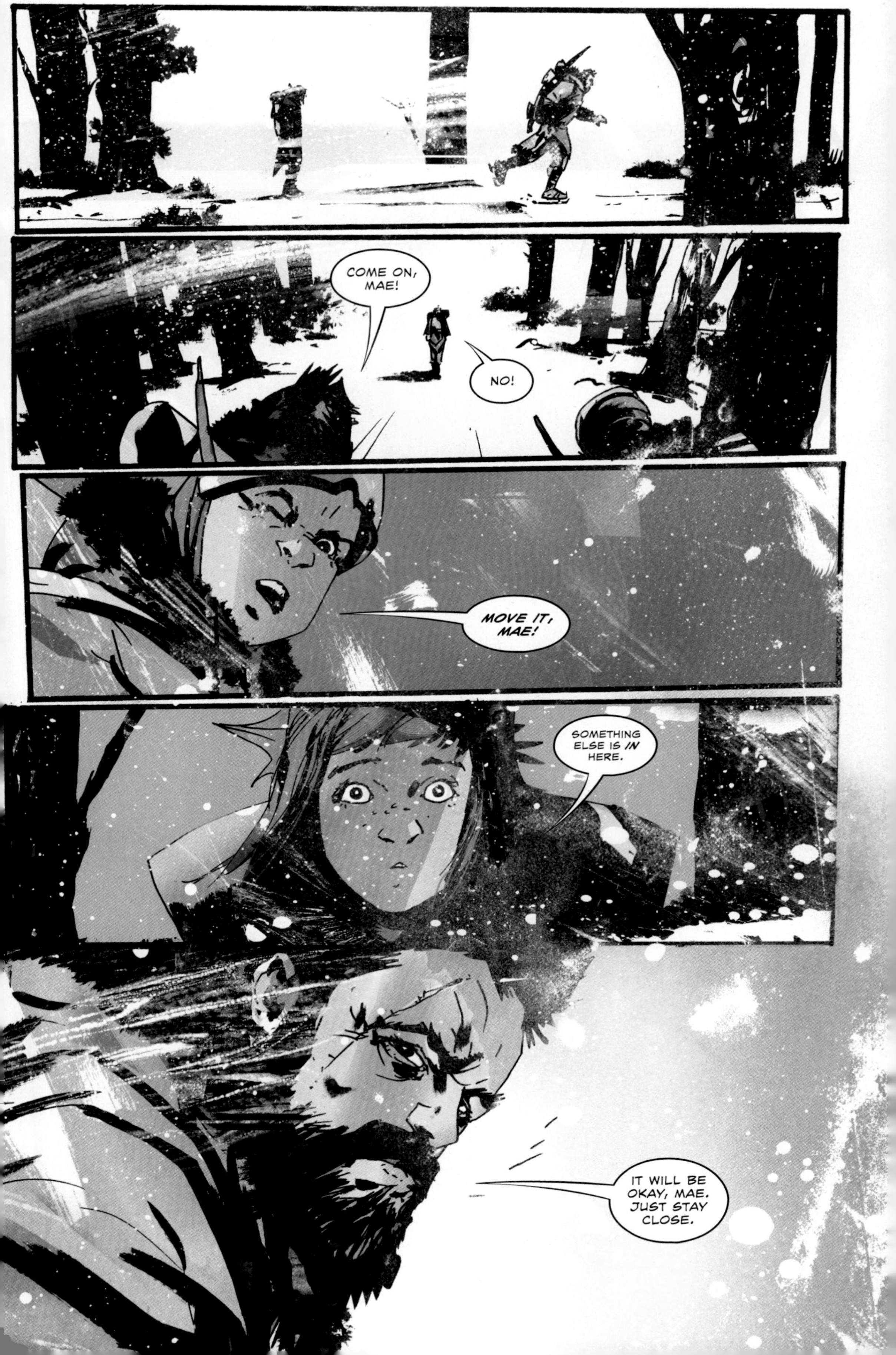
COME ON, MAE!
NO!
MOVE IT, MAE!
SOMETHING ELSE IS IN HERE.
IT WILL BE OKAY, MAE. JUST STAY CLOSE.

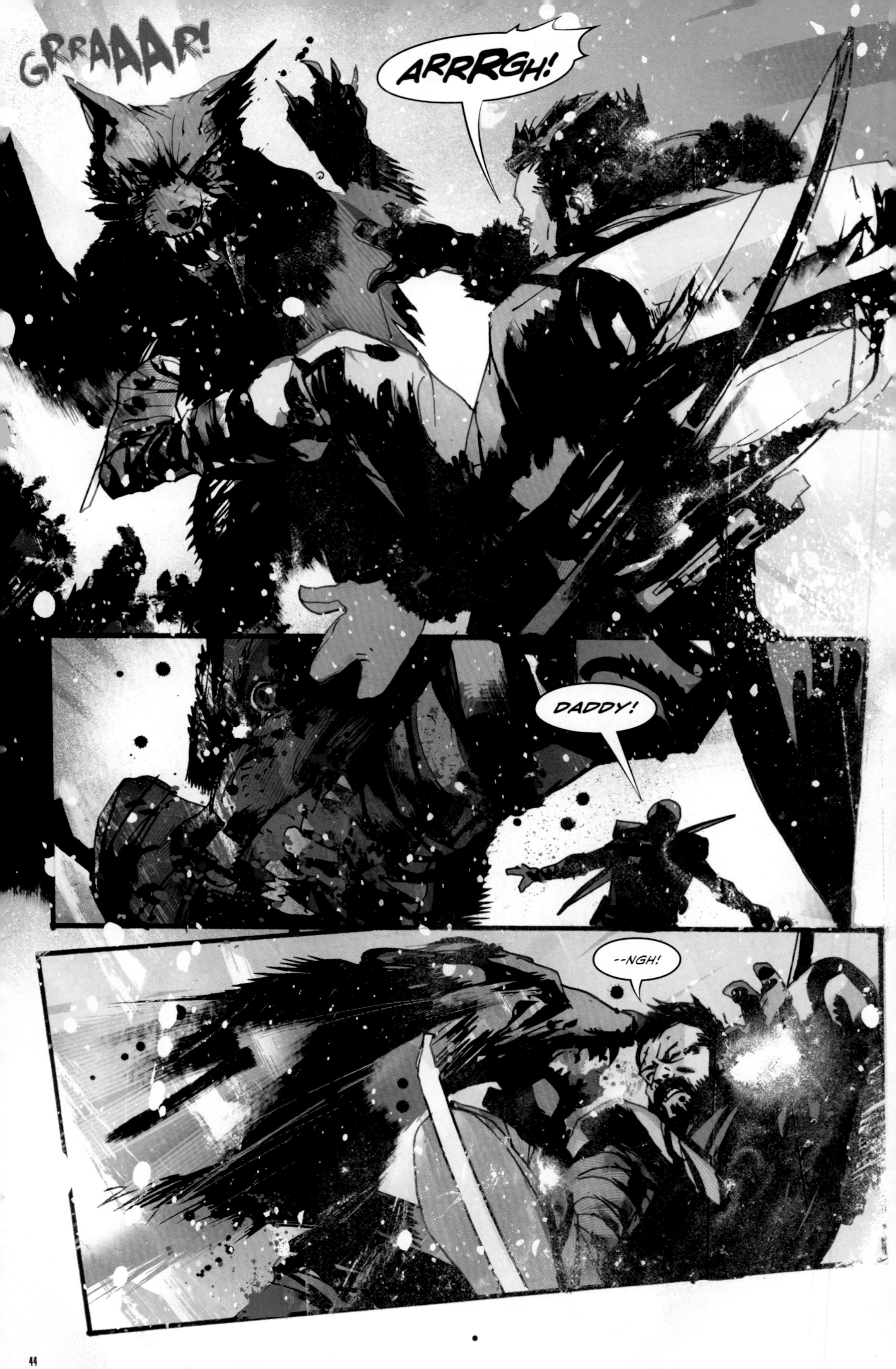
GRRAAAR!
ARRRGH!
DADDY!
--NGH!

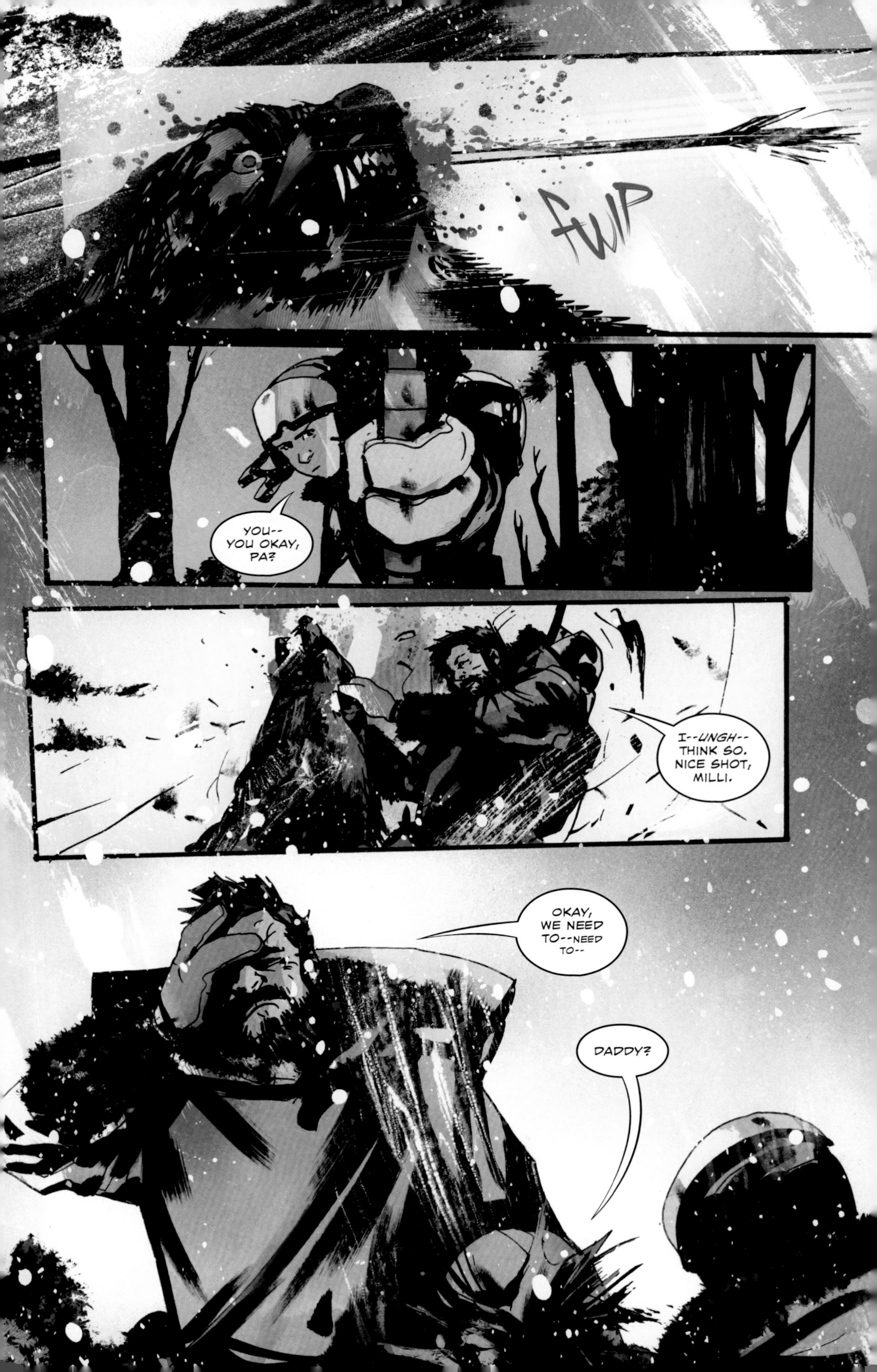
FWIP
YOU-- YOU OKAY, PA?
I--UNGH-- THINK SO. NICE SHOT, MILLI.
OKAY, WE NEED TO--NEED TO--
DADDY?

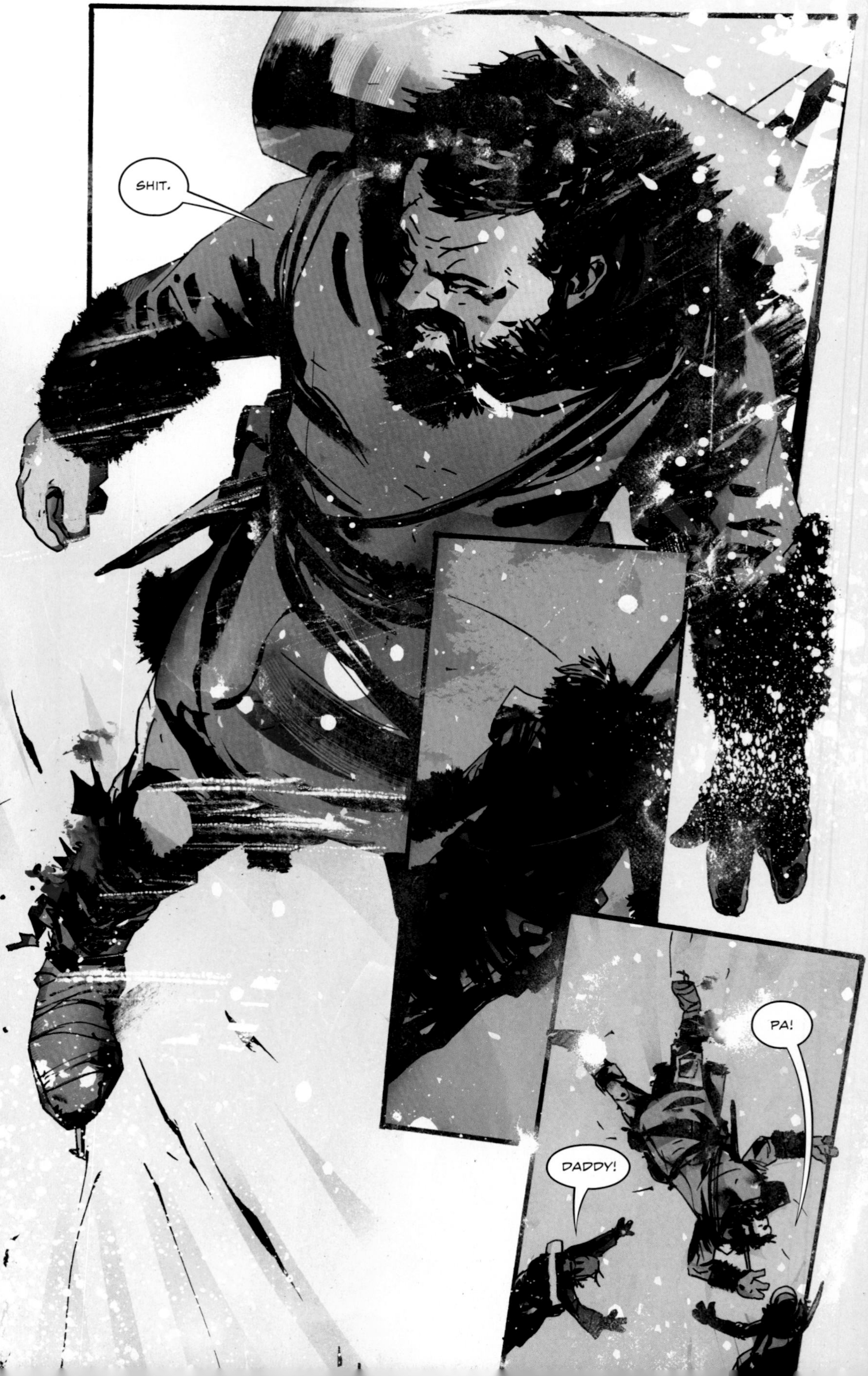
SHIT.
PA!
DADDY!

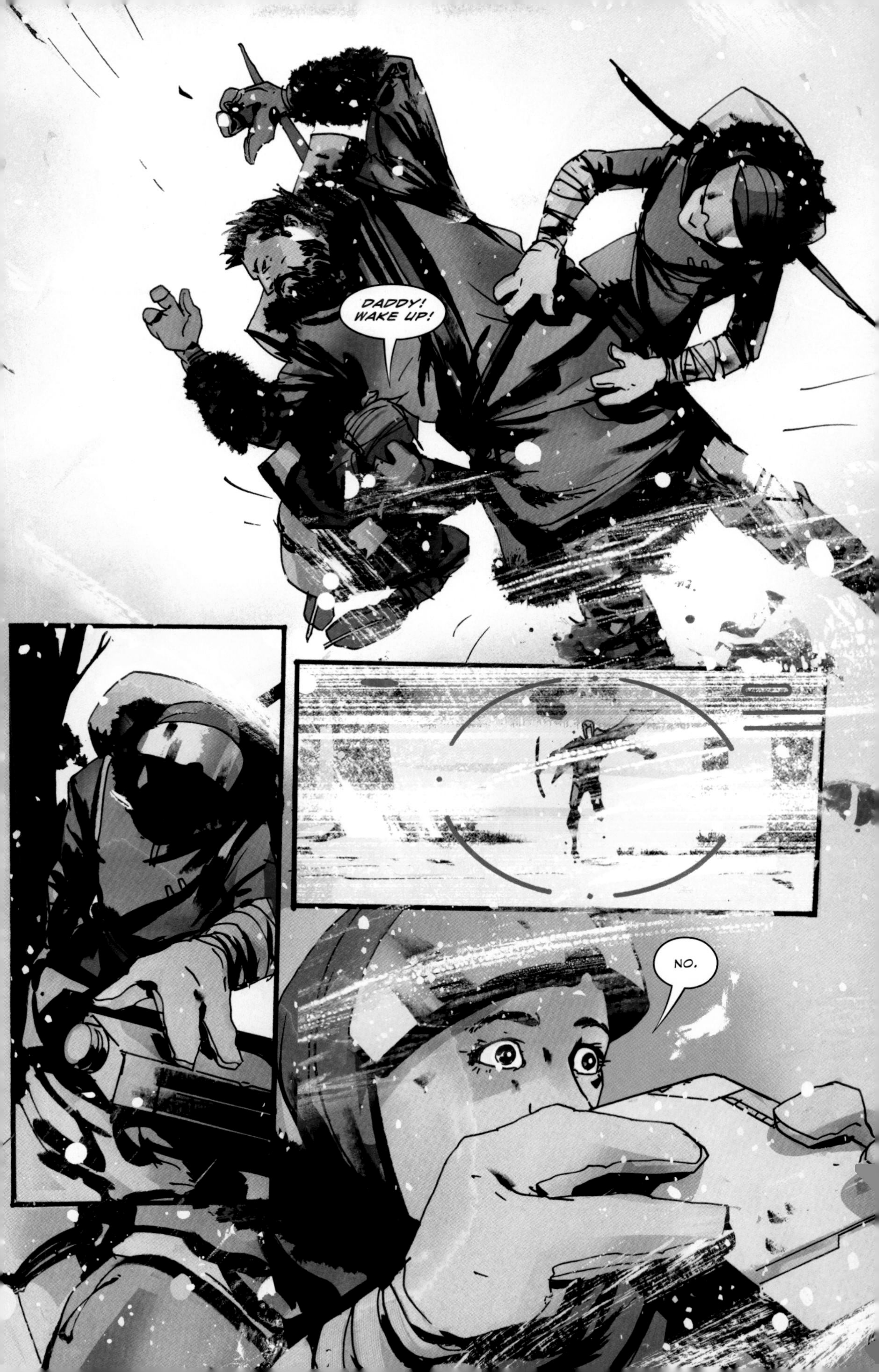
DADDY! WAKE UP!
NO.

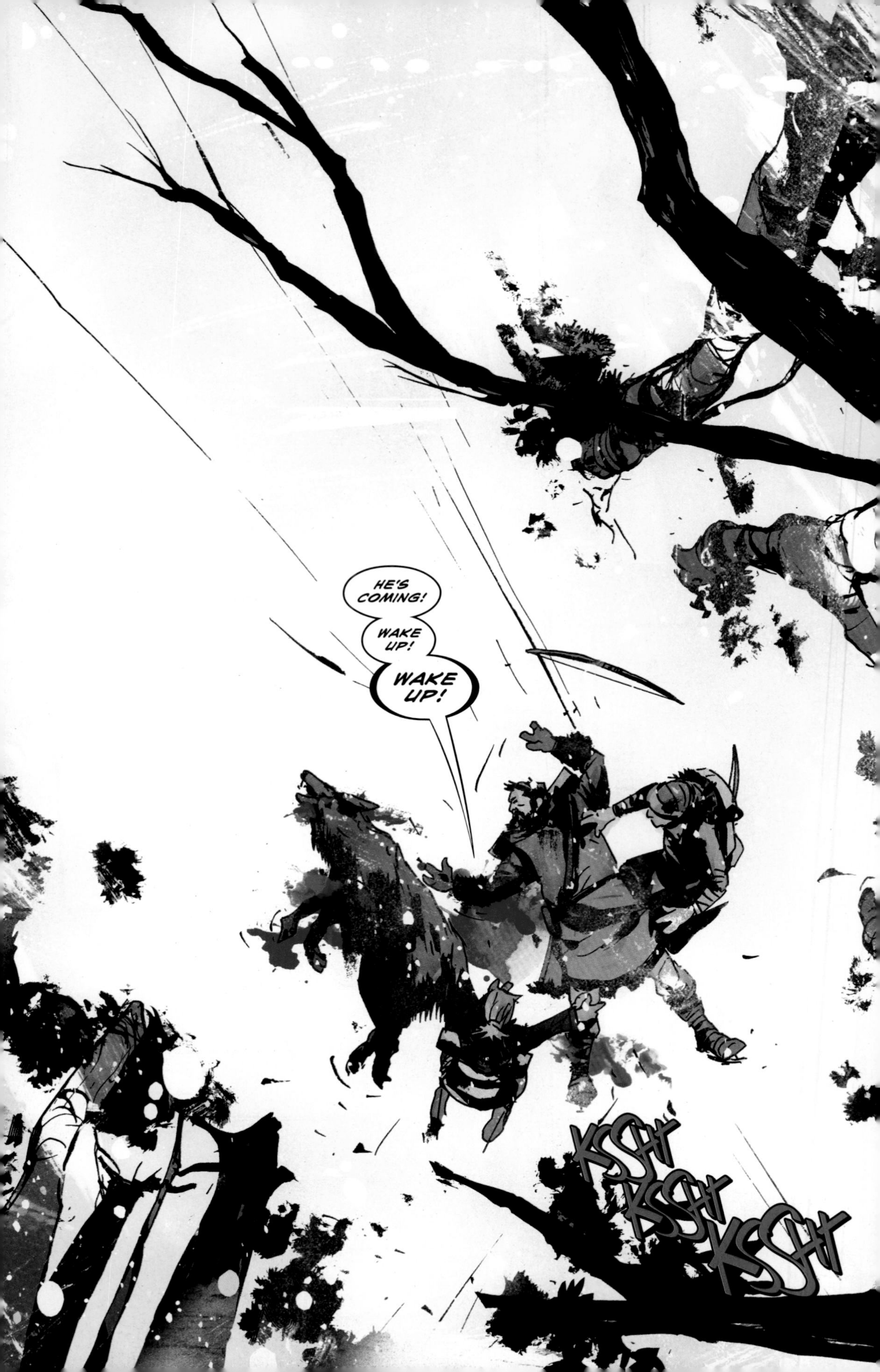
HE'S COMING!
WAKE UP!
WAKE UP!
KSSHT KSSHT KSSHT

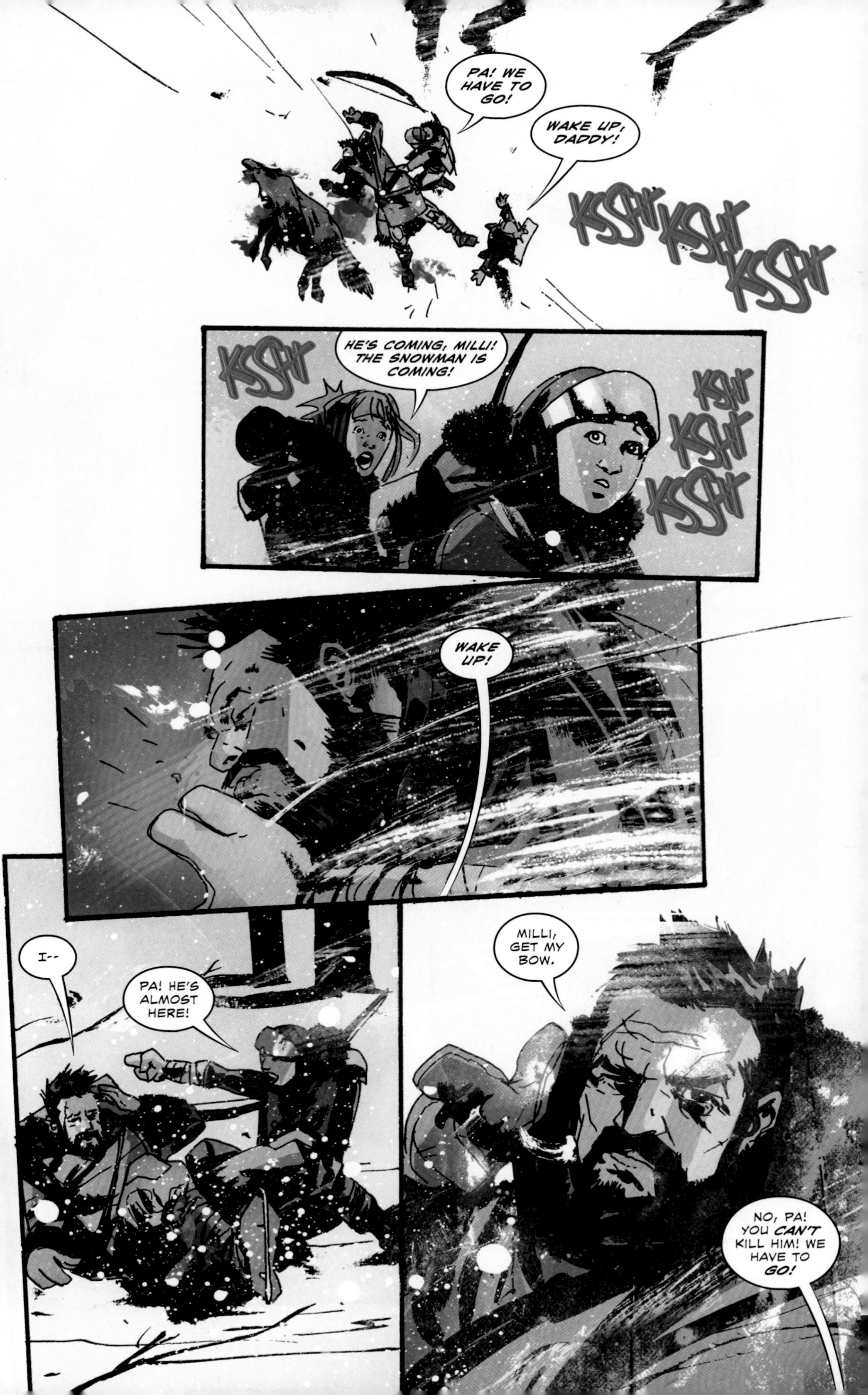
PA! WE HAVE TO GO!
WAKE UP, DADDY!
KSSHT KSHT KSSHT
KSSHT
HE'S COMING, MILLI! THE SNOWMAN IS COMING!
KSHT KSHT KSSHT
WAKE UP!
I--
PA! HE'S ALMOST HERE!
MILLI, GET MY BOW.
NO, PA! YOU CAN'T KILL HIM! WE HAVE TO GO!

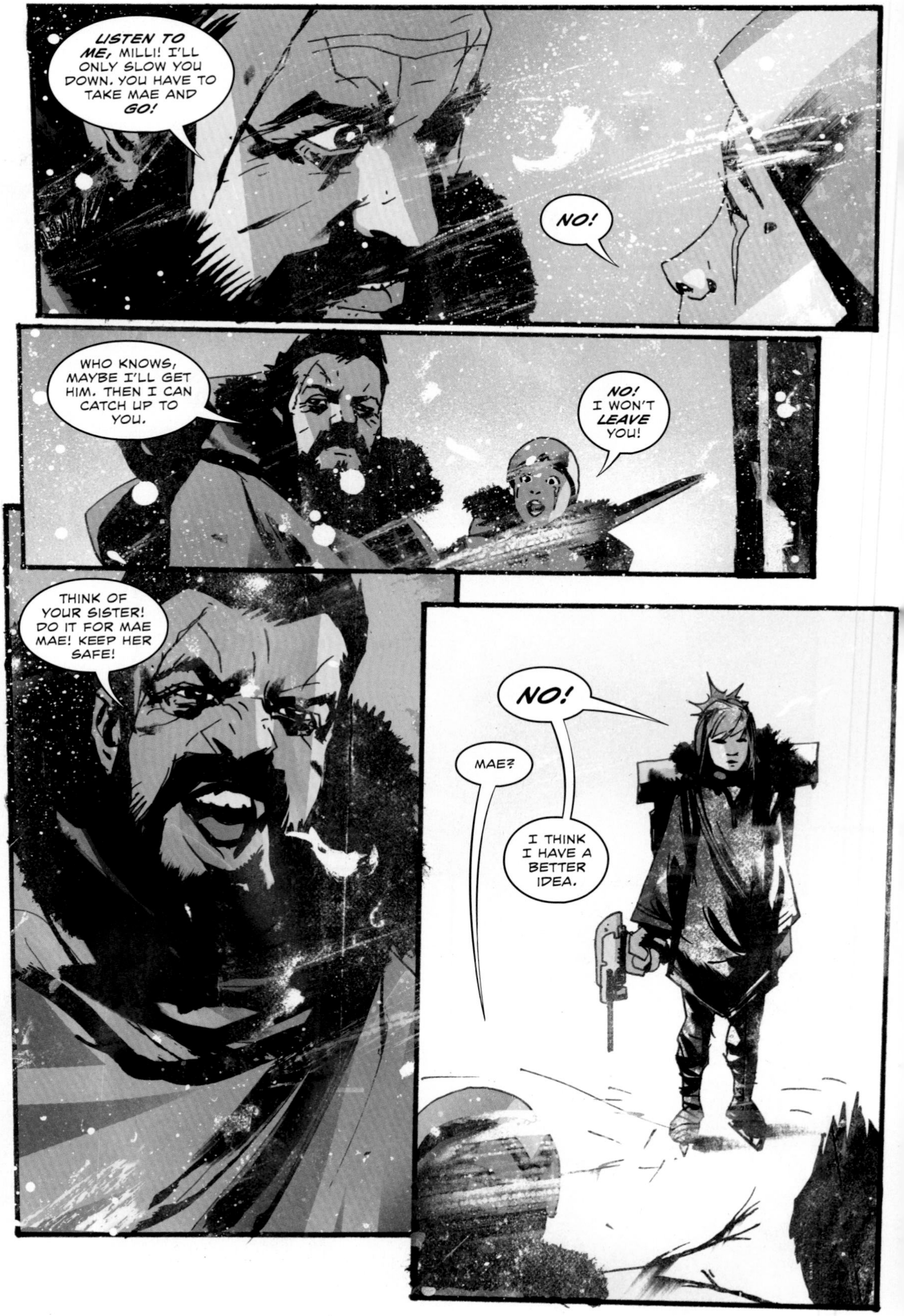
LISTEN TO ME, MILLI! I'LL ONLY SLOW YOU DOWN. YOU HAVE TO TAKE MAE AND GO!
NO!
WHO KNOWS, MAYBE I'LL GET HIM. THEN I CAN CATCH UP TO YOU.
NO! I WON'T LEAVE YOU!
THINK OF YOUR SISTER! DO IT FOR MAE MAE! KEEP HER SAFE!
NO!
MAE?
I THINK I HAVE A BETTER IDEA.

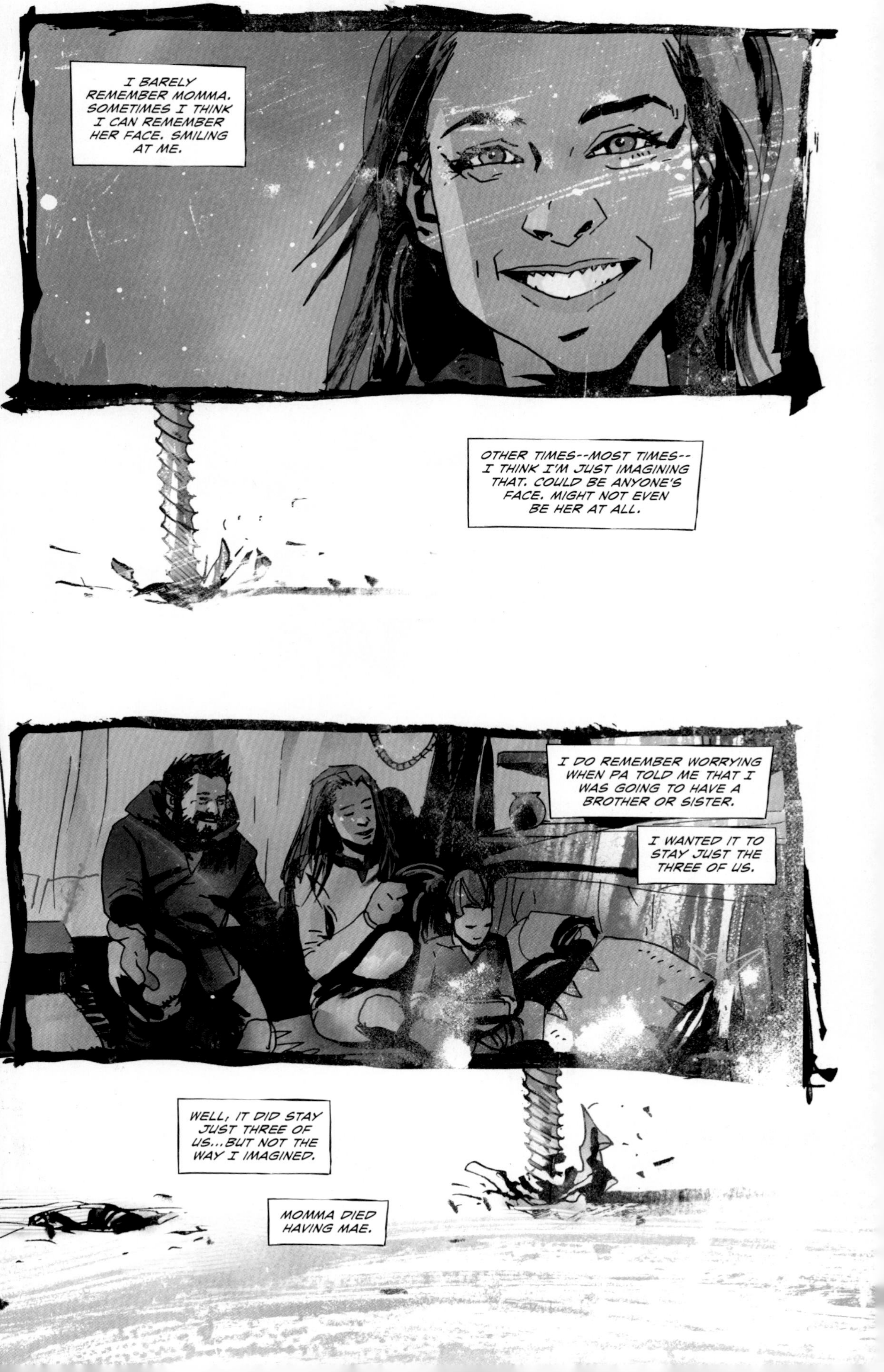
I BARELY REMEMBER MOMMA. SOMETIMES I THINK I CAN REMEMBER HER FACE. SMILING AT ME.
OTHER TIMES--MOST TIMES--I THINK I'M JUST IMAGINING THAT. COULD BE ANYONE'S FACE. MIGHT NOT EVEN BE HER AT ALL.
I DO REMEMBER WORRYING WHEN PA TOLD ME THAT I WAS GOING TO HAVE A BROTHER OR SISTER.
I WANTED IT TO STAY JUST THE THREE OF US.
WELL, IT DID STAY JUST THREE OF US...BUT NOT THE WAY I IMAGINED.
MOMMA DIED HAVING MAE.

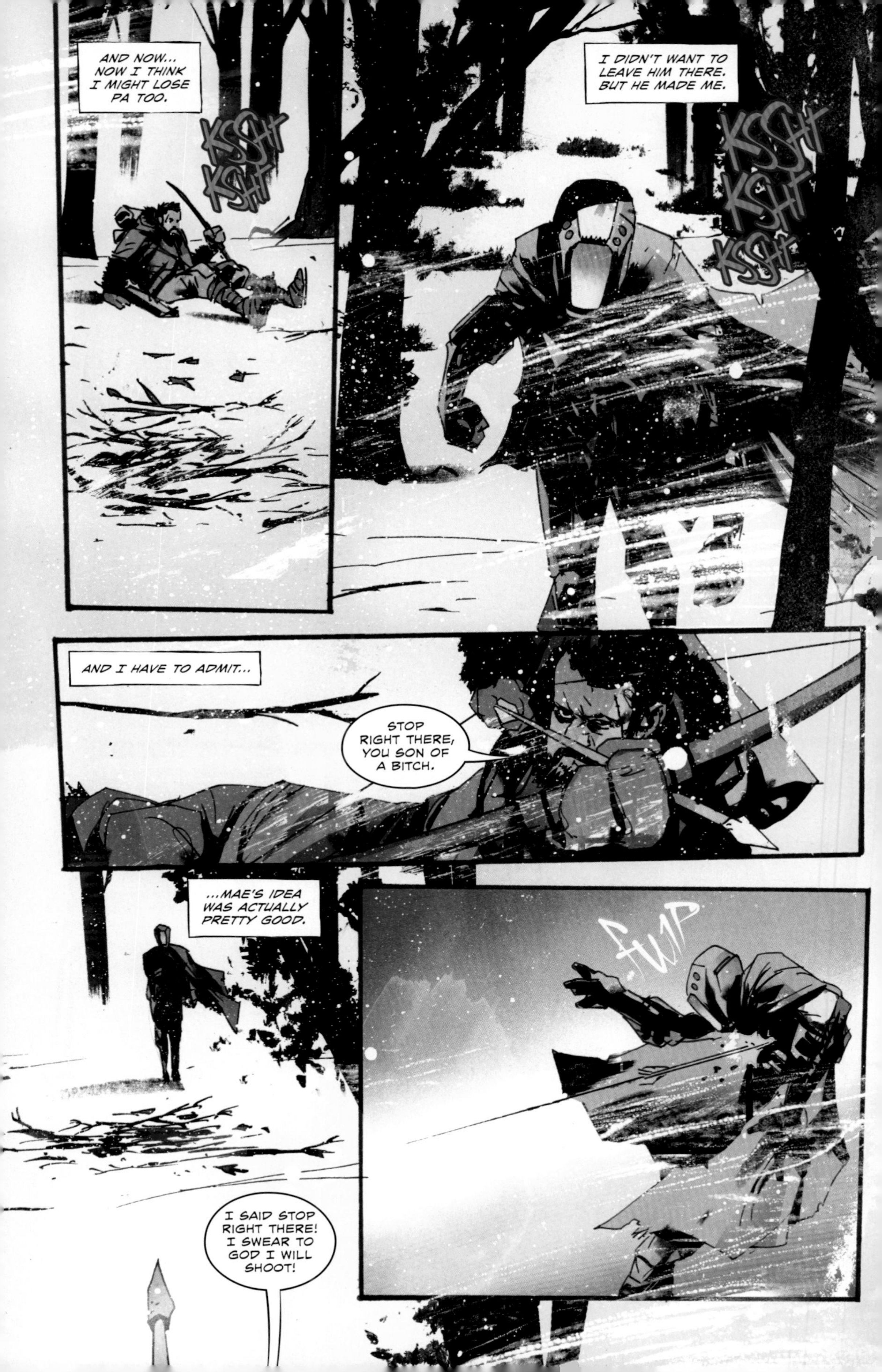
AND NOW... NOW I THINK I MIGHT LOSE PA TOO.
KSSHT KSHT
I DIDN'T WANT TO LEAVE HIM THERE. BUT HE MADE ME.
KSSHT KSHT KSSHT
AND I HAVE TO ADMIT...
STOP RIGHT THERE, YOU SON OF A BITCH.
...MAE'S IDEA WAS ACTUALLY PRETTY GOOD.
FWIP
I SAID STOP RIGHT THERE! I SWEAR TO GOD I WILL SHOOT!

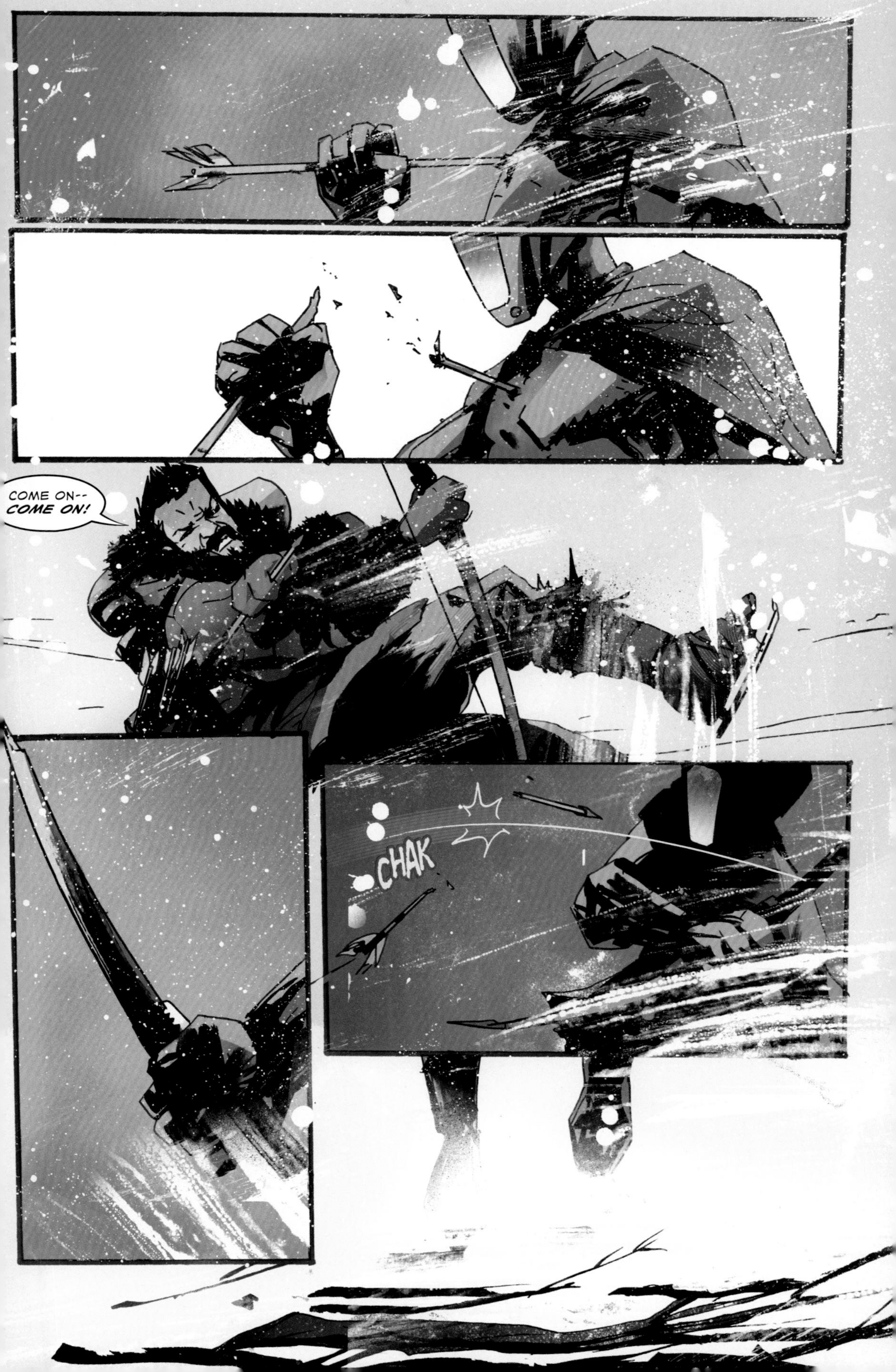
COME ON--
COME ON!
CHAK

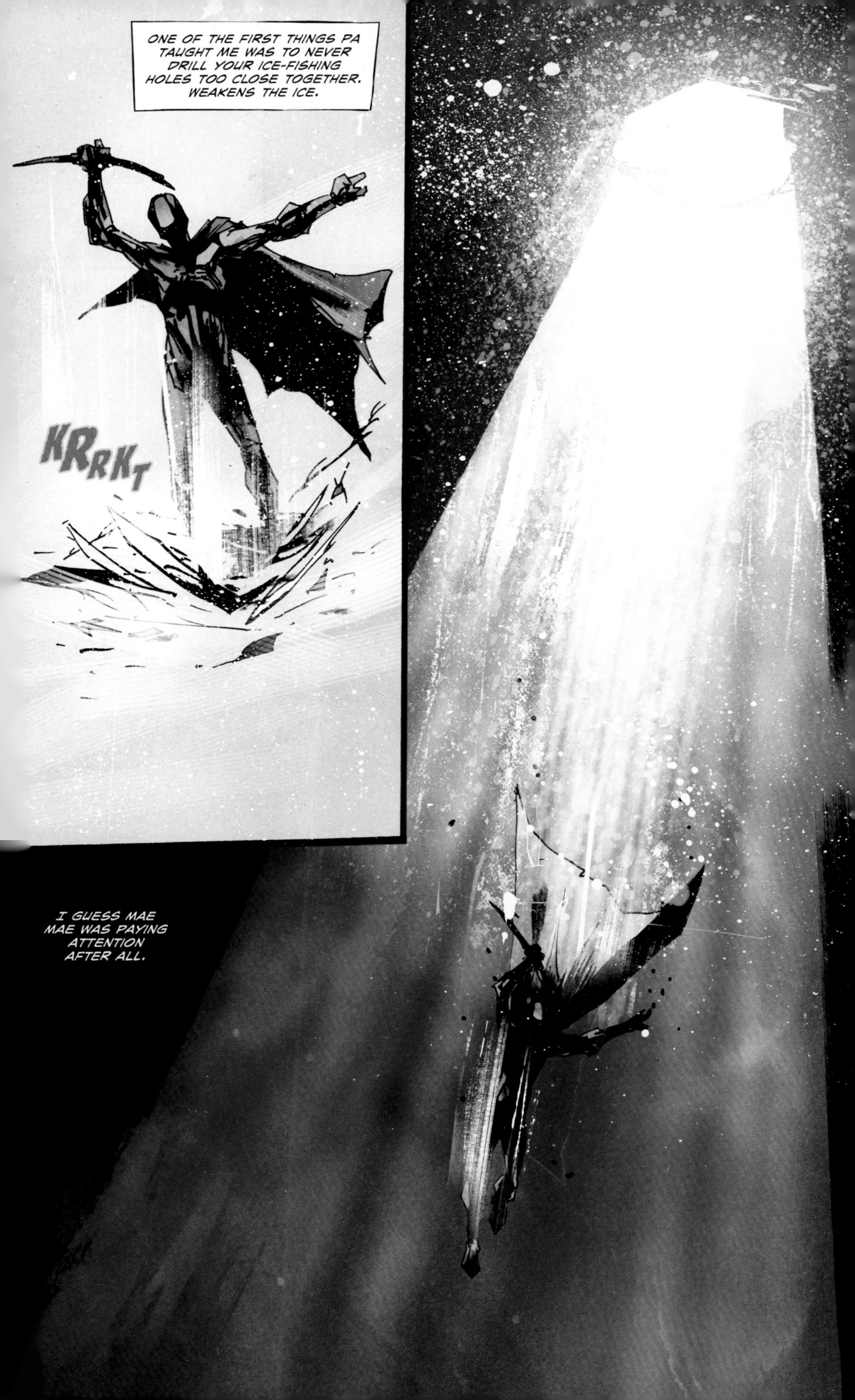
ONE OF THE FIRST THINGS PA TAUGHT ME WAS TO NEVER DRILL YOUR ICE-FISHING HOLES TOO CLOSE TOGETHER. WEAKENS THE ICE.
KRRKT
I GUESS MAE MAE WAS PAYING ATTENTION AFTER ALL.

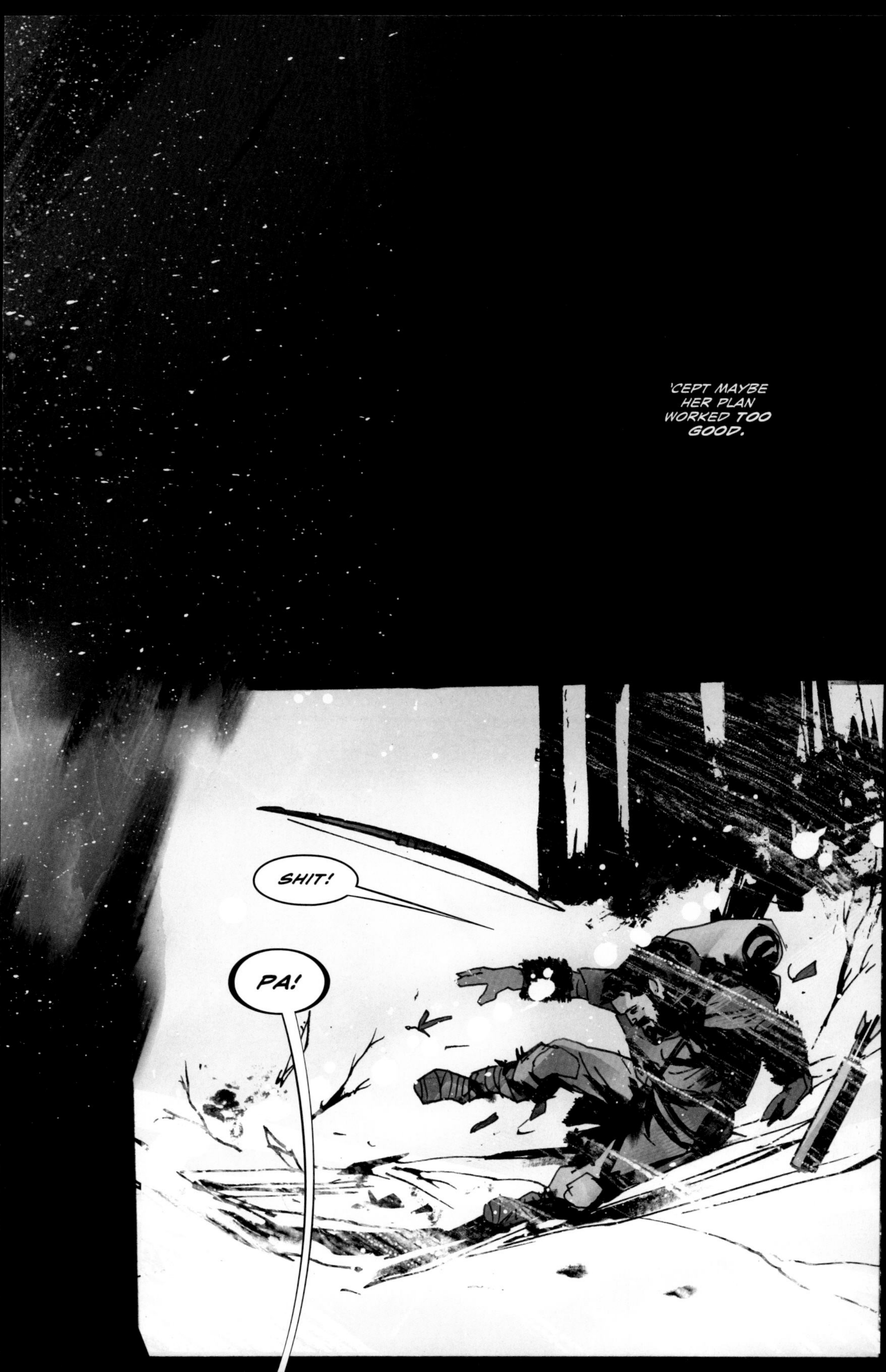
'CEPT MAYBE HER PLAN WORKED TOO GOOD.
SHIT!
PA!

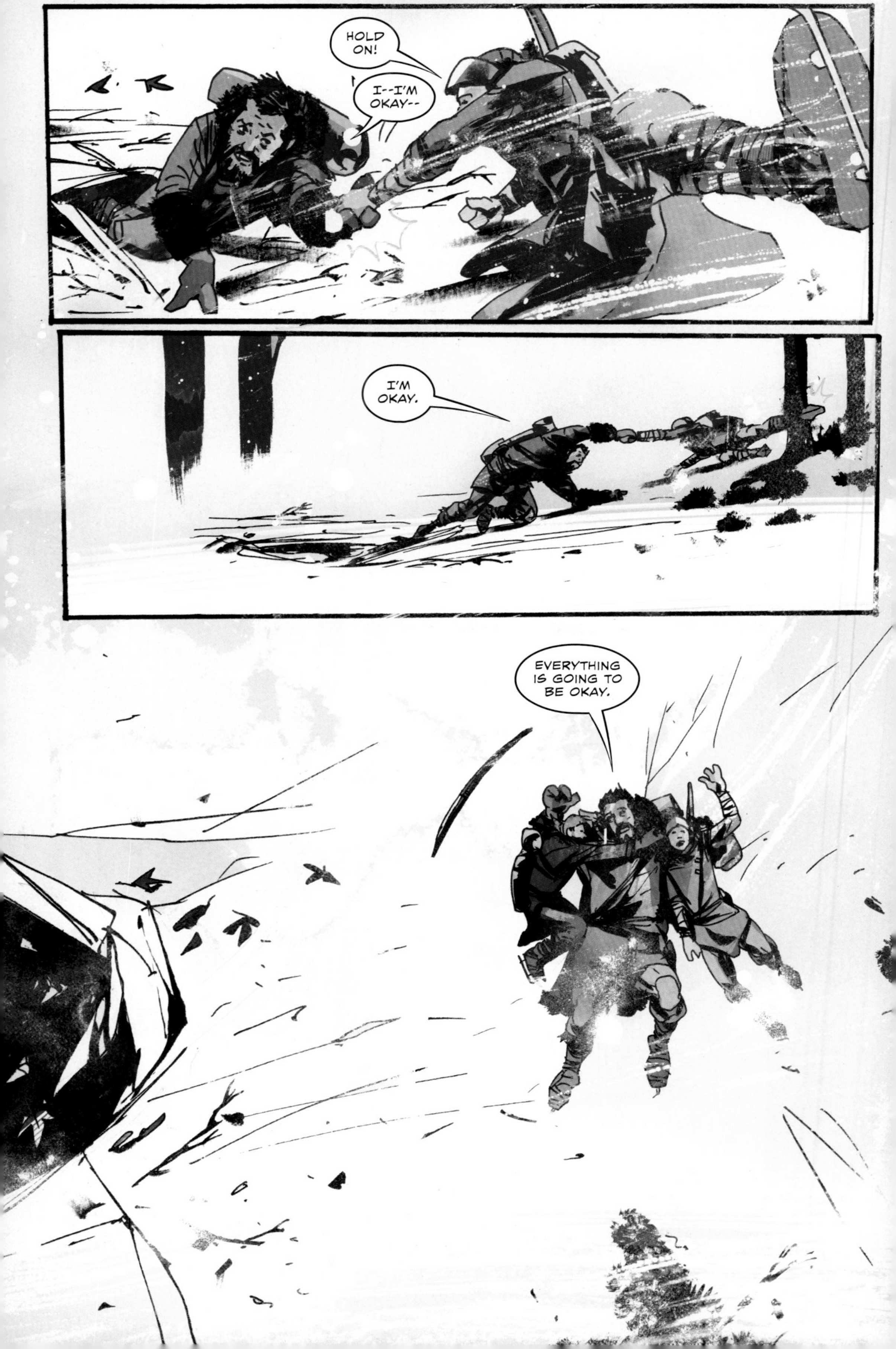
HOLD ON!
I--I'M OKAY--
I'M OKAY.
EVERYTHING IS GOING TO BE OKAY.

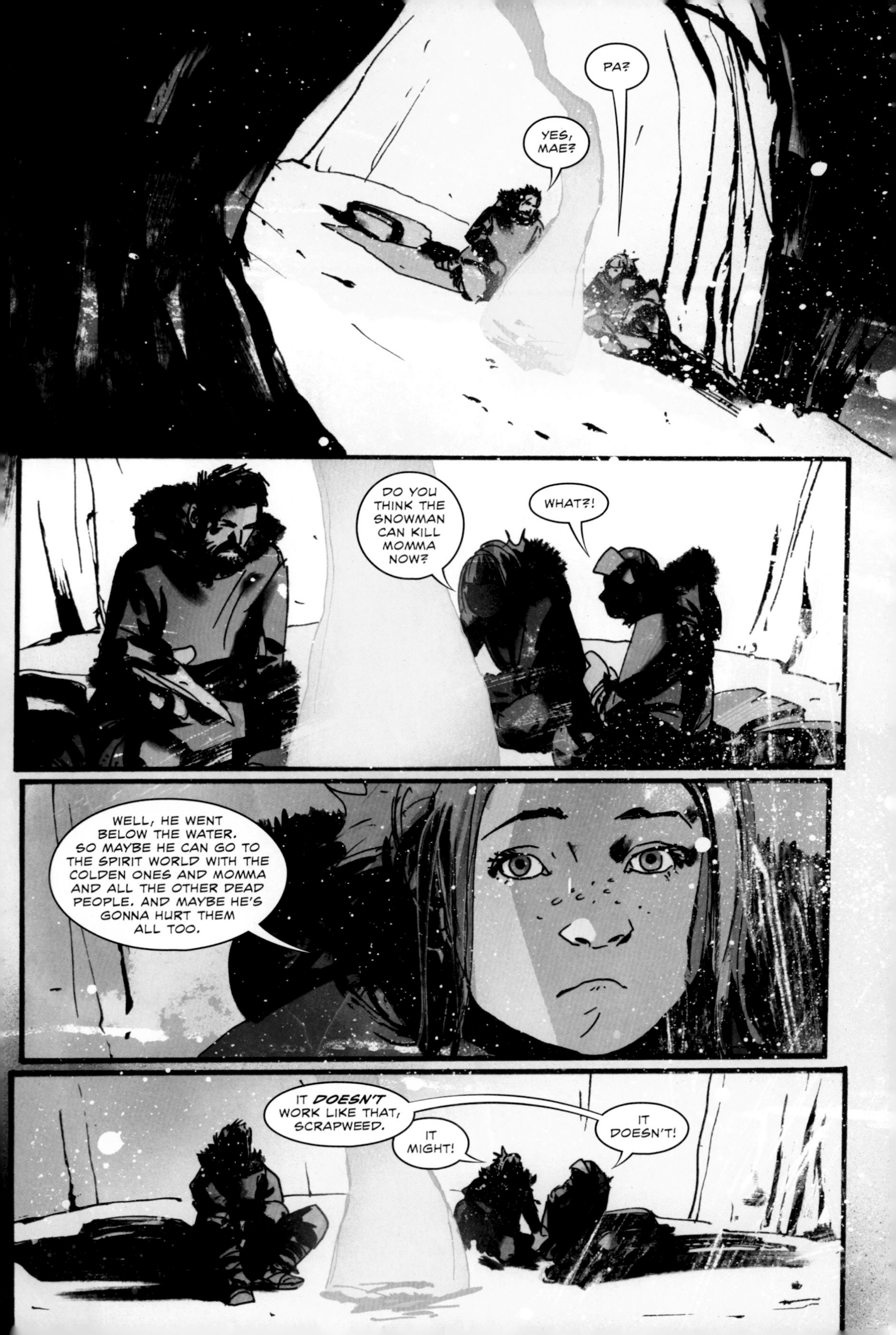
PA?
YES, MAE?
DO YOU THINK THE SNOWMAN CAN KILL MOMMA NOW?
WHAT?!
WELL, HE WENT BELOW THE WATER. SO MAYBE HE CAN GO TO THE SPIRIT WORLD WITH THE GOLDEN ONES AND MOMMA AND ALL THE OTHER DEAD PEOPLE. AND MAYBE HE'S GONNA HURT THEM ALL TOO.
IT DOESN'T WORK LIKE THAT, SCRAPWEED.
IT MIGHT!
IT DOESN'T!

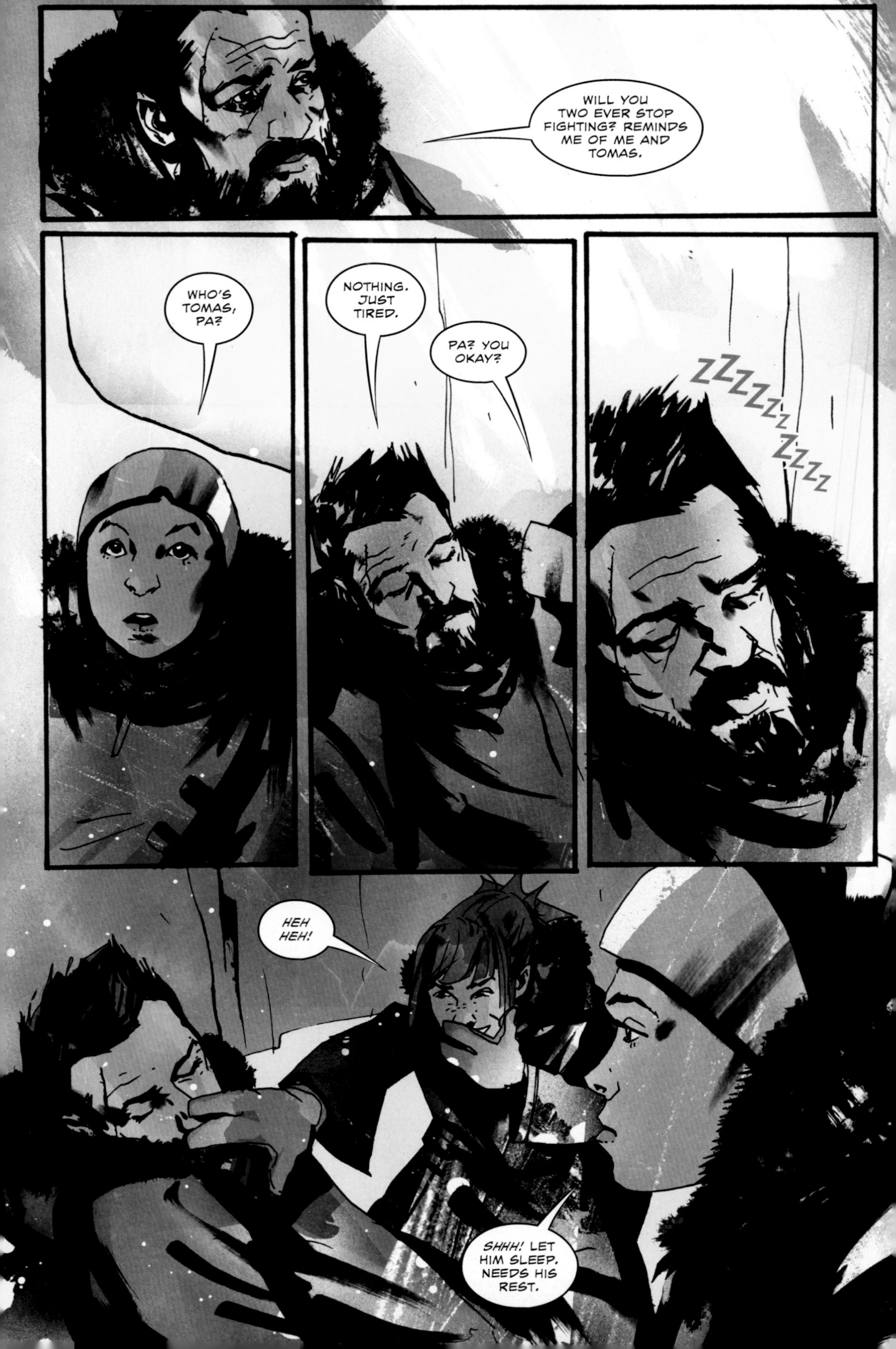
WILL YOU TWO EVER STOP FIGHTING? REMINDS ME OF ME AND TOMAS.
WHO'S TOMAS, PA?
NOTHING. JUST TIRED.
PA? YOU OKAY?
ZZZZZZ ZZZZ
HEH HEH!
SHHH! LET HIM SLEEP. NEEDS HIS REST.

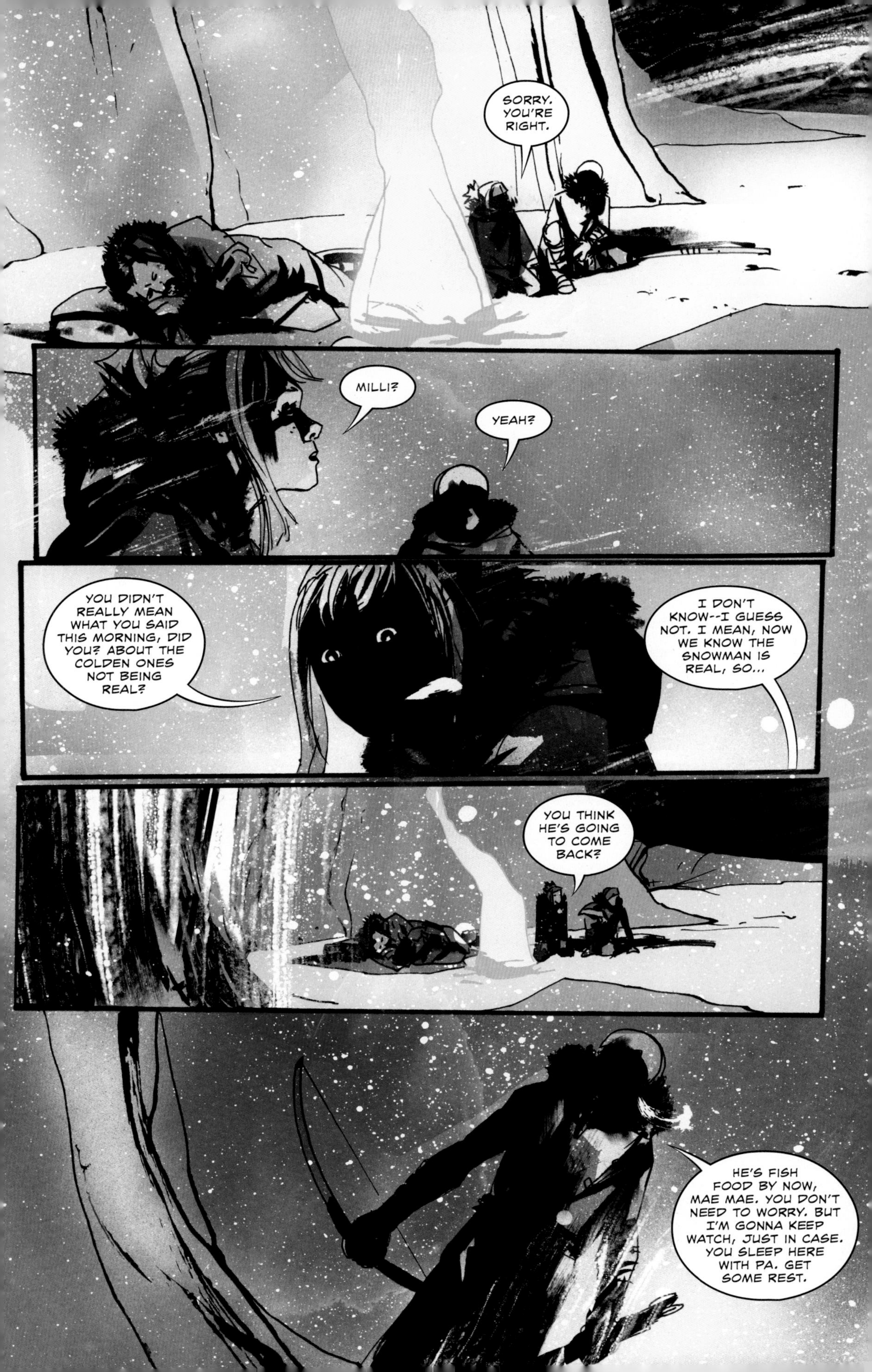
SORRY. YOU'RE RIGHT.
MILLI?
YEAH?
YOU DIDN'T REALLY MEAN WHAT YOU SAID THIS MORNING, DID YOU? ABOUT THE COLDEN ONES NOT BEING REAL?
I DON'T KNOW--I GUESS NOT. I MEAN, NOW WE KNOW THE SNOWMAN IS REAL, SO...
YOU THINK HE'S GOING TO COME BACK?
HE'S FISH FOOD BY NOW, MAE MAE. YOU DON'T NEED TO WORRY. BUT I'M GONNA KEEP WATCH, JUST IN CASE. YOU SLEEP HERE WITH PA. GET SOME REST.

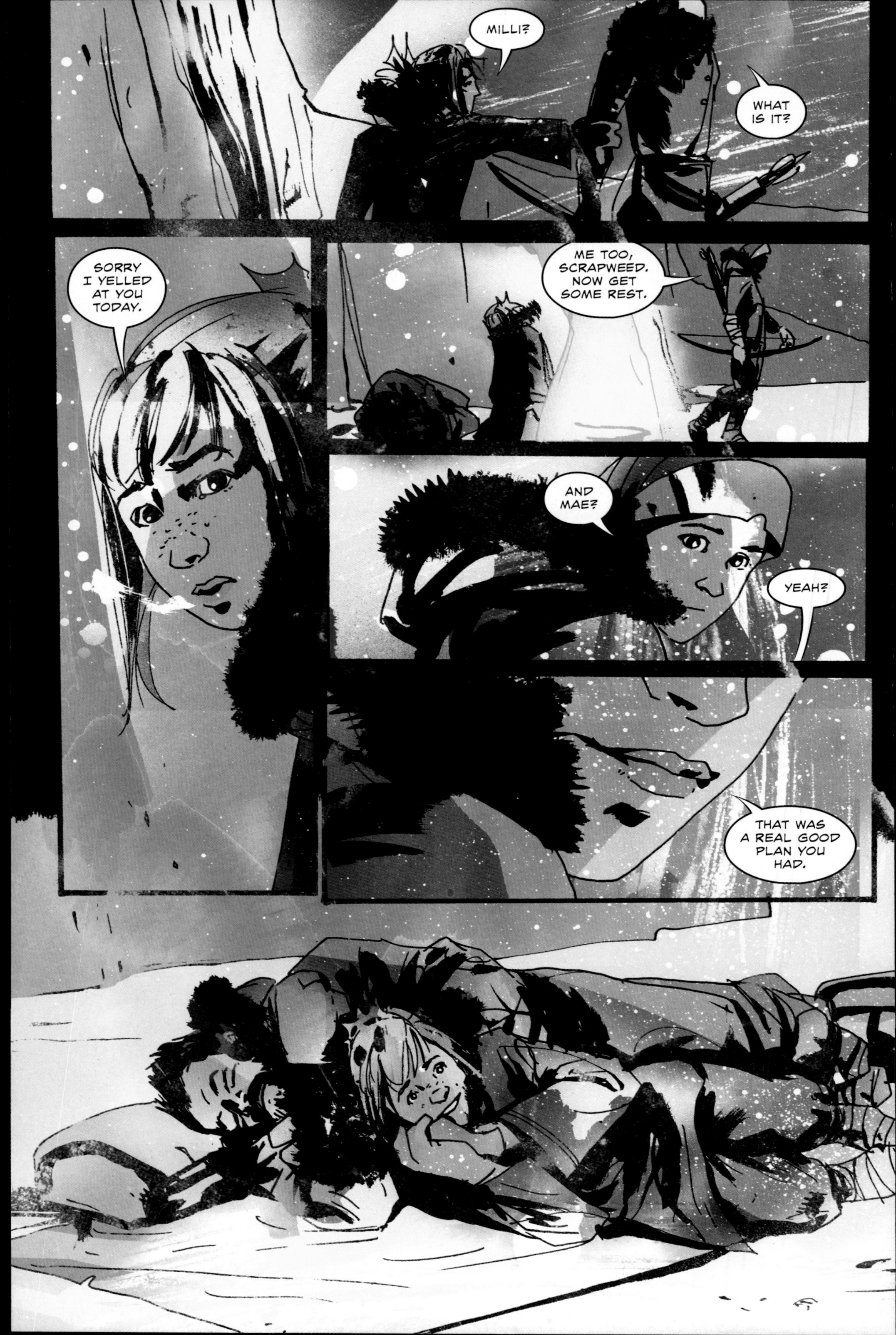
MILLI?
WHAT IS IT?
SORRY I YELLED AT YOU TODAY.
ME TOO, SCRAPWEED. NOW GET SOME REST.
AND MAE?
YEAH?
THAT WAS A REAL GOOD PLAN YOU HAD.

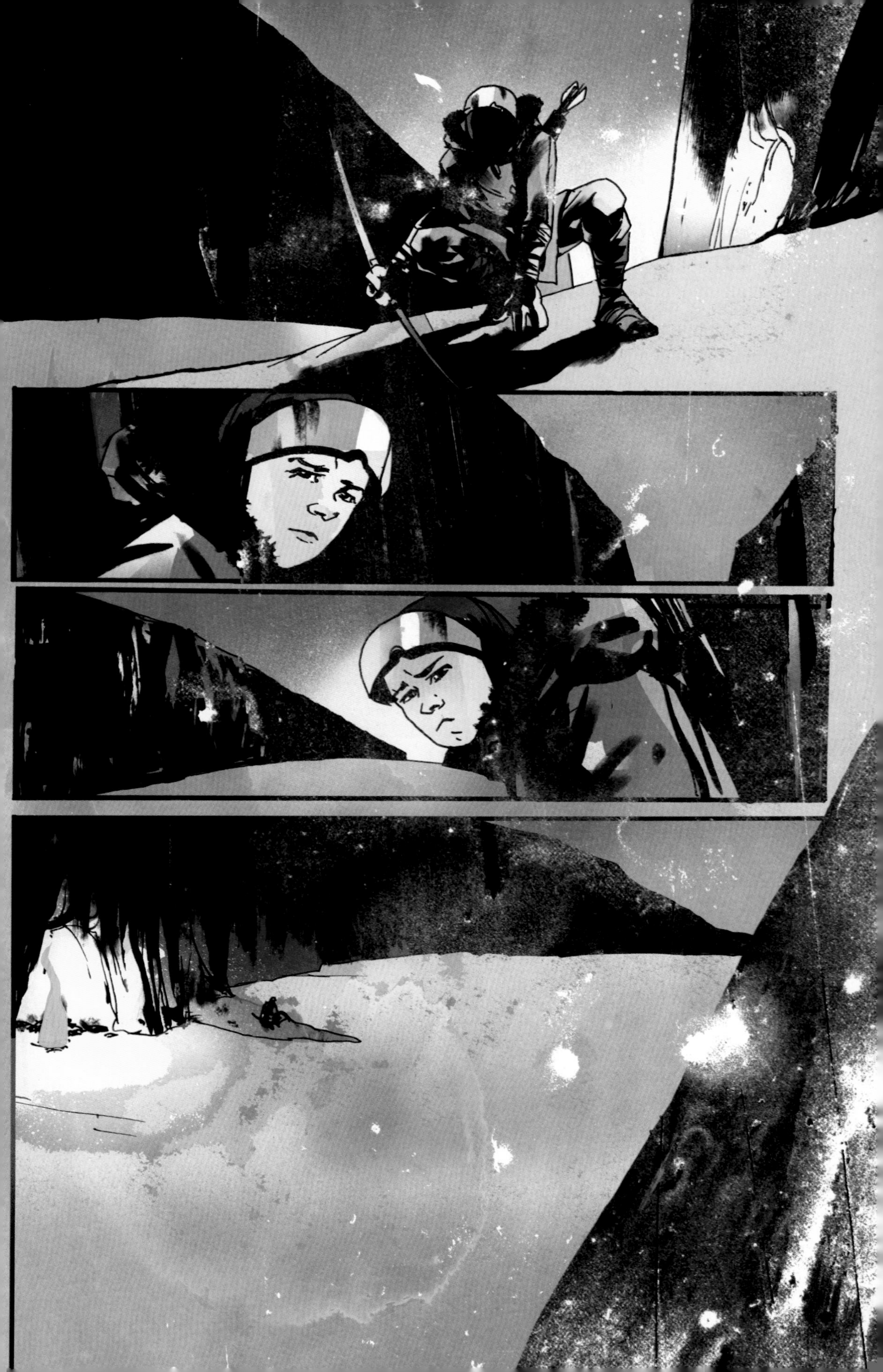

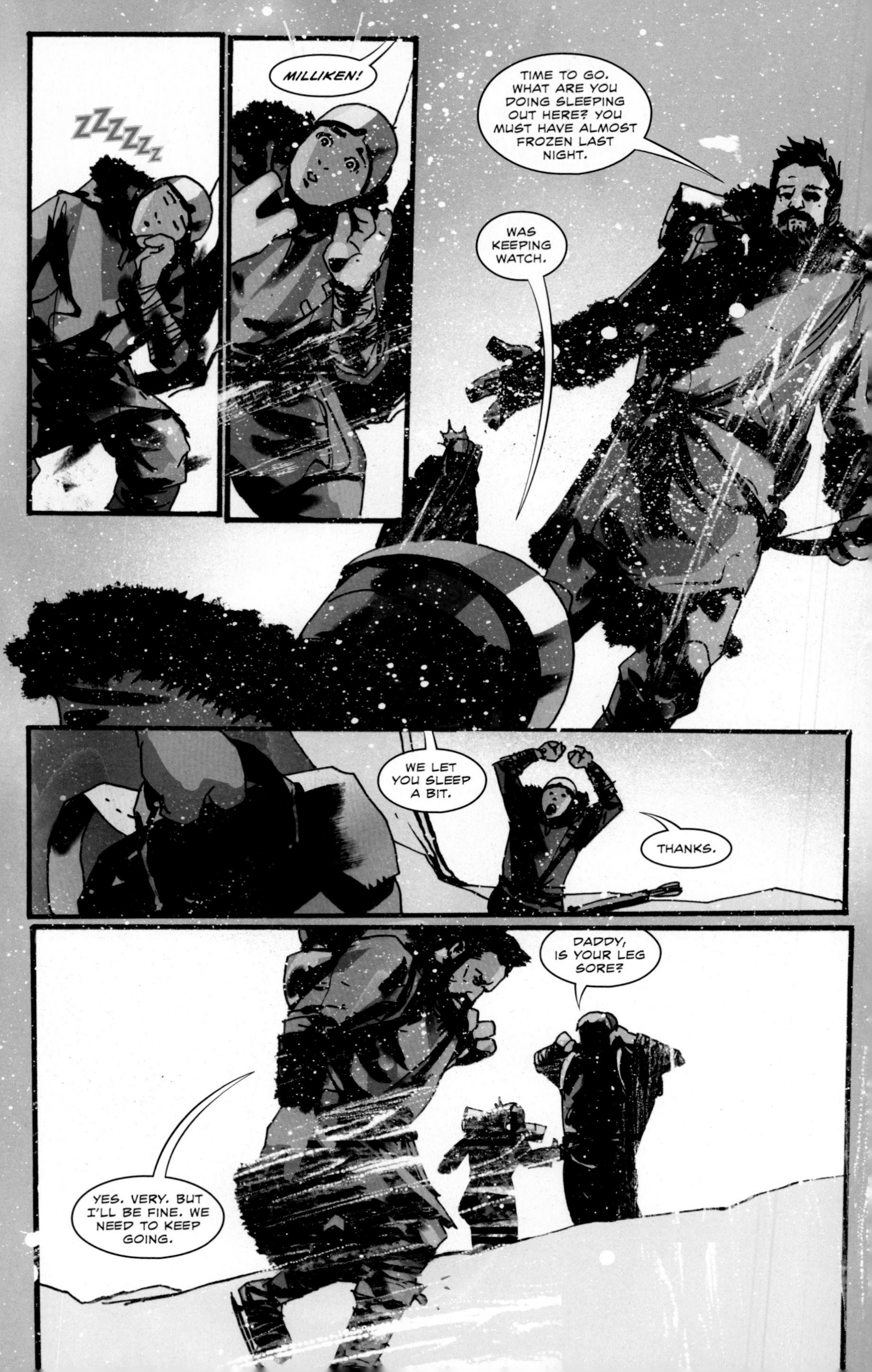
ZZZZZZZ
MILLIKEN!
TIME TO GO. WHAT ARE YOU DOING SLEEPING OUT HERE? YOU MUST HAVE ALMOST FROZEN LAST NIGHT.
WAS KEEPING WATCH.
WE LET YOU SLEEP A BIT.
THANKS.
DADDY, IS YOUR LEG SORE?
YES. VERY. BUT I'LL BE FINE. WE NEED TO KEEP GOING.

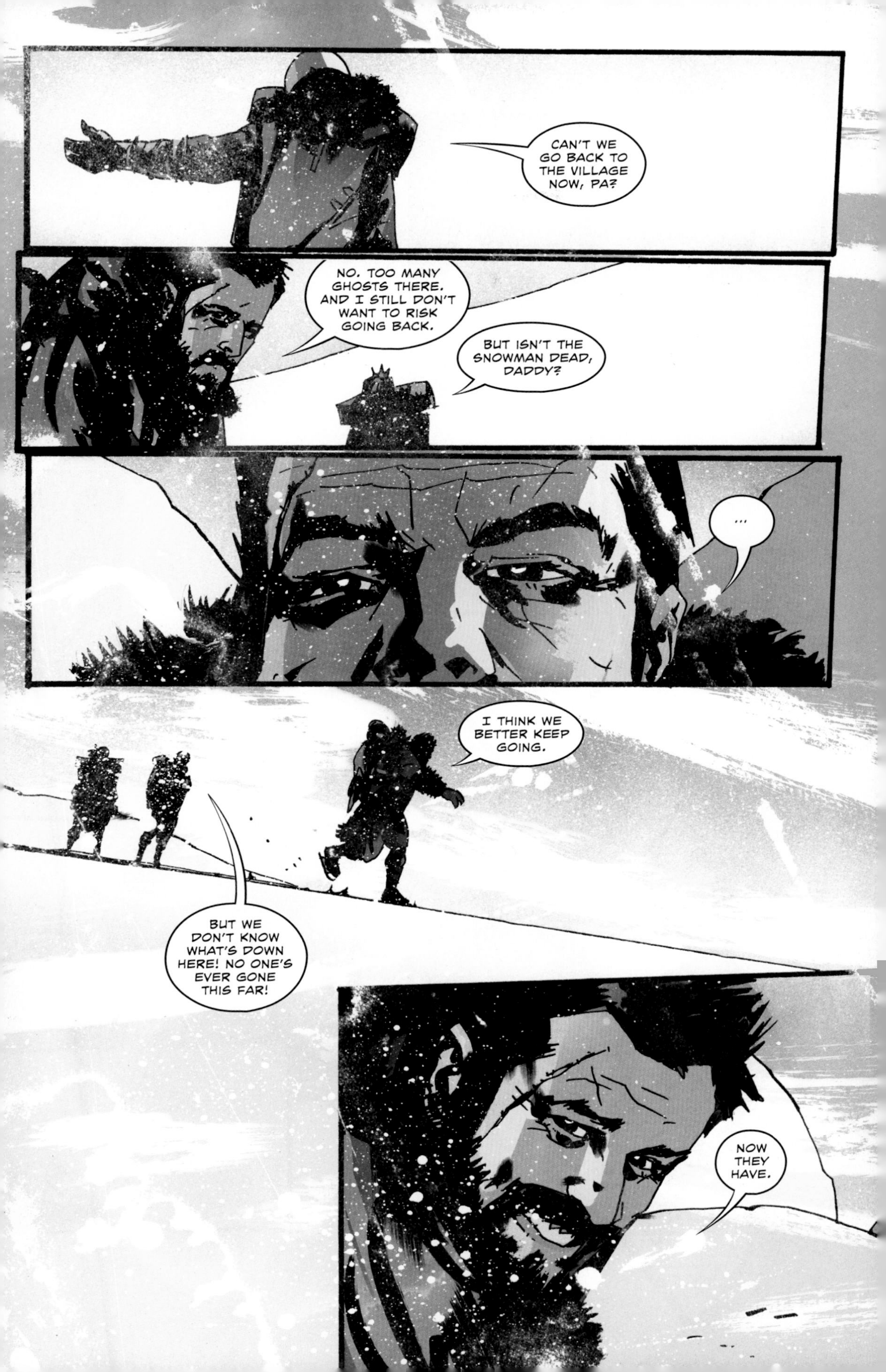
CAN'T WE GO BACK TO THE VILLAGE NOW, PA?
NO. TOO MANY GHOSTS THERE. AND I STILL DON'T WANT TO RISK GOING BACK.
BUT ISN'T THE SNOWMAN DEAD, DADDY?
...
I THINK WE BETTER KEEP GOING.
BUT WE DON'T KNOW WHAT'S DOWN HERE! NO ONE'S EVER GONE THIS FAR!
NOW THEY HAVE.

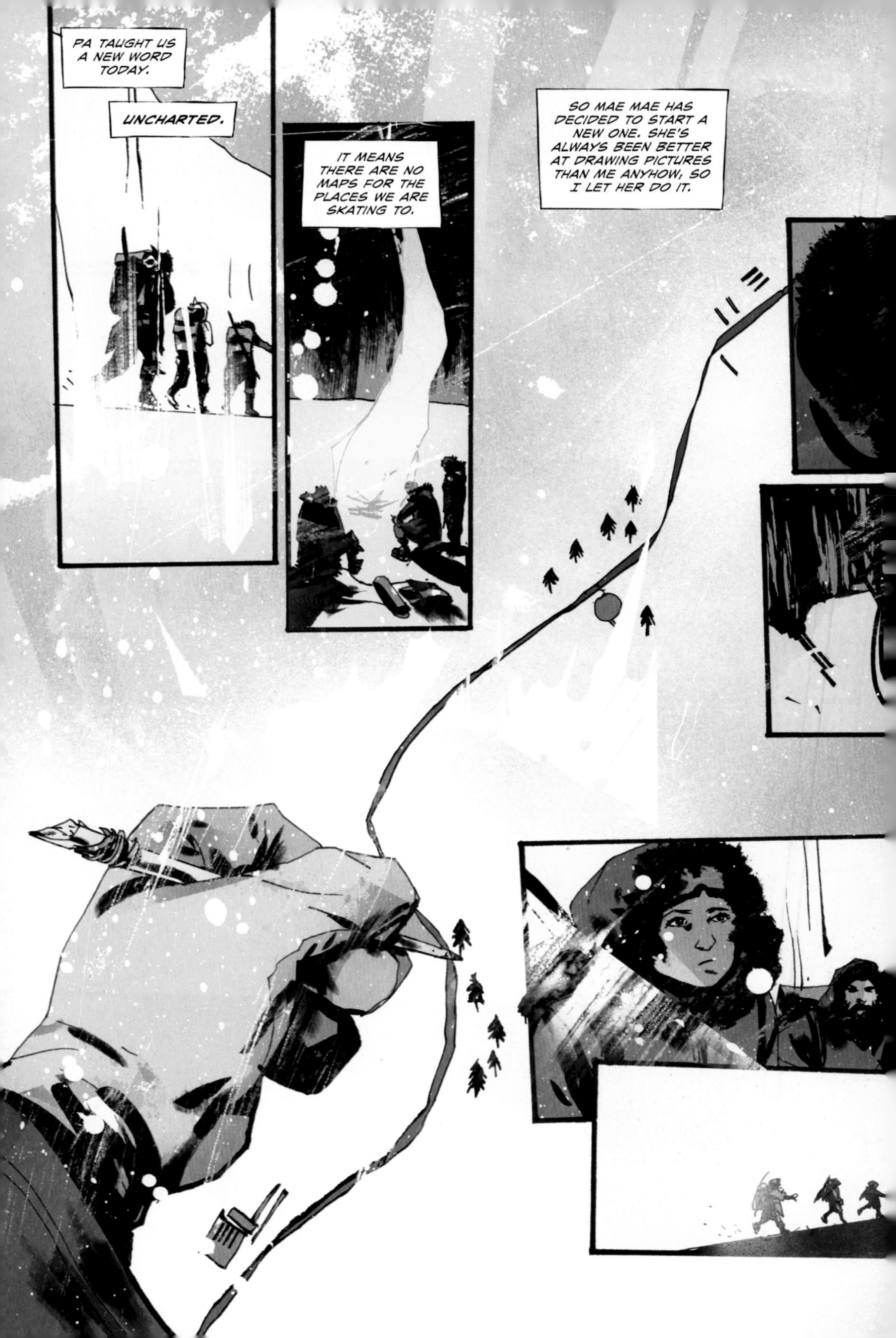
PA TAUGHT US A NEW WORD TODAY.
UNCHARTED.
IT MEANS THERE ARE NO MAPS FOR THE PLACES WE ARE SKATING TO.
SO MAE MAE HAS DECIDED TO START A NEW ONE. SHE'S ALWAYS BEEN BETTER AT DRAWING PICTURES THAN ME ANYHOW, SO I LET HER DO IT.

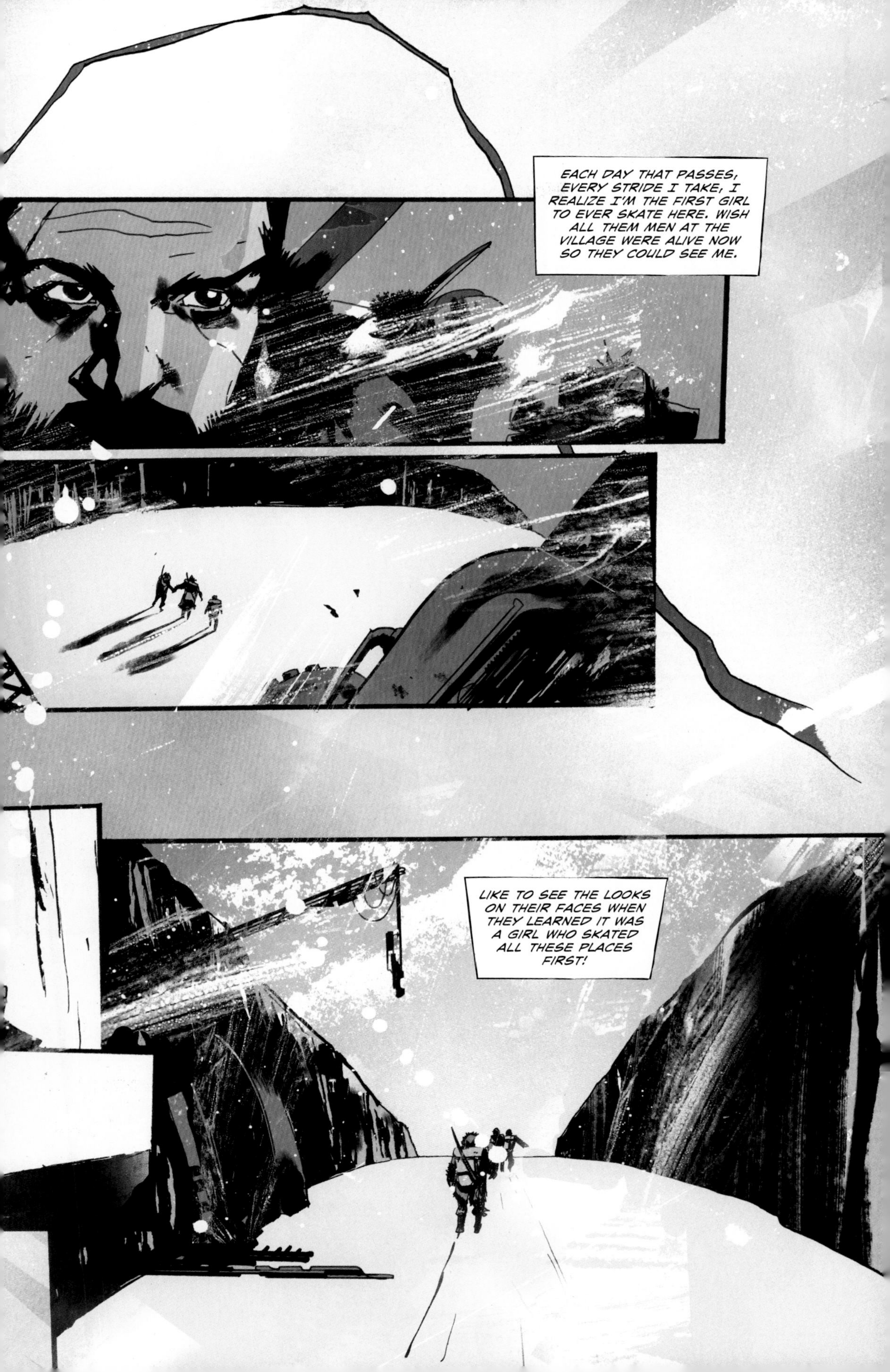
EACH DAY THAT PASSES, EVERY STRIDE I TAKE, I REALIZE I'M THE FIRST GIRL TO EVER SKATE HERE. WISH ALL THEM MEN AT THE VILLAGE WERE ALIVE NOW SO THEY COULD SEE ME.
LIKE TO SEE THE LOOKS ON THEIR FACES WHEN THEY LEARNED IT WAS A GIRL WHO SKATED ALL THESE PLACES FIRST!

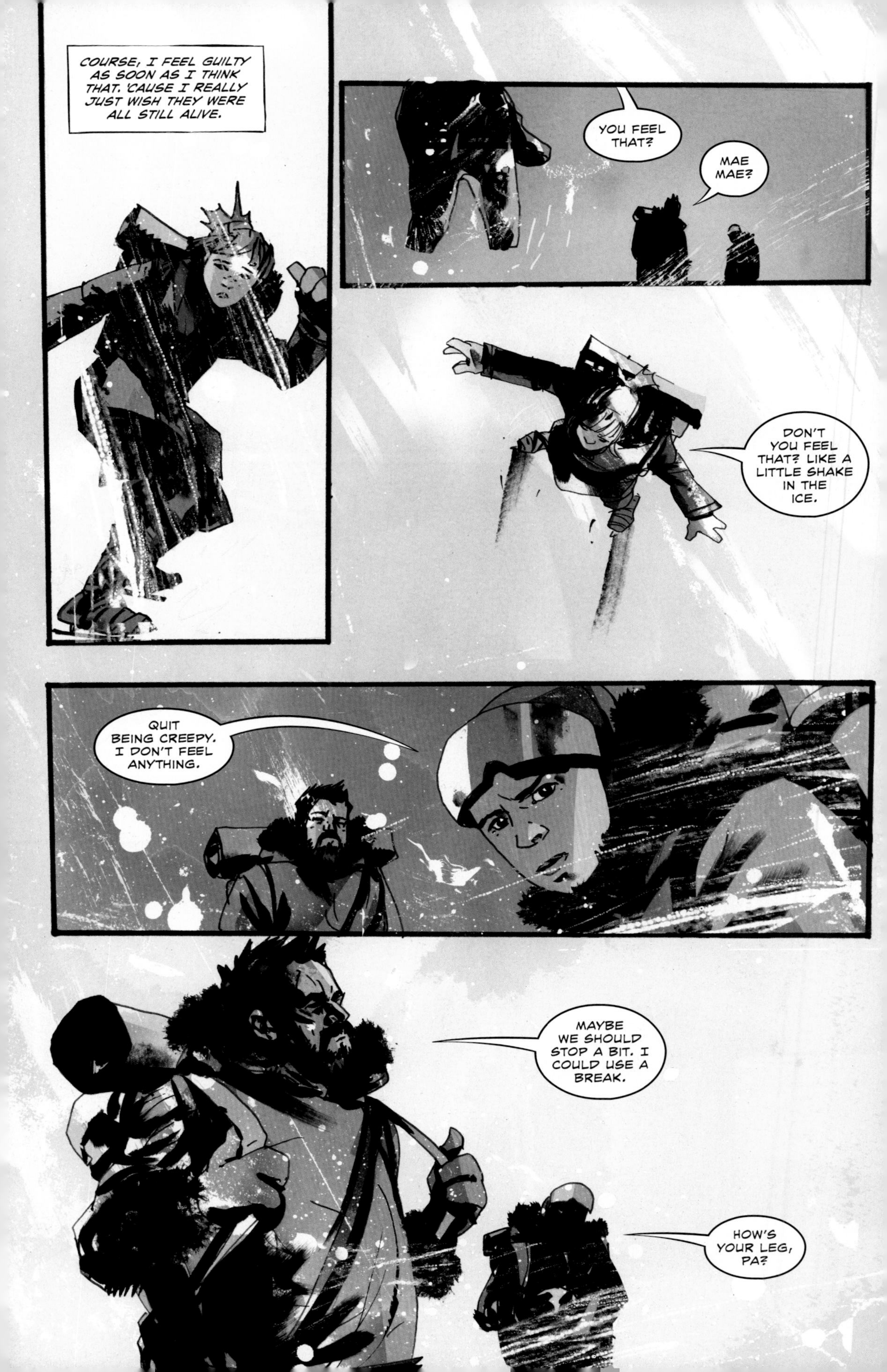
COURSE, I FEEL GUILTY AS SOON AS I THINK THAT. 'CAUSE I REALLY JUST WISH THEY WERE ALL STILL ALIVE.
YOU FEEL THAT?
MAE MAE?
DON'T YOU FEEL THAT? LIKE A LITTLE SHAKE IN THE ICE.
QUIT BEING CREEPY. I DON'T FEEL ANYTHING.
MAYBE WE SHOULD STOP A BIT. I COULD USE A BREAK.
HOW'S YOUR LEG, PA?

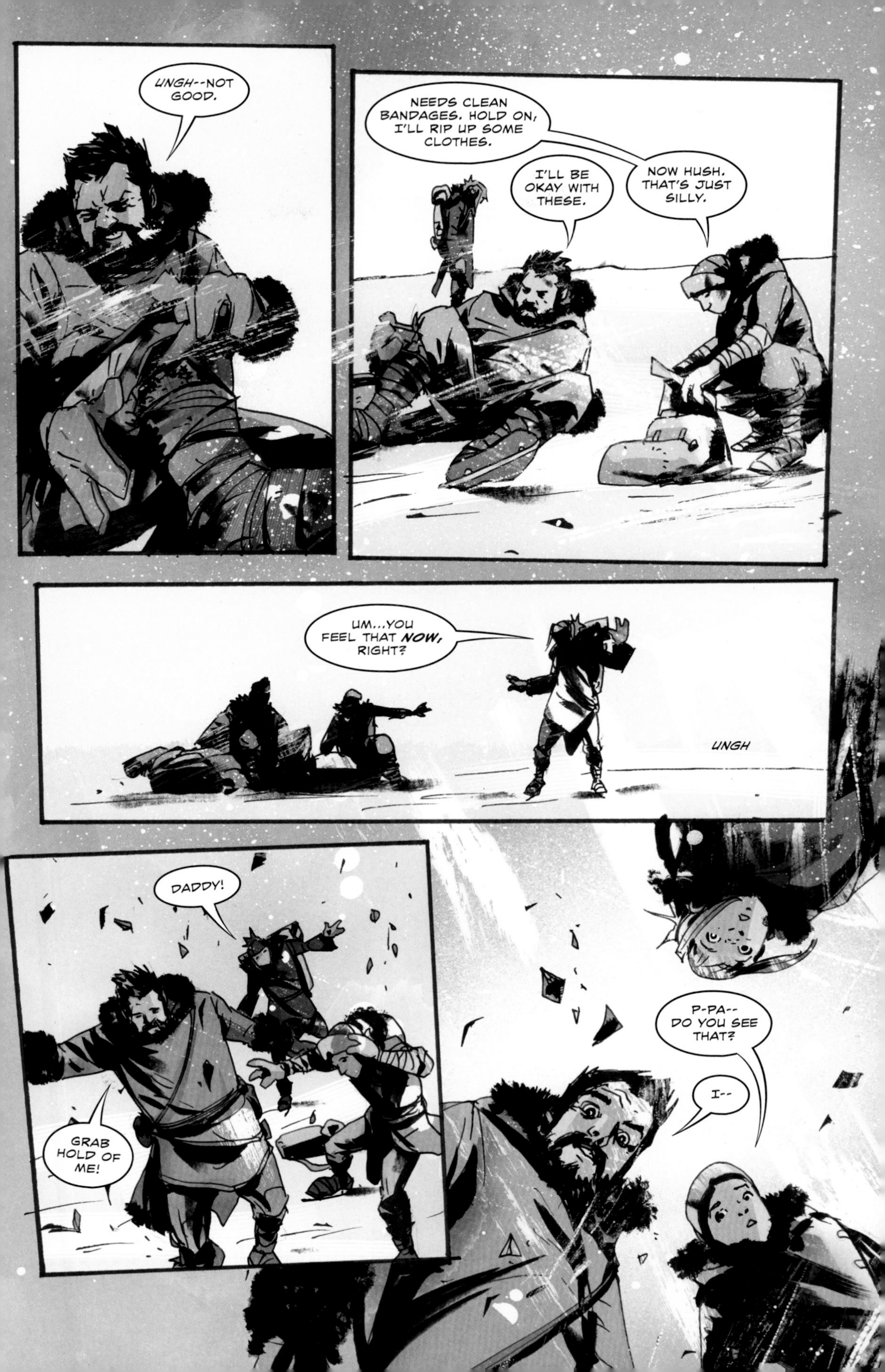
UNGH--NOT GOOD.
NEEDS CLEAN BANDAGES. HOLD ON, I'LL RIP UP SOME CLOTHES.
I'LL BE OKAY WITH THESE.
NOW HUSH. THAT'S JUST SILLY.
UM...YOU FEEL THAT ***NOW,*** RIGHT?
UNGH
DADDY!
GRAB HOLD OF ME!
P-PA-- DO YOU SEE THAT?
I--

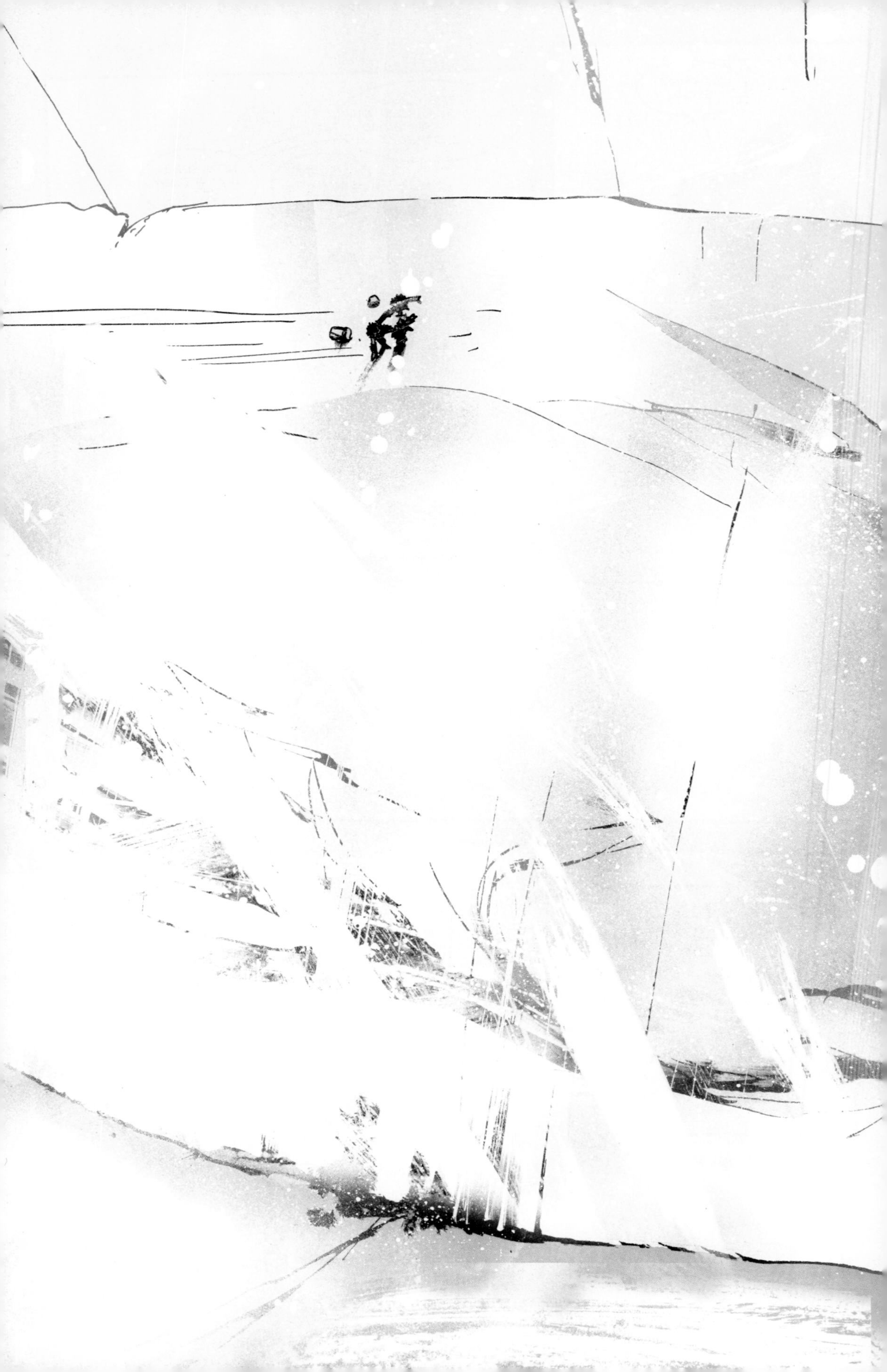

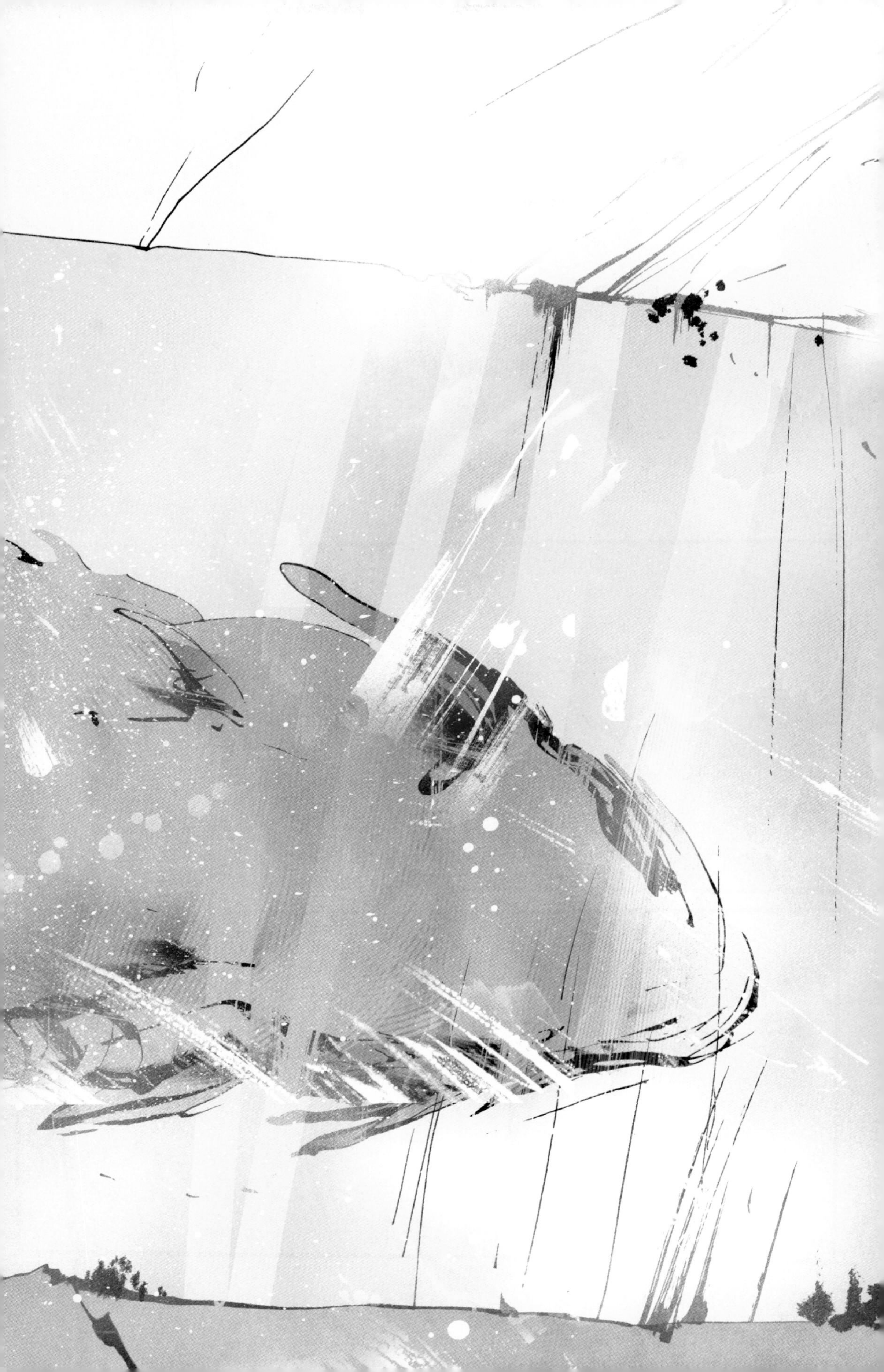

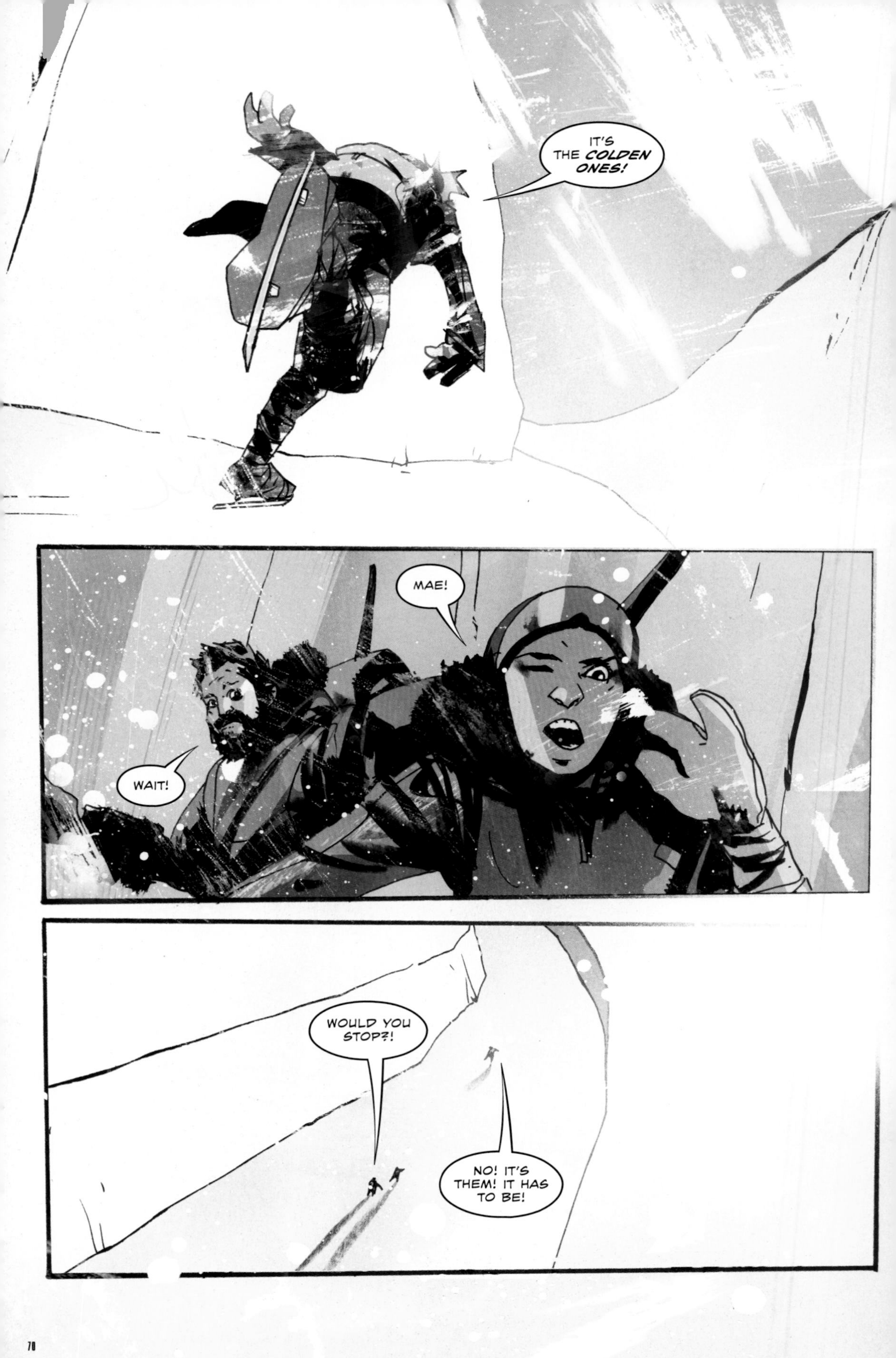
IT'S THE *COLDEN ONES!*
MAE!
WAIT!
WOULD YOU STOP?!
NO! IT'S THEM! IT HAS TO BE!

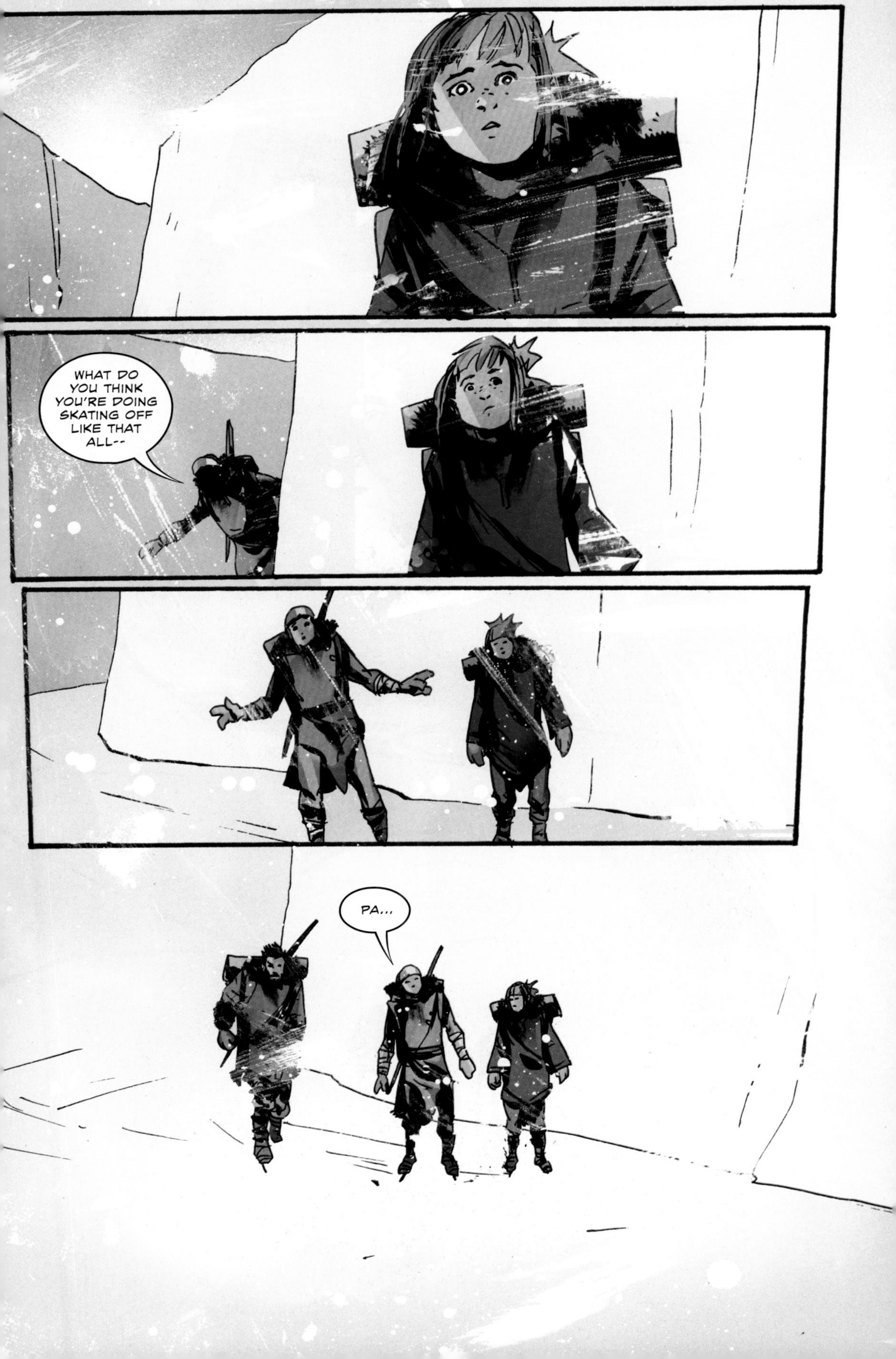
WHAT DO YOU THINK YOU'RE DOING SKATING OFF LIKE THAT ALL--
PA...

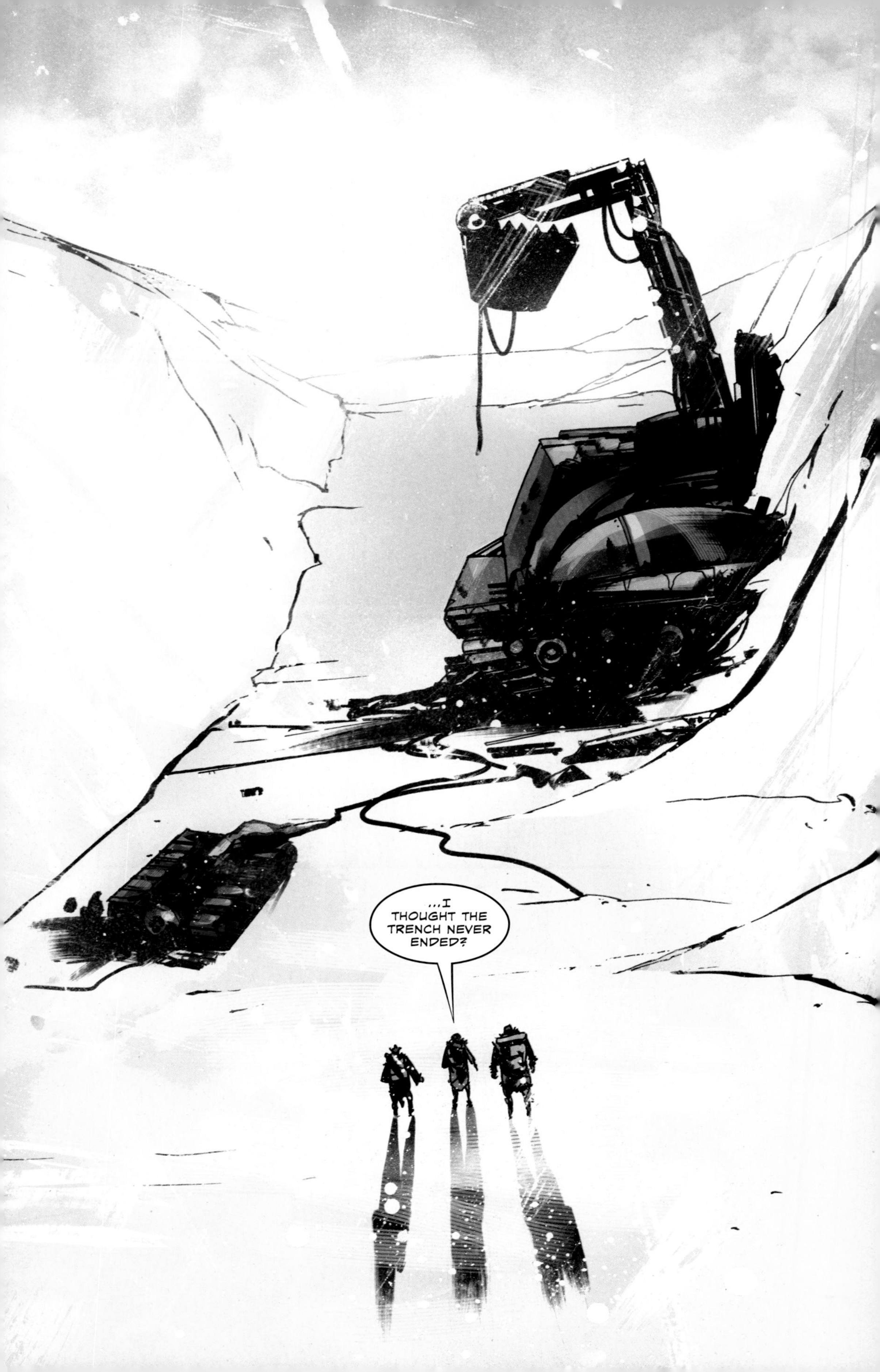
...I THOUGHT THE TRENCH NEVER ENDED?

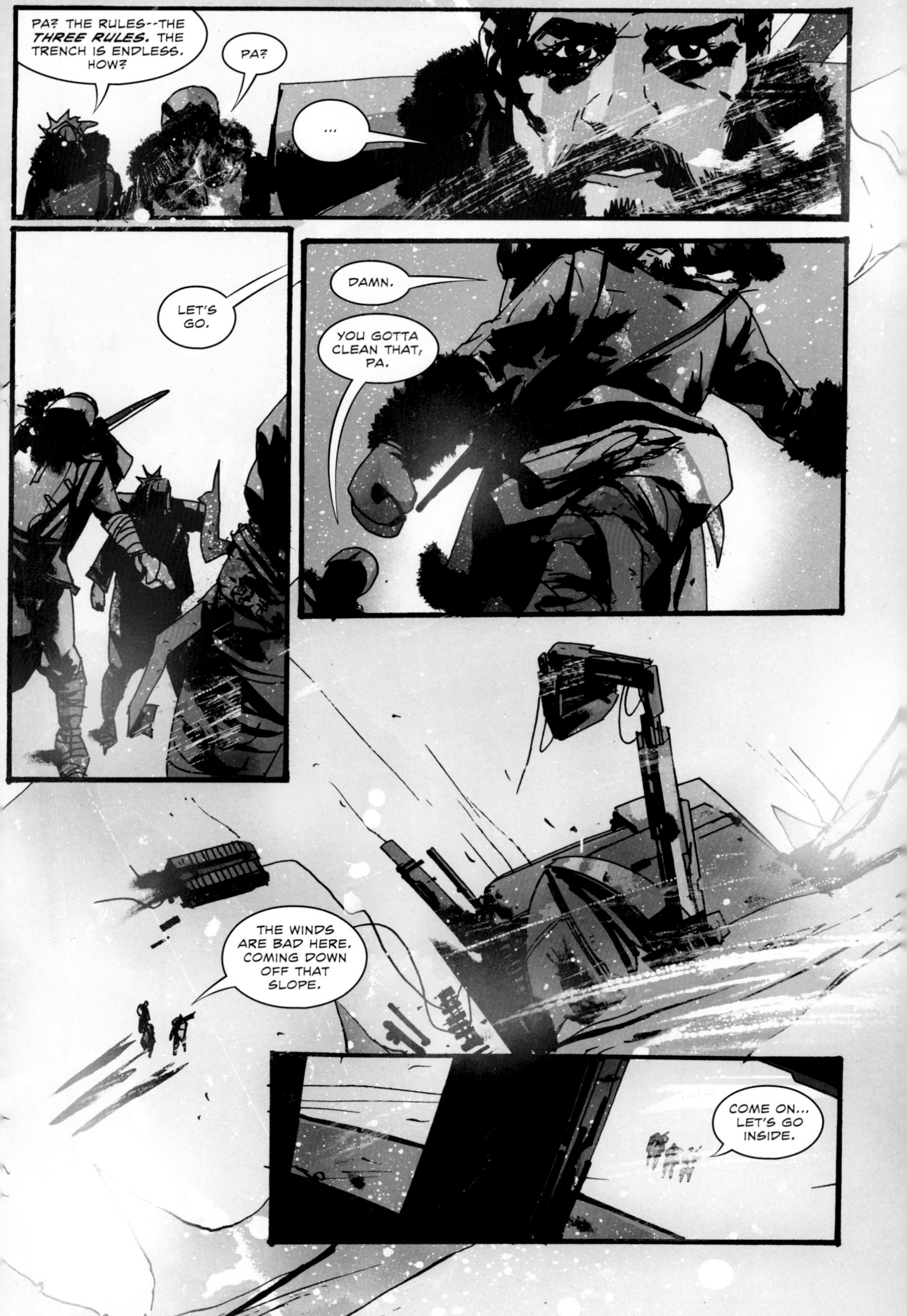
PA? THE RULES--THE *THREE RULES.* THE TRENCH IS ENDLESS. HOW?
PA?
...
LET'S GO.
DAMN.
YOU GOTTA CLEAN THAT, PA.
THE WINDS ARE BAD HERE. COMING DOWN OFF THAT SLOPE.
COME ON... LET'S GO INSIDE.

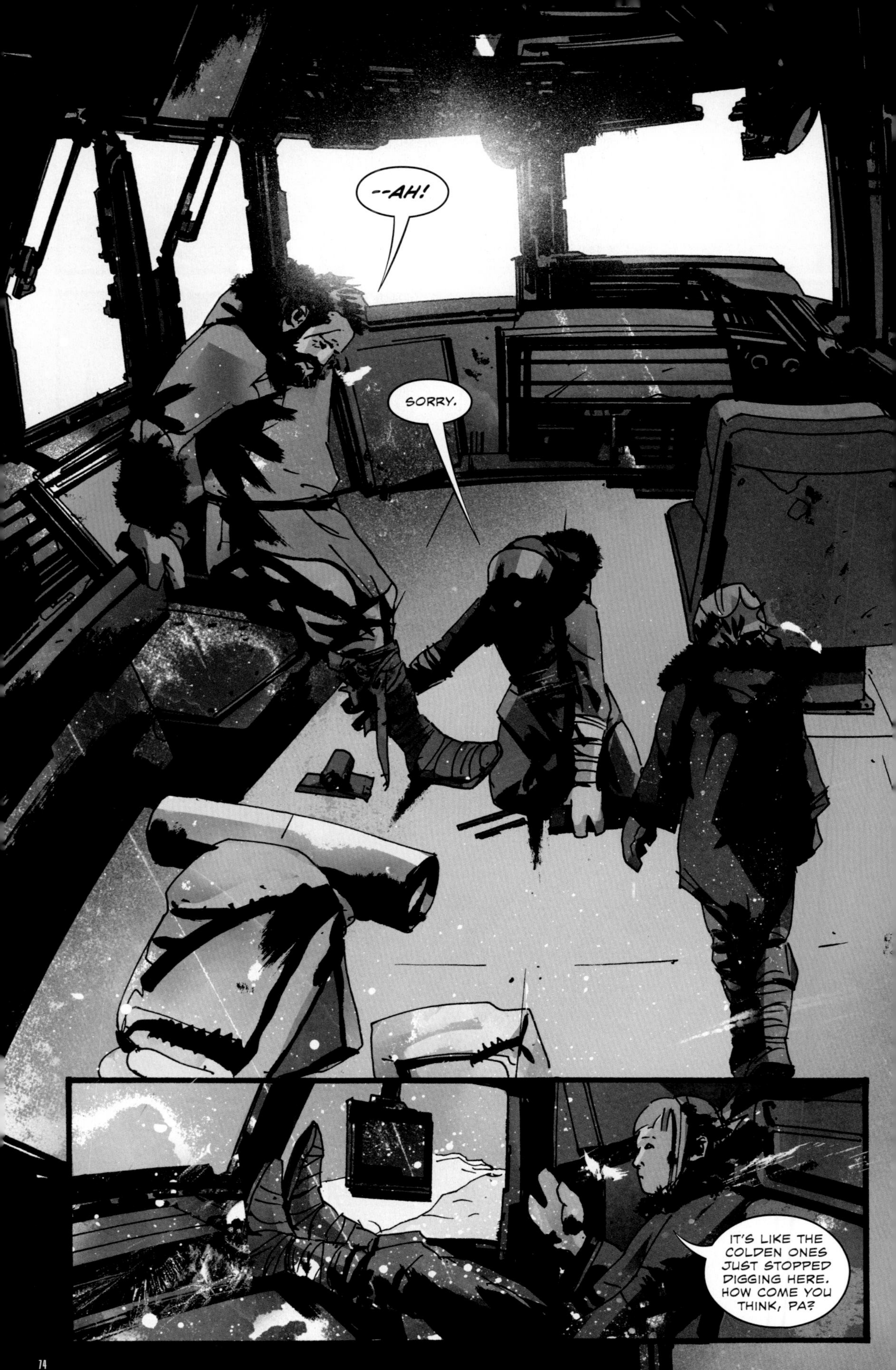
--AH!
SORRY.
IT'S LIKE THE COLDEN ONES JUST STOPPED DIGGING HERE. HOW COME YOU THINK, PA?

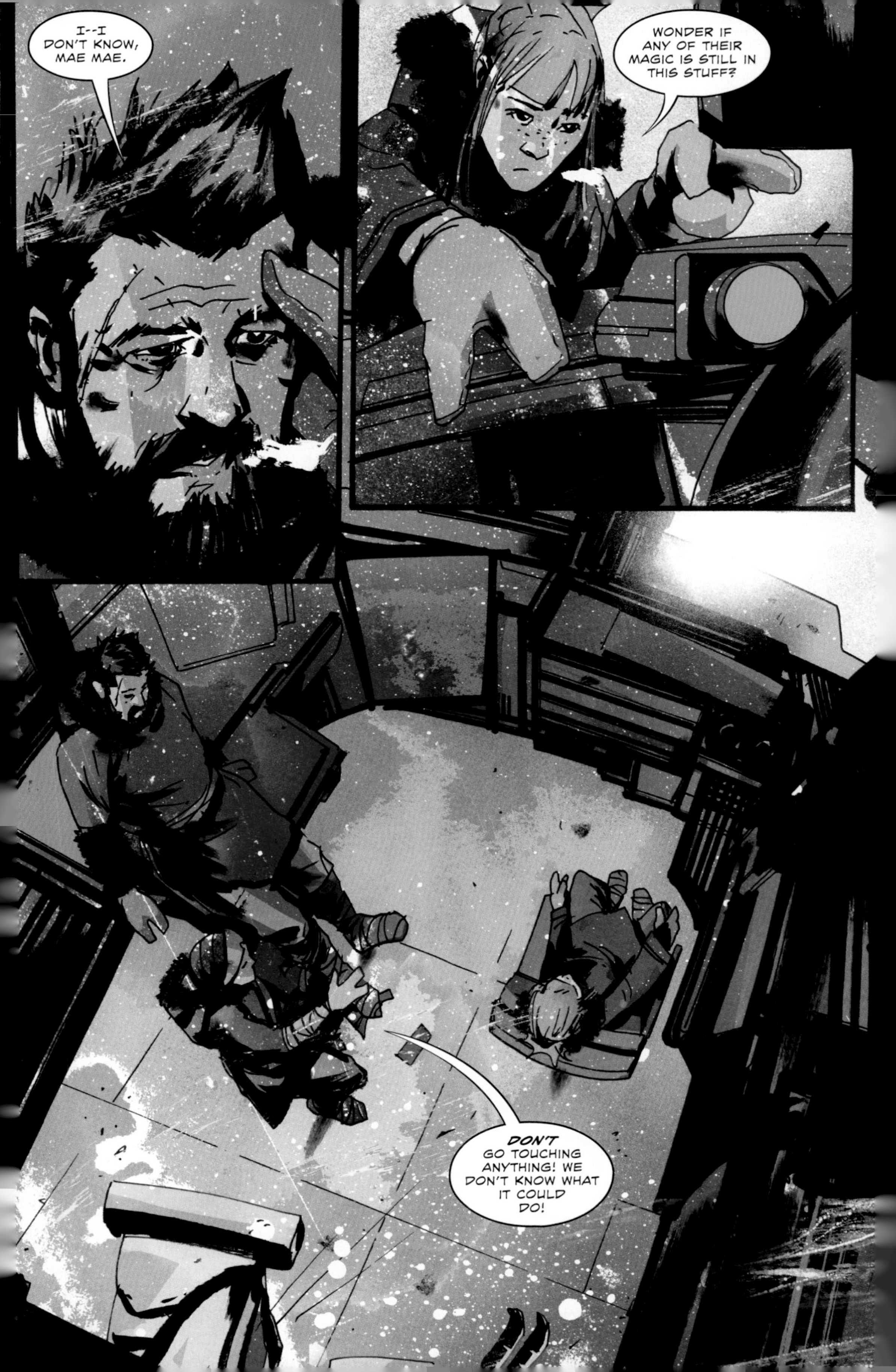
I--I DON'T KNOW, MAE MAE.
WONDER IF ANY OF THEIR MAGIC IS STILL IN THIS STUFF?
DON'T GO TOUCHING ANYTHING! WE DON'T KNOW WHAT IT COULD DO!

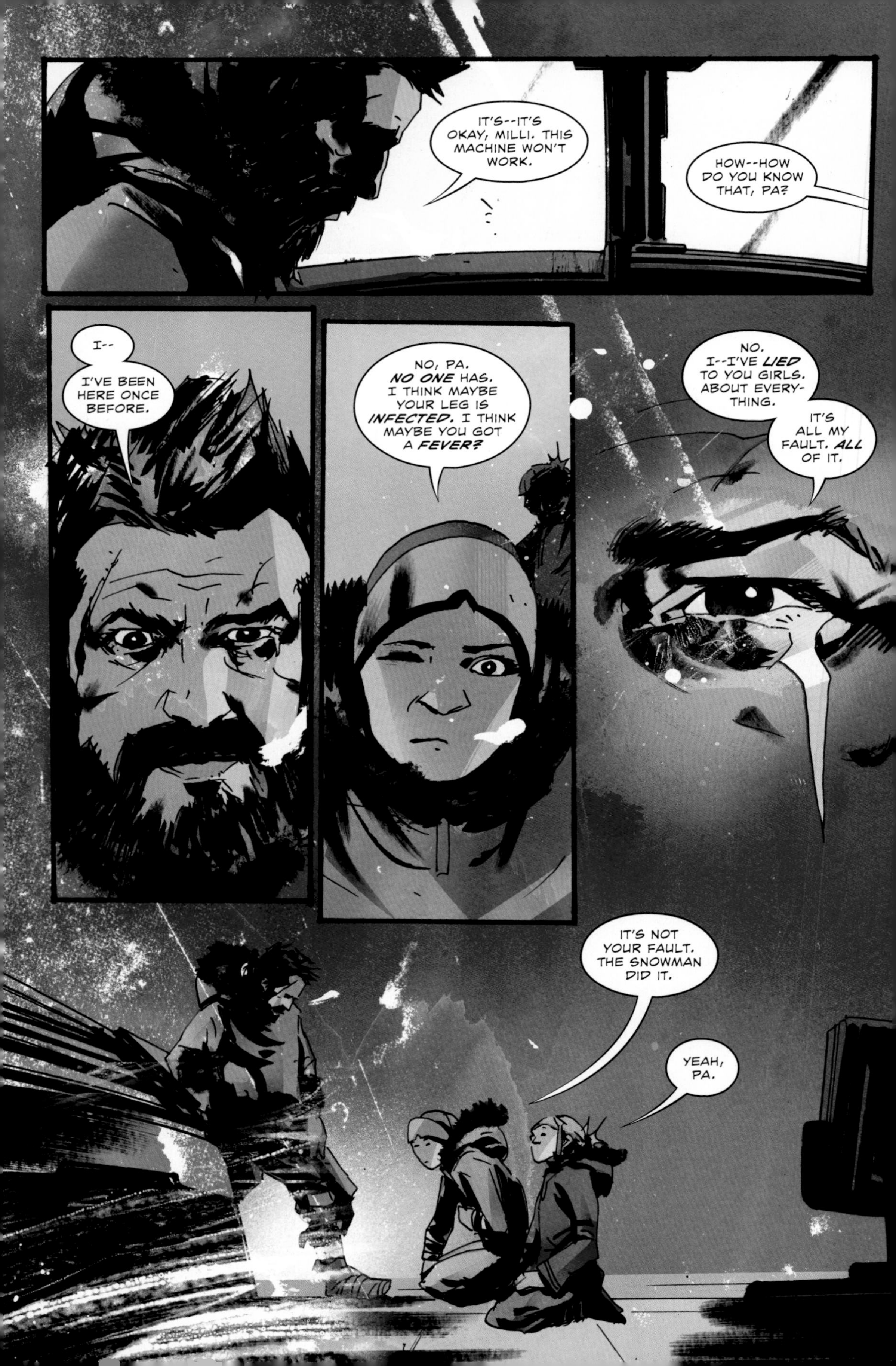
IT'S--IT'S OKAY, MILLI. THIS MACHINE WON'T WORK.
HOW--HOW DO YOU KNOW THAT, PA?
I--
I'VE BEEN HERE ONCE BEFORE.
NO, PA. NO ONE HAS. I THINK MAYBE YOUR LEG IS INFECTED. I THINK MAYBE YOU GOT A FEVER?
NO. I--I'VE LIED TO YOU GIRLS. ABOUT EVERYTHING.
IT'S ALL MY FAULT. ALL OF IT.
IT'S NOT YOUR FAULT. THE SNOWMAN DID IT.
YEAH, PA.

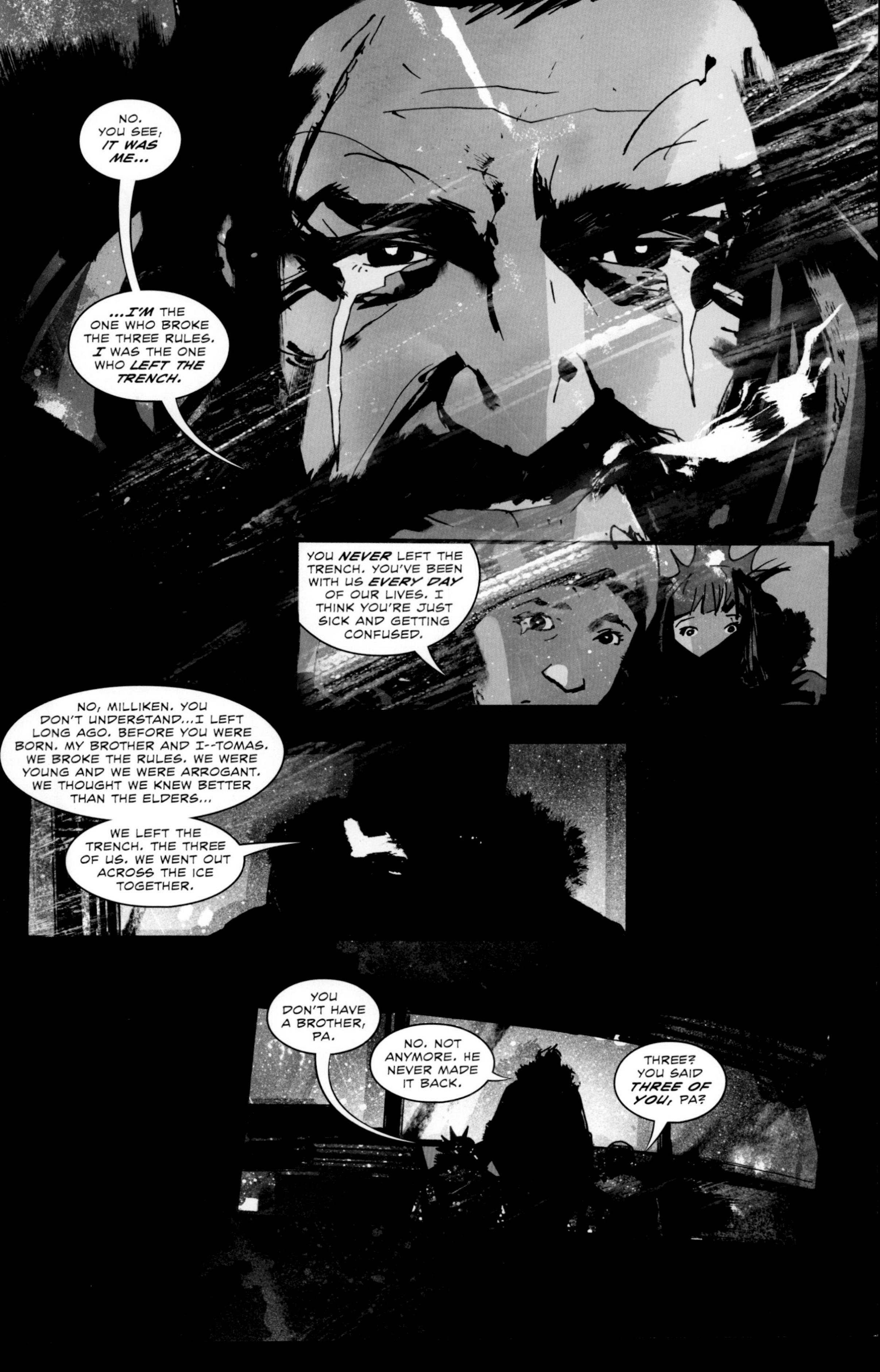
NO. YOU SEE, IT WAS ME...
...I'M THE ONE WHO BROKE THE THREE RULES. I WAS THE ONE WHO LEFT THE TRENCH.
YOU NEVER LEFT THE TRENCH. YOU'VE BEEN WITH US EVERY DAY OF OUR LIVES. I THINK YOU'RE JUST SICK AND GETTING CONFUSED.
NO, MILLIKEN. YOU DON'T UNDERSTAND...I LEFT LONG AGO. BEFORE YOU WERE BORN. MY BROTHER AND I--TOMAS. WE BROKE THE RULES. WE WERE YOUNG AND WE WERE ARROGANT. WE THOUGHT WE KNEW BETTER THAN THE ELDERS...
WE LEFT THE TRENCH. THE THREE OF US. WE WENT OUT ACROSS THE ICE TOGETHER.
YOU DON'T HAVE A BROTHER, PA.
NO. NOT ANYMORE. HE NEVER MADE IT BACK.
THREE? YOU SAID THREE OF YOU, PA?

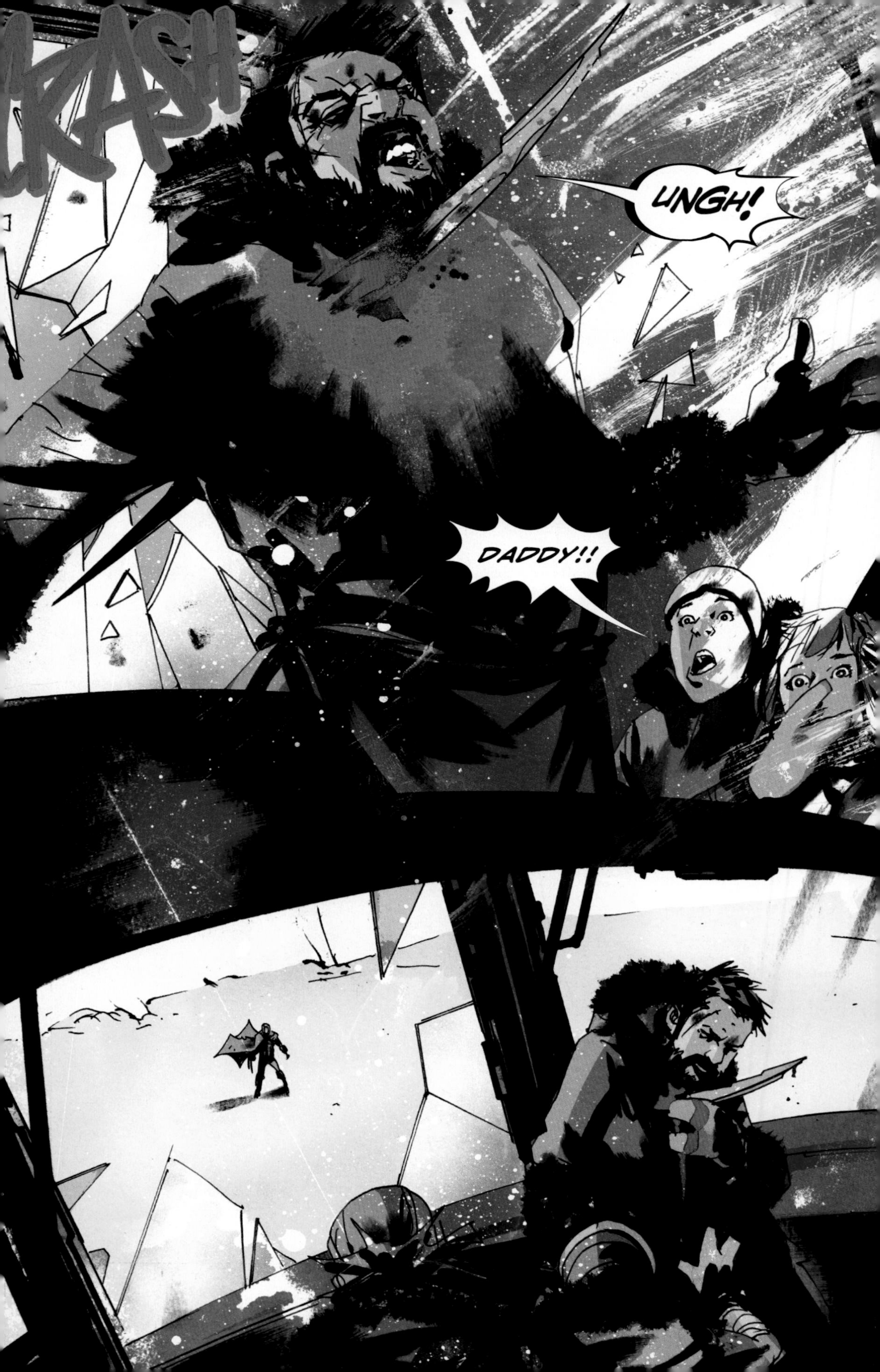
KRASH
UNGH!
DADDY!!

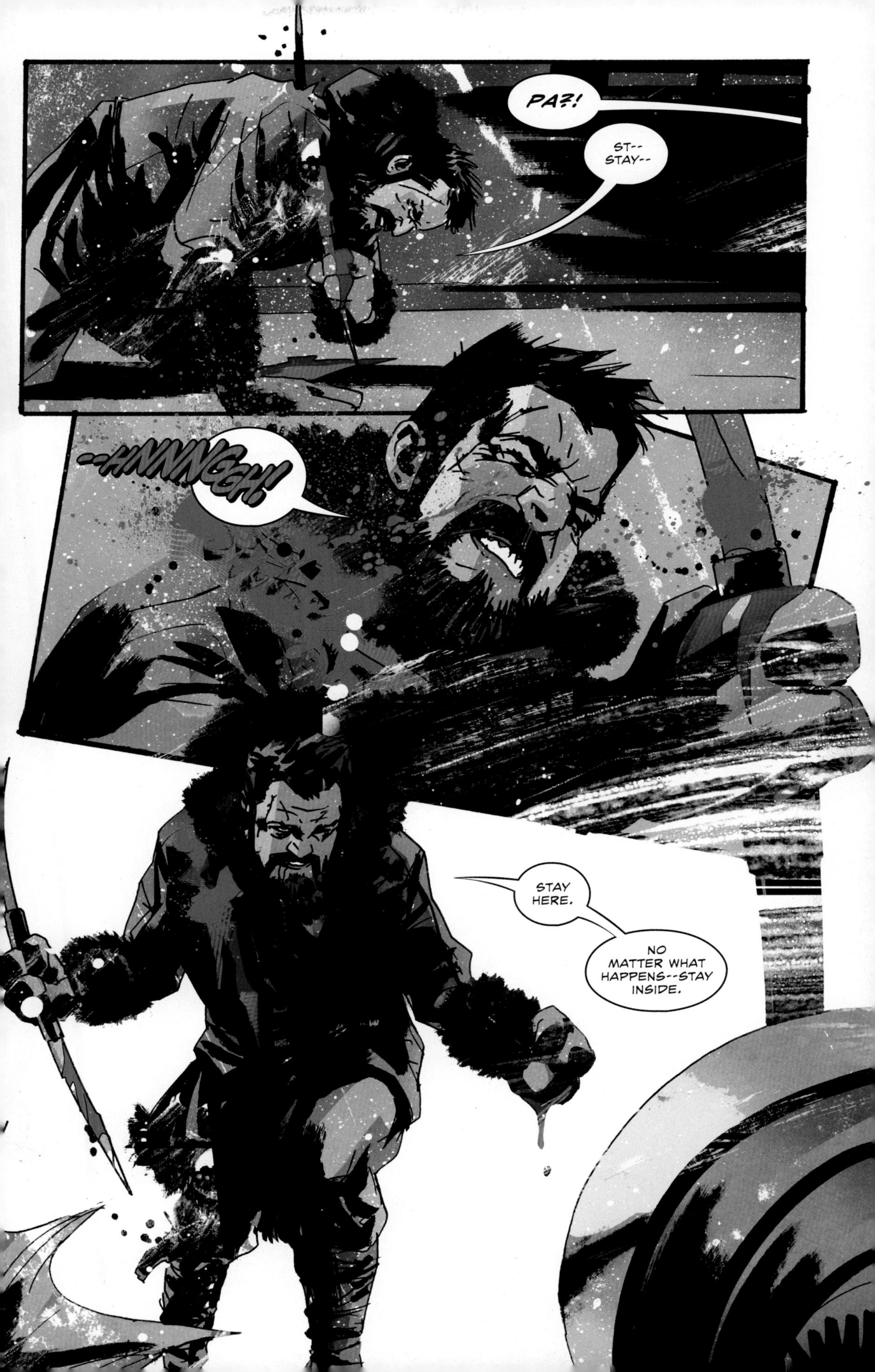
PA?!
ST--
STAY--
--HNNNGGH!
STAY HERE.
NO MATTER WHAT HAPPENS--STAY INSIDE.

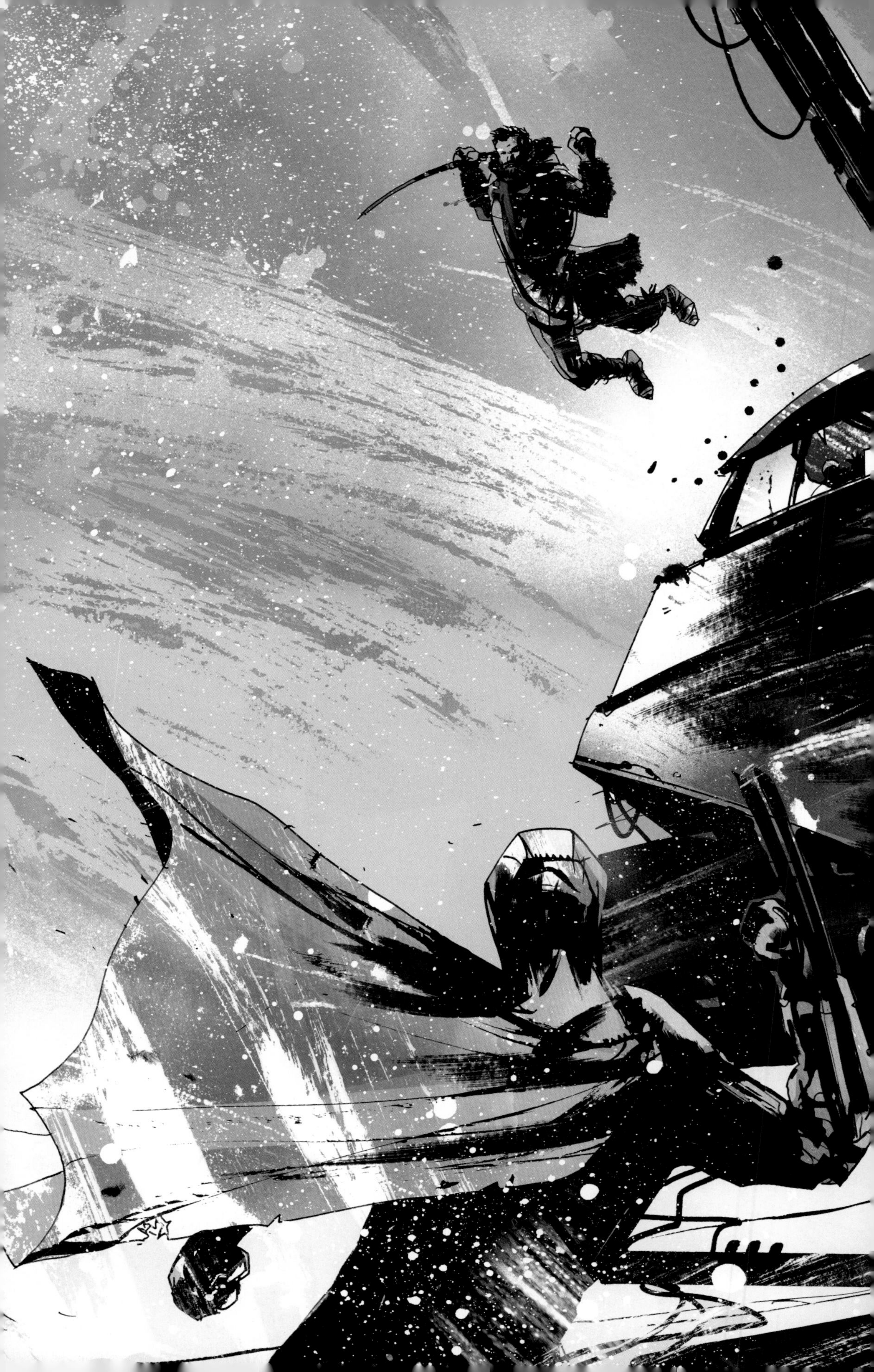

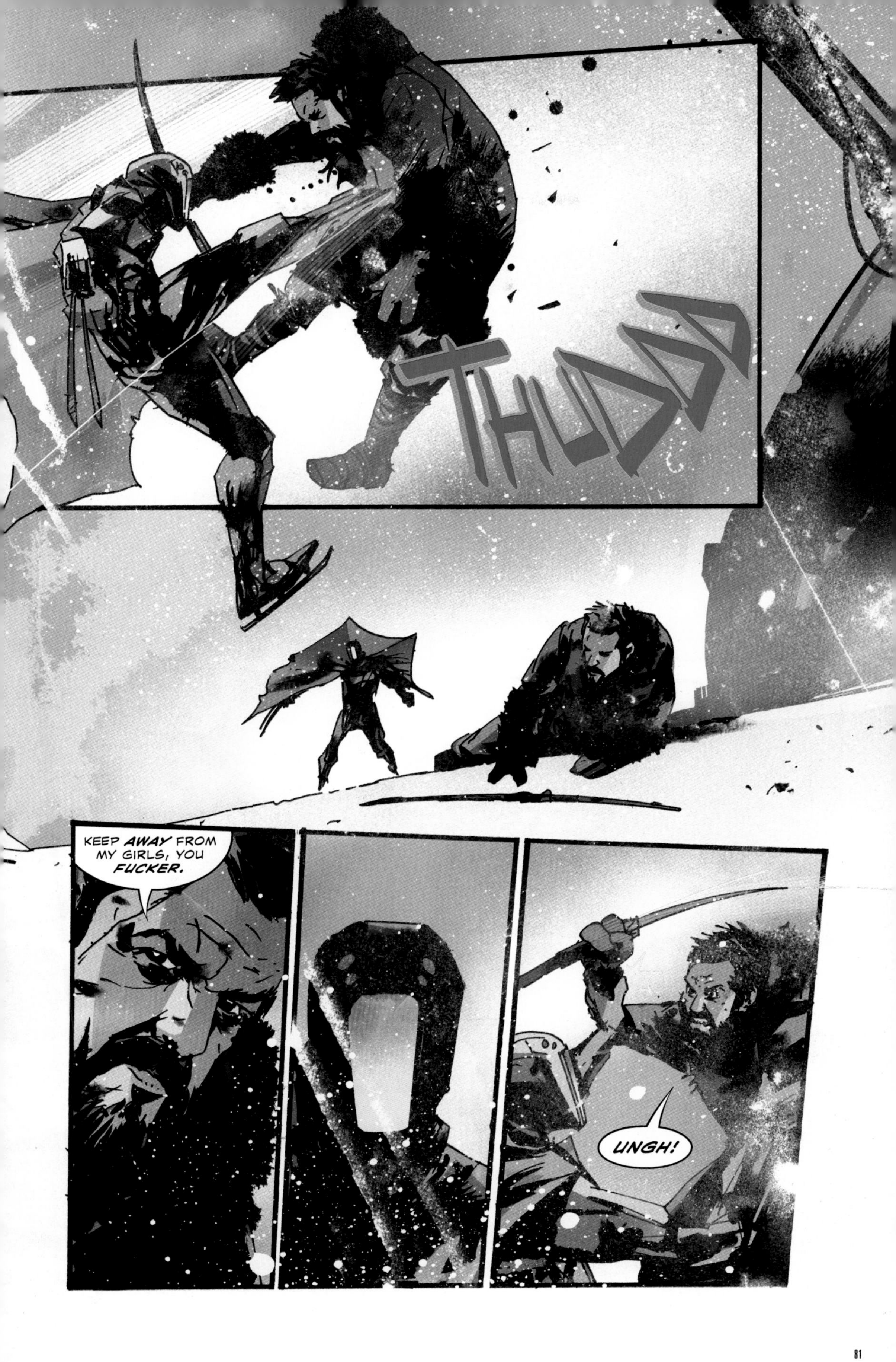
THUDD
KEEP AWAY FROM MY GIRLS, YOU FUCKER.
UNGH!

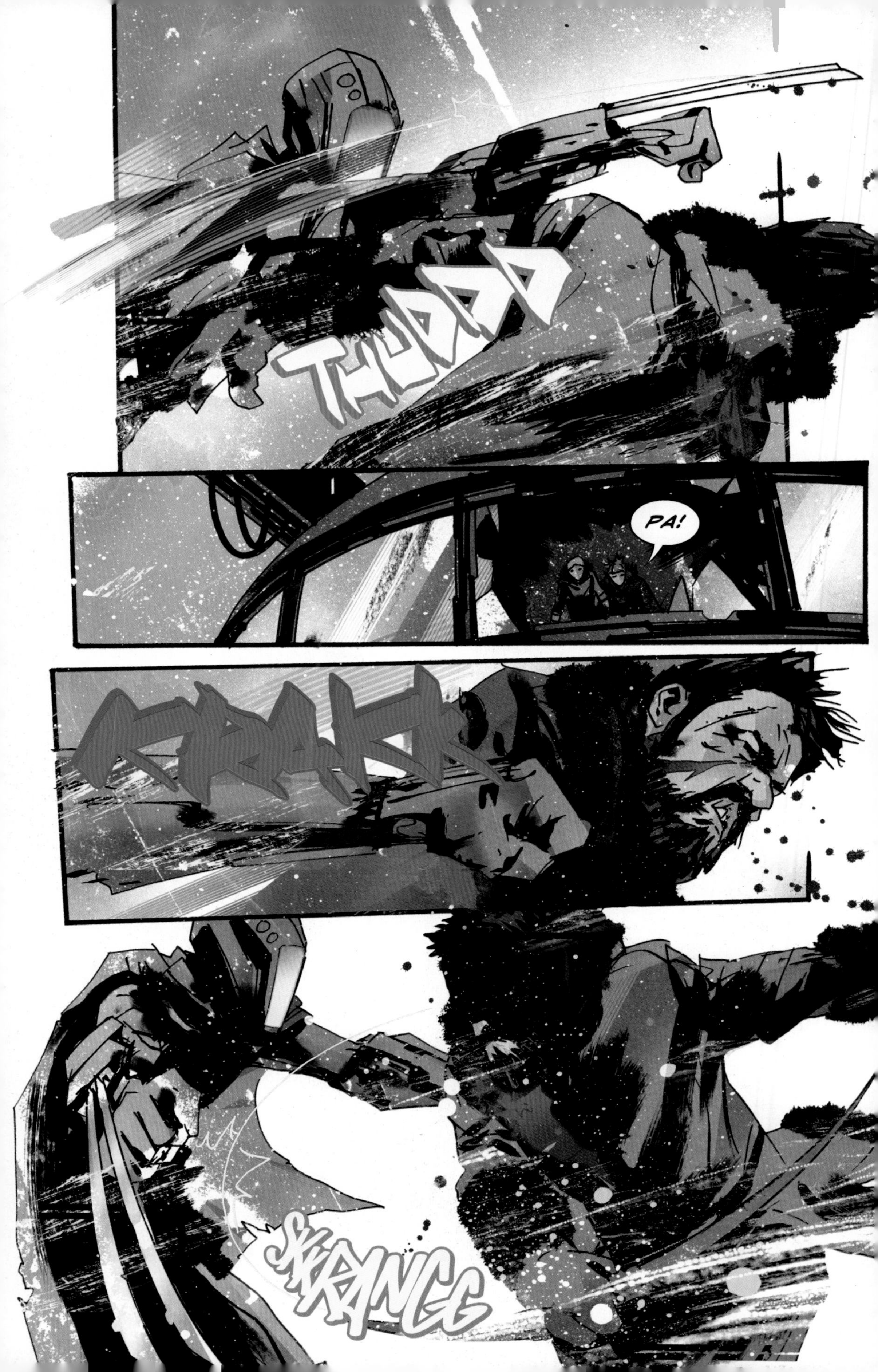
THUDDD
PA!
SKRANGG

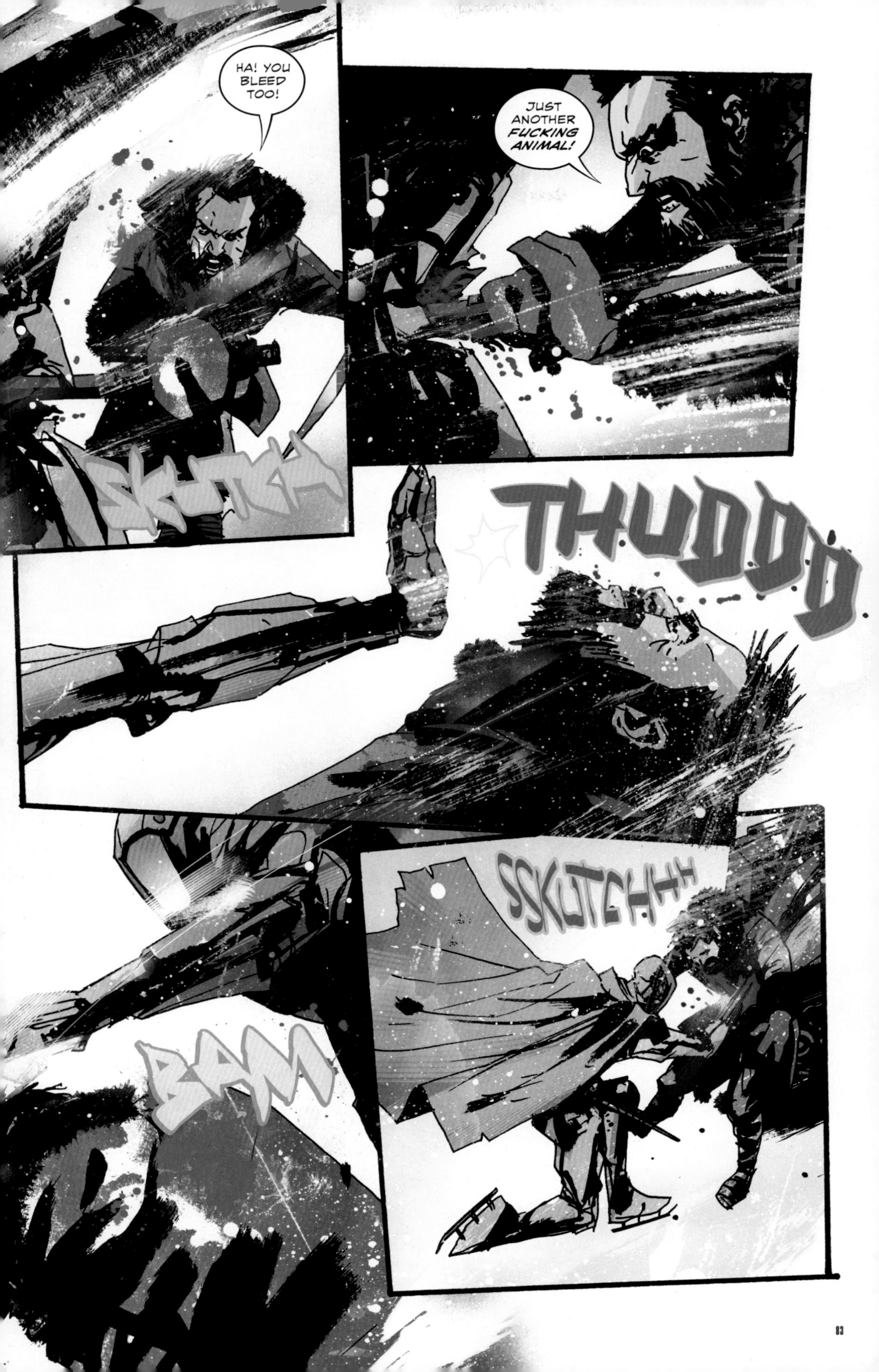
HA! YOU BLEED TOO!
SKUTCH
JUST ANOTHER FUCKING ANIMAL!
THUDDD
SSKUTCHHH
BAM

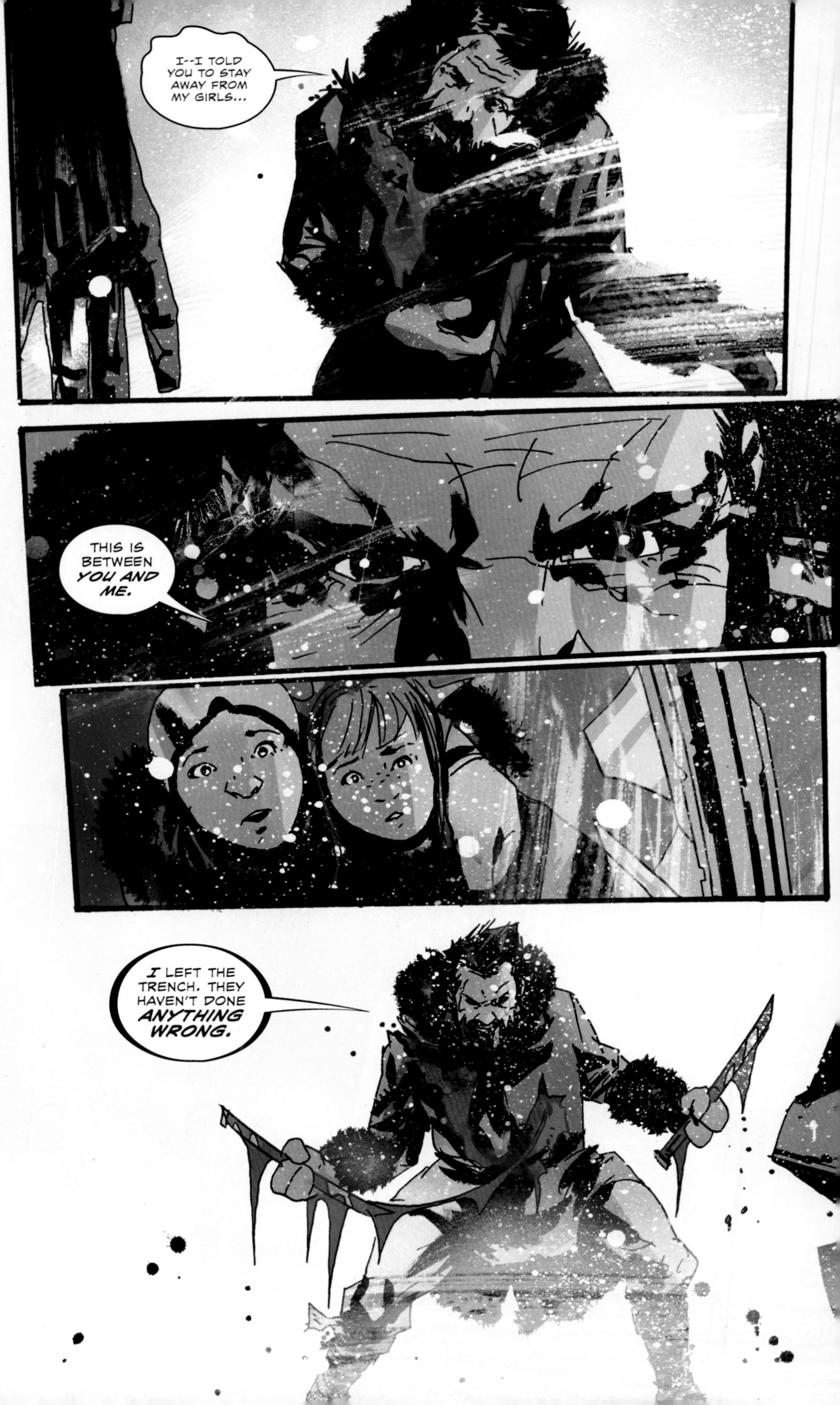
I--I TOLD YOU TO STAY AWAY FROM MY GIRLS...
THIS IS BETWEEN YOU AND ME.
I LEFT THE TRENCH. THEY HAVEN'T DONE ANYTHING WRONG.

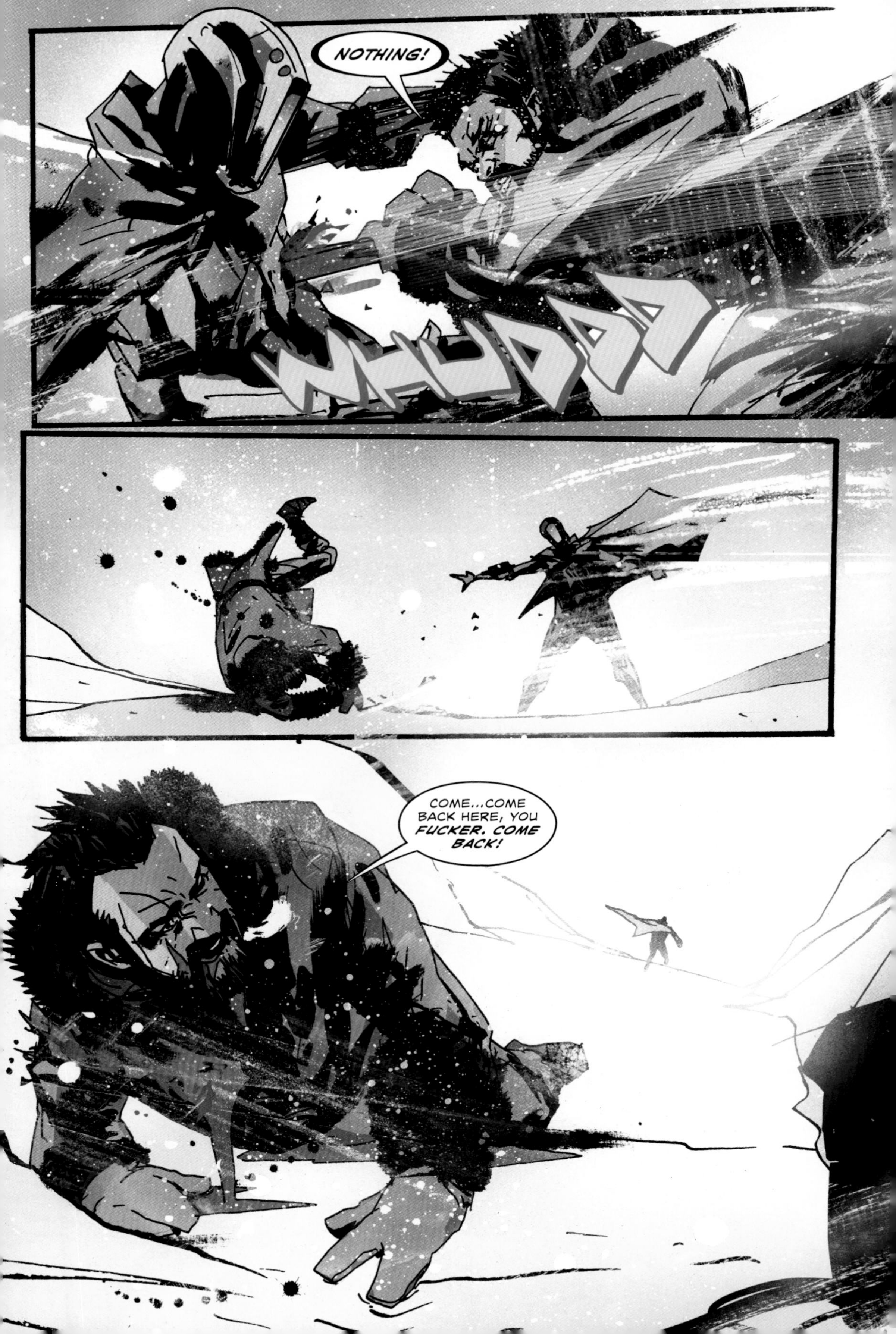
NOTHING!
WHUDDD
COME...COME BACK HERE, YOU FUCKER. COME BACK!

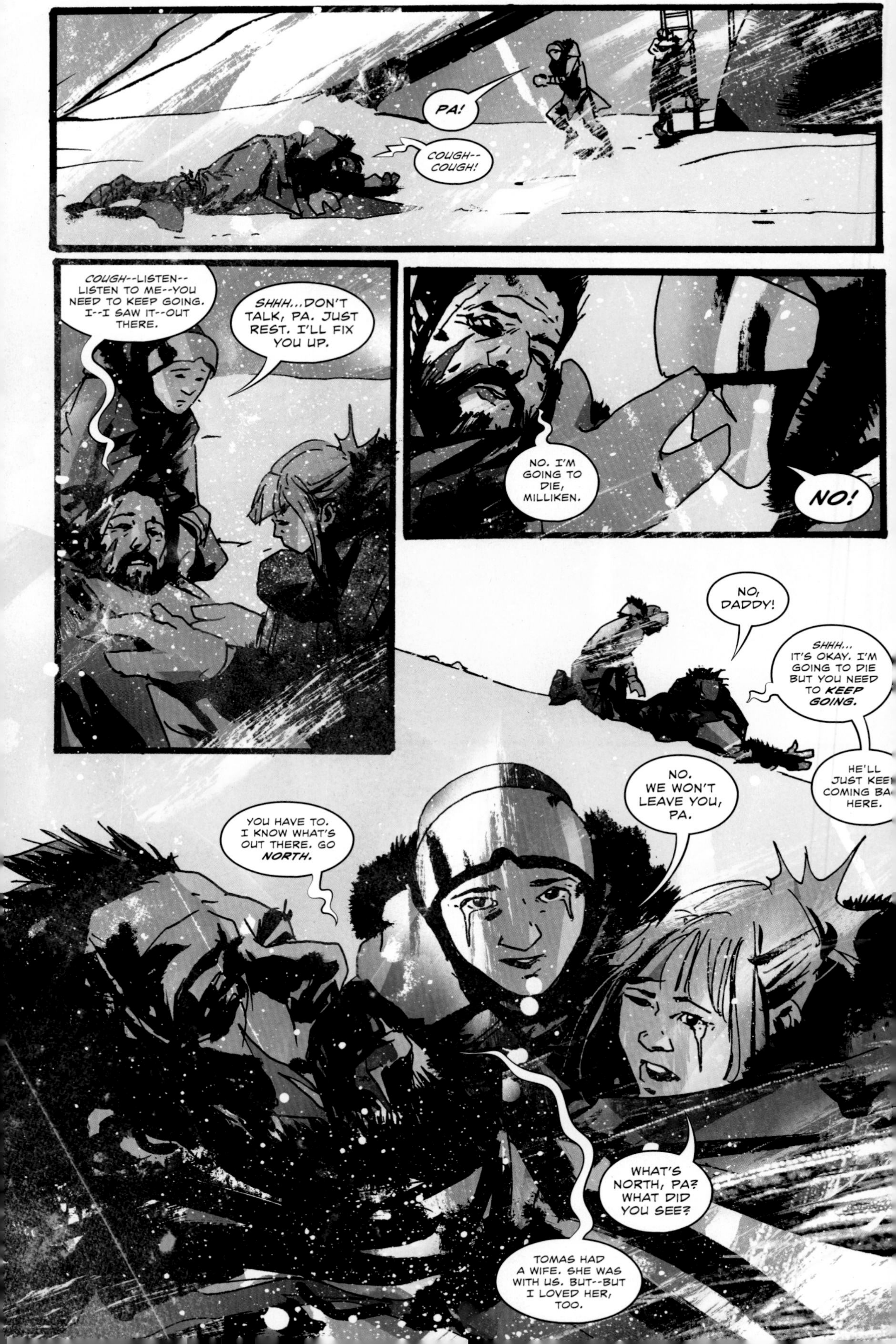
PA!
COUGH--COUGH!
COUGH--LISTEN--LISTEN TO ME--YOU NEED TO KEEP GOING. I--I SAW IT--OUT THERE.
SHHH...DON'T TALK, PA. JUST REST. I'LL FIX YOU UP.
NO. I'M GOING TO DIE, MILLIKEN.
NO!
NO, DADDY!
SHHH... IT'S OKAY. I'M GOING TO DIE BUT YOU NEED TO KEEP GOING.
HE'LL JUST KEE COMING BA HERE.
NO. WE WON'T LEAVE YOU, PA.
YOU HAVE TO. I KNOW WHAT'S OUT THERE. GO NORTH.
WHAT'S NORTH, PA? WHAT DID YOU SEE?
TOMAS HAD A WIFE. SHE WAS WITH US. BUT--BUT I LOVED HER, TOO.

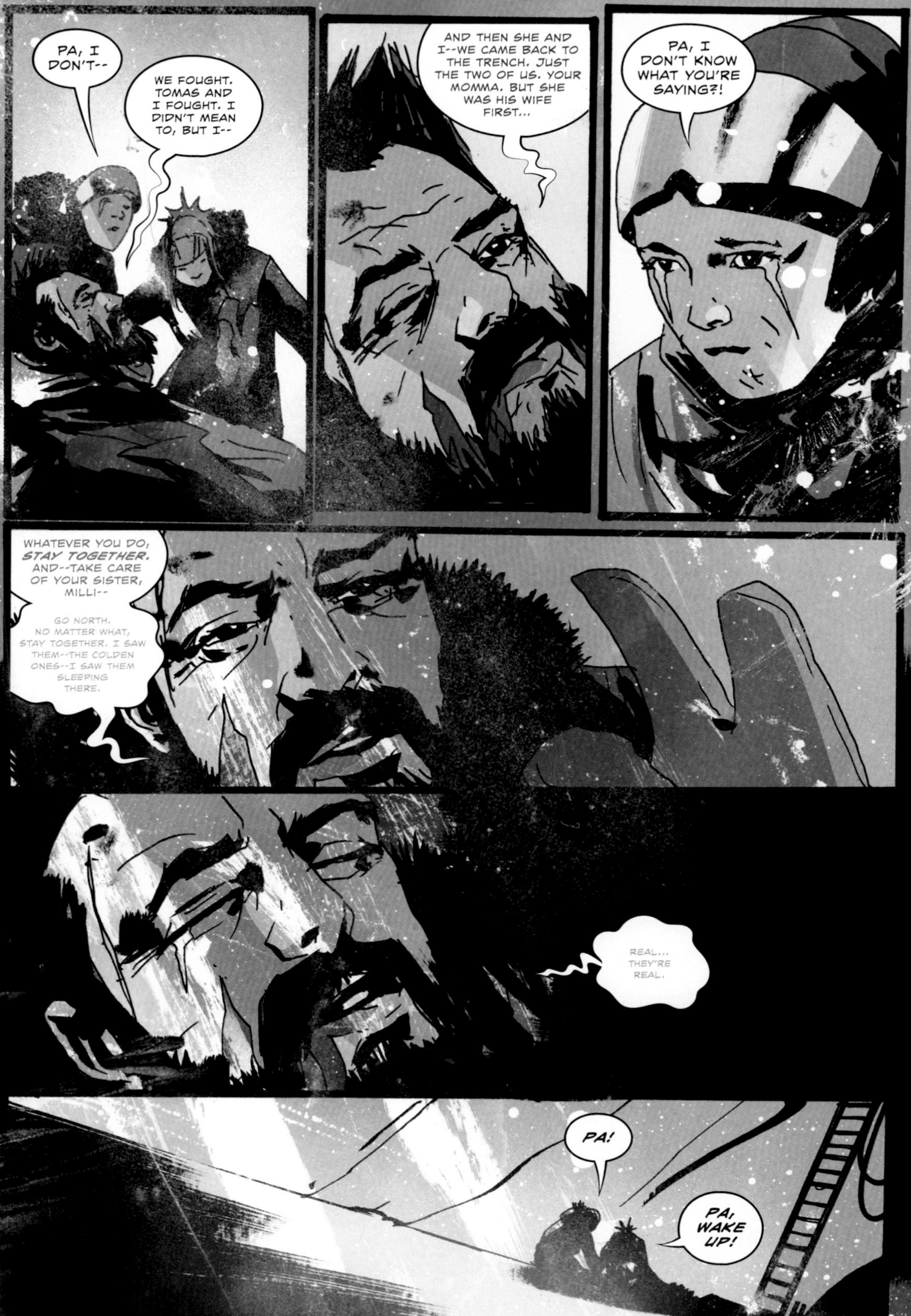
PA, I DON'T--
WE FOUGHT. TOMAS AND I FOUGHT. I DIDN'T MEAN TO, BUT I--
AND THEN SHE AND I--WE CAME BACK TO THE TRENCH. JUST THE TWO OF US. YOUR MOMMA. BUT SHE WAS HIS WIFE FIRST...
PA, I DON'T KNOW WHAT YOU'RE SAYING?!
WHATEVER YOU DO, *STAY TOGETHER.* AND--TAKE CARE OF YOUR SISTER, MILLI--
GO NORTH. NO MATTER WHAT, STAY TOGETHER. I SAW THEM--THE COLDEN ONES--I SAW THEM SLEEPING THERE.
REAL... THEY'RE REAL.
PA!
PA, WAKE UP!

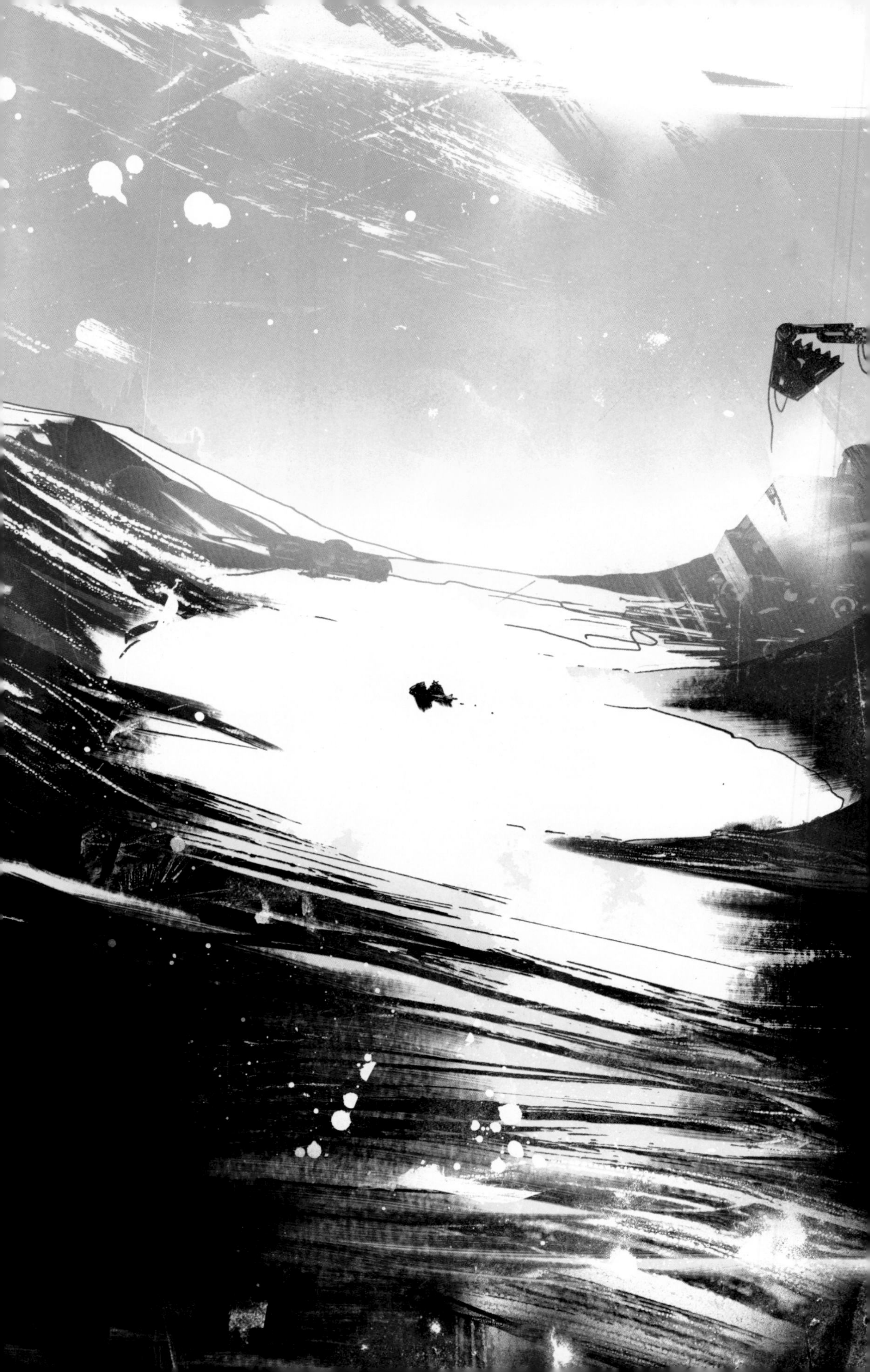

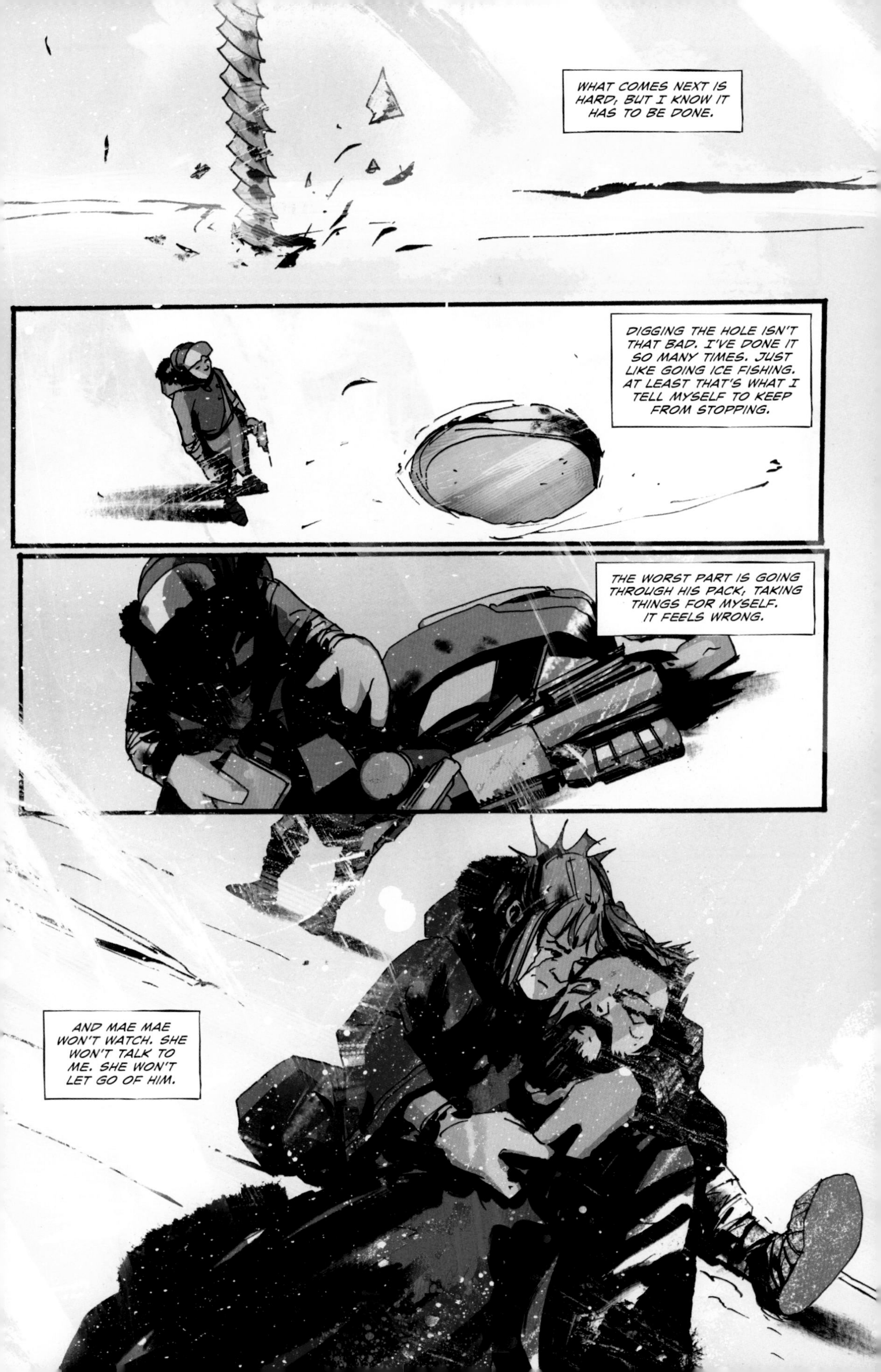
WHAT COMES NEXT IS HARD; BUT I KNOW IT HAS TO BE DONE.
DIGGING THE HOLE ISN'T THAT BAD. I'VE DONE IT SO MANY TIMES. JUST LIKE GOING ICE FISHING. AT LEAST THAT'S WHAT I TELL MYSELF TO KEEP FROM STOPPING.
THE WORST PART IS GOING THROUGH HIS PACK, TAKING THINGS FOR MYSELF. IT FEELS WRONG.
AND MAE MAE WON'T WATCH. SHE WON'T TALK TO ME. SHE WON'T LET GO OF HIM.

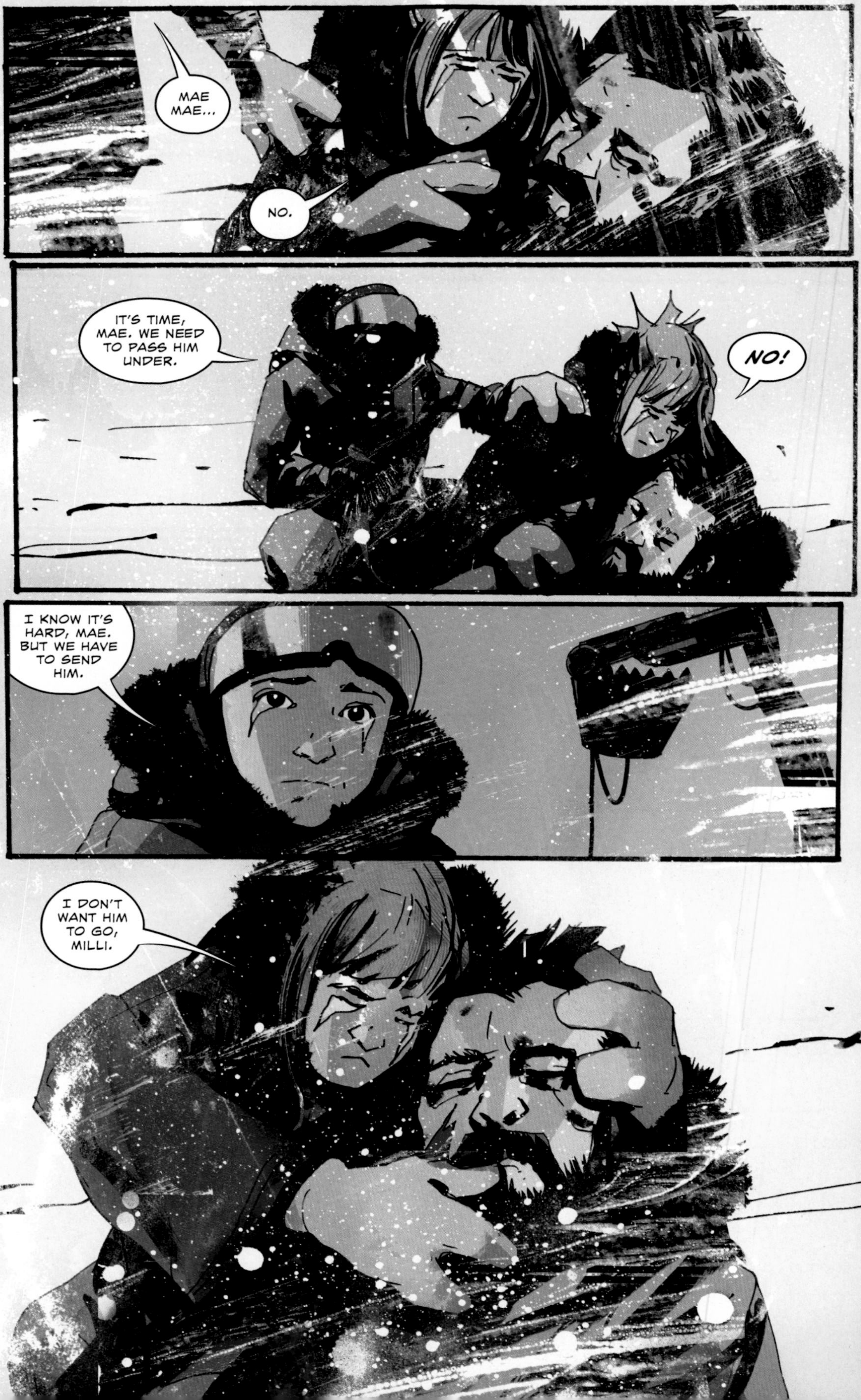
MAE MAE...
NO.
IT'S TIME, MAE. WE NEED TO PASS HIM UNDER.
NO!
I KNOW IT'S HARD, MAE. BUT WE HAVE TO SEND HIM.
I DON'T WANT HIM TO GO, MILLI.

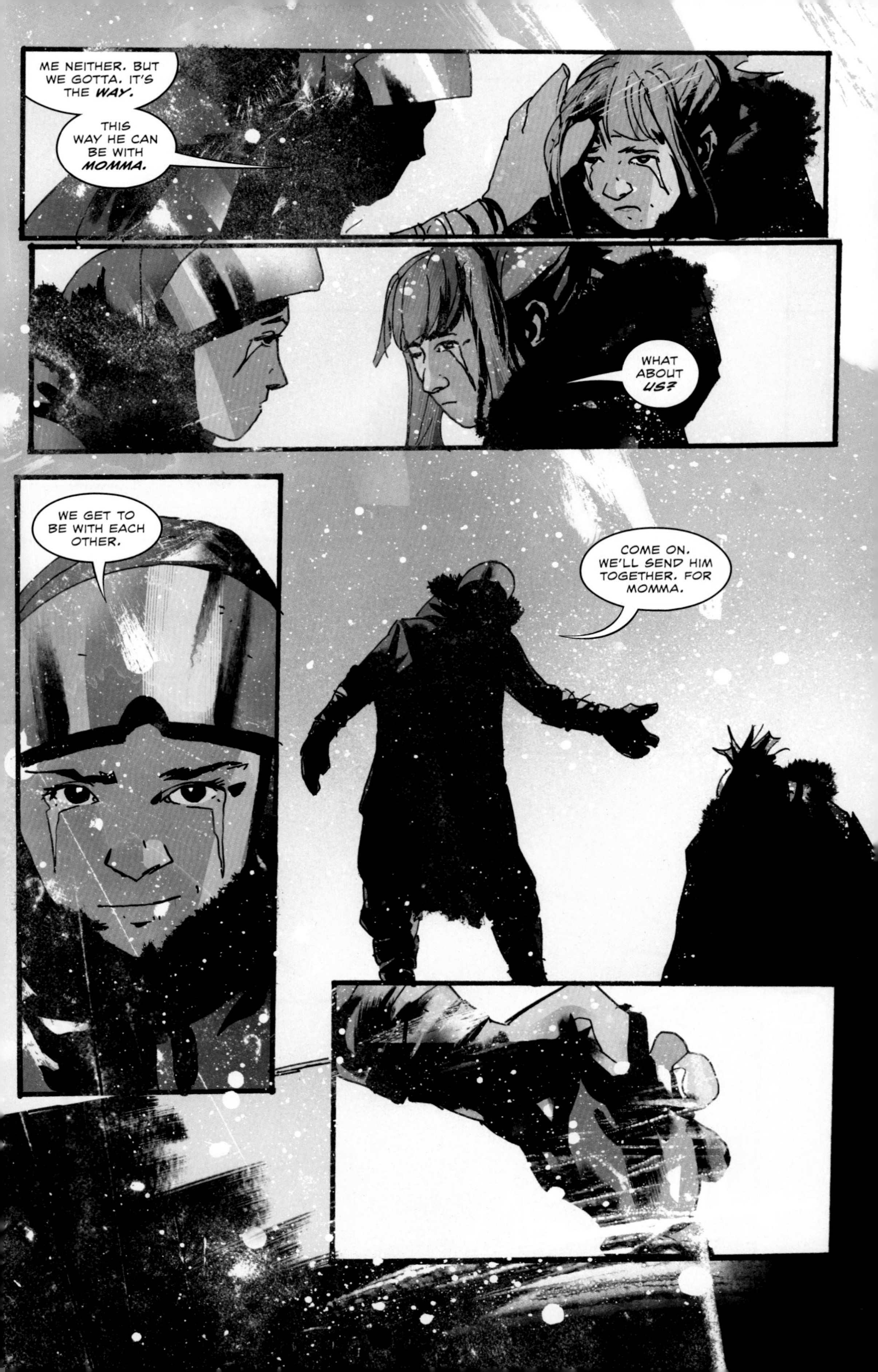
ME NEITHER. BUT WE GOTTA. IT'S THE *WAY.*
THIS WAY HE CAN BE WITH *MOMMA.*
WHAT ABOUT *US?*
WE GET TO BE WITH EACH OTHER.
COME ON. WE'LL SEND HIM TOGETHER. FOR MOMMA.

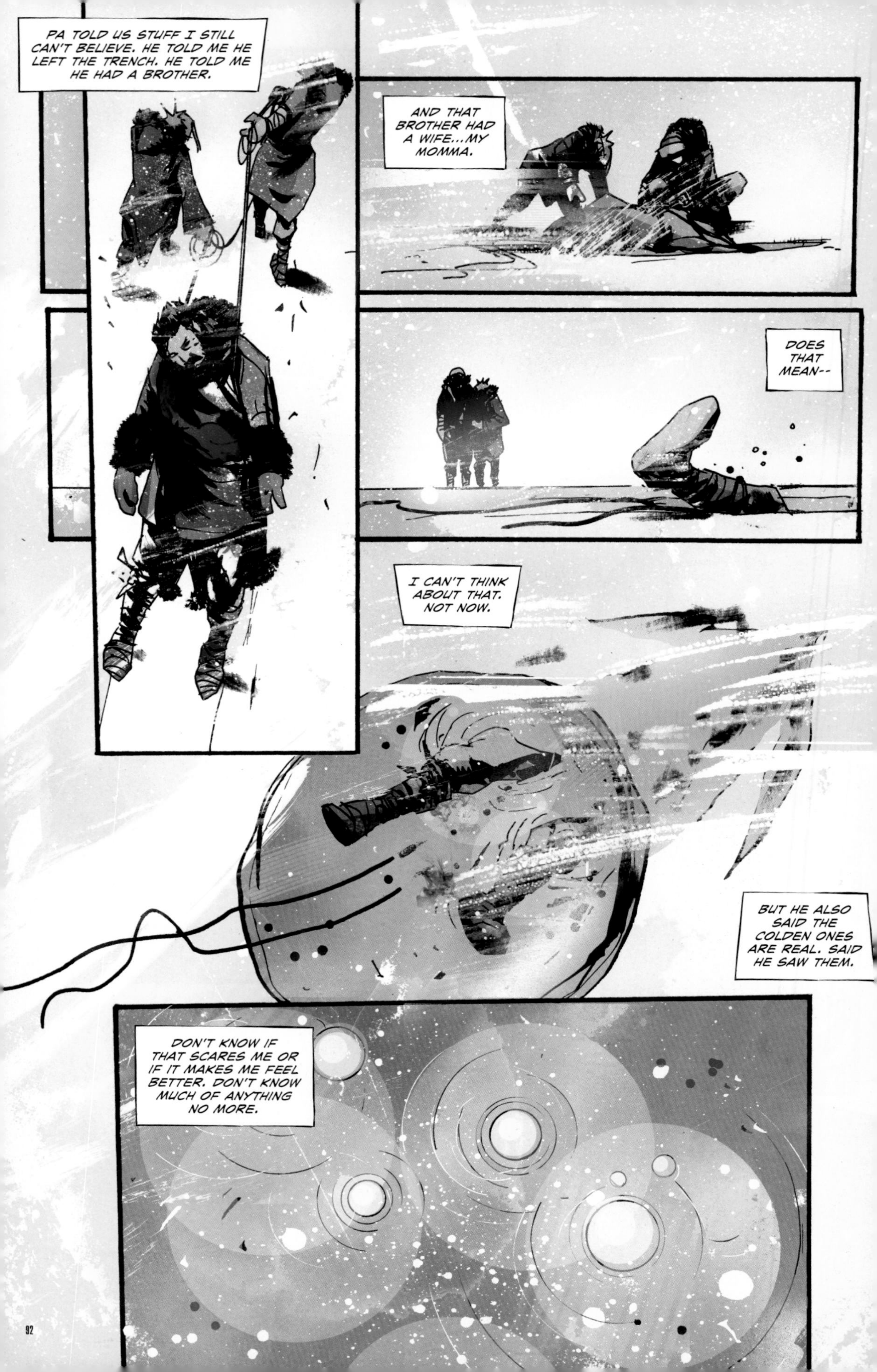
PA TOLD US STUFF I STILL CAN'T BELIEVE. HE TOLD ME HE LEFT THE TRENCH. HE TOLD ME HE HAD A BROTHER.
AND THAT BROTHER HAD A WIFE...MY MOMMA.
DOES THAT MEAN--
I CAN'T THINK ABOUT THAT. NOT NOW.
BUT HE ALSO SAID THE COLDEN ONES ARE REAL. SAID HE SAW THEM.
DON'T KNOW IF THAT SCARES ME OR IF IT MAKES ME FEEL BETTER. DON'T KNOW MUCH OF ANYTHING NO MORE.

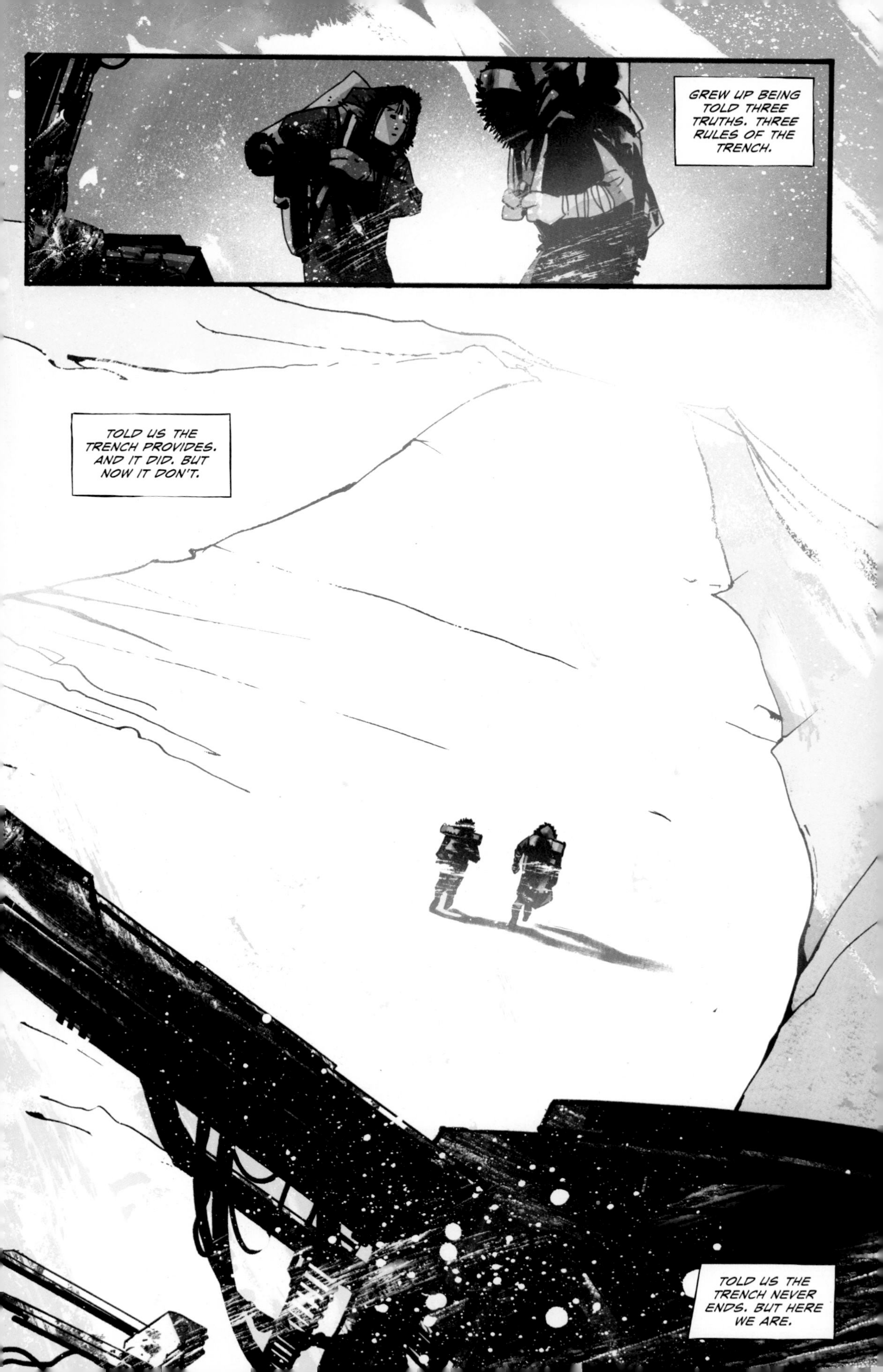
GREW UP BEING TOLD THREE TRUTHS. THREE RULES OF THE TRENCH.
TOLD US THE TRENCH PROVIDES. AND IT DID. BUT NOW IT DON'T.
TOLD US THE TRENCH NEVER ENDS. BUT HERE WE ARE.

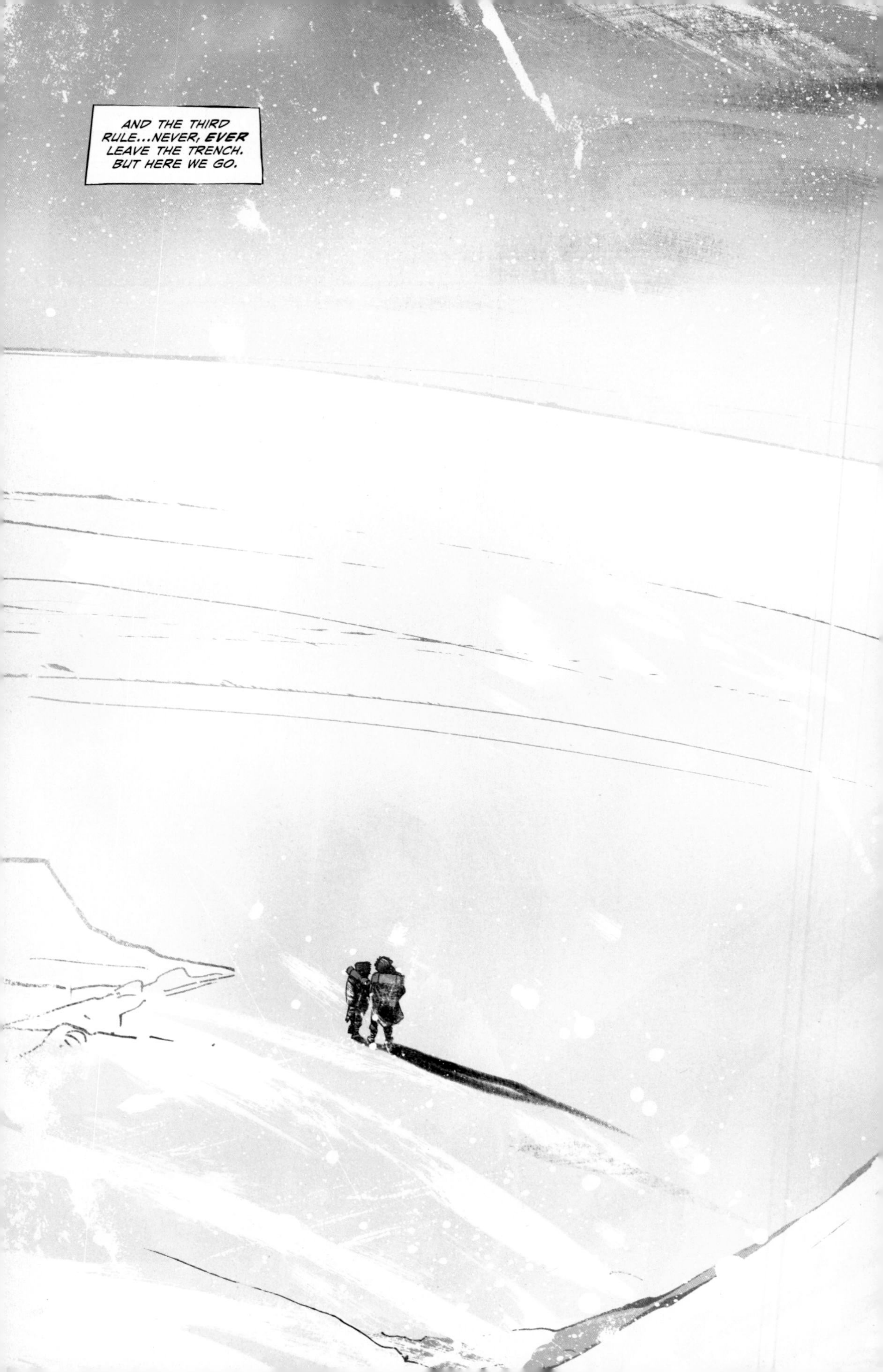
AND THE THIRD RULE...NEVER, EVER LEAVE THE TRENCH. BUT HERE WE GO.

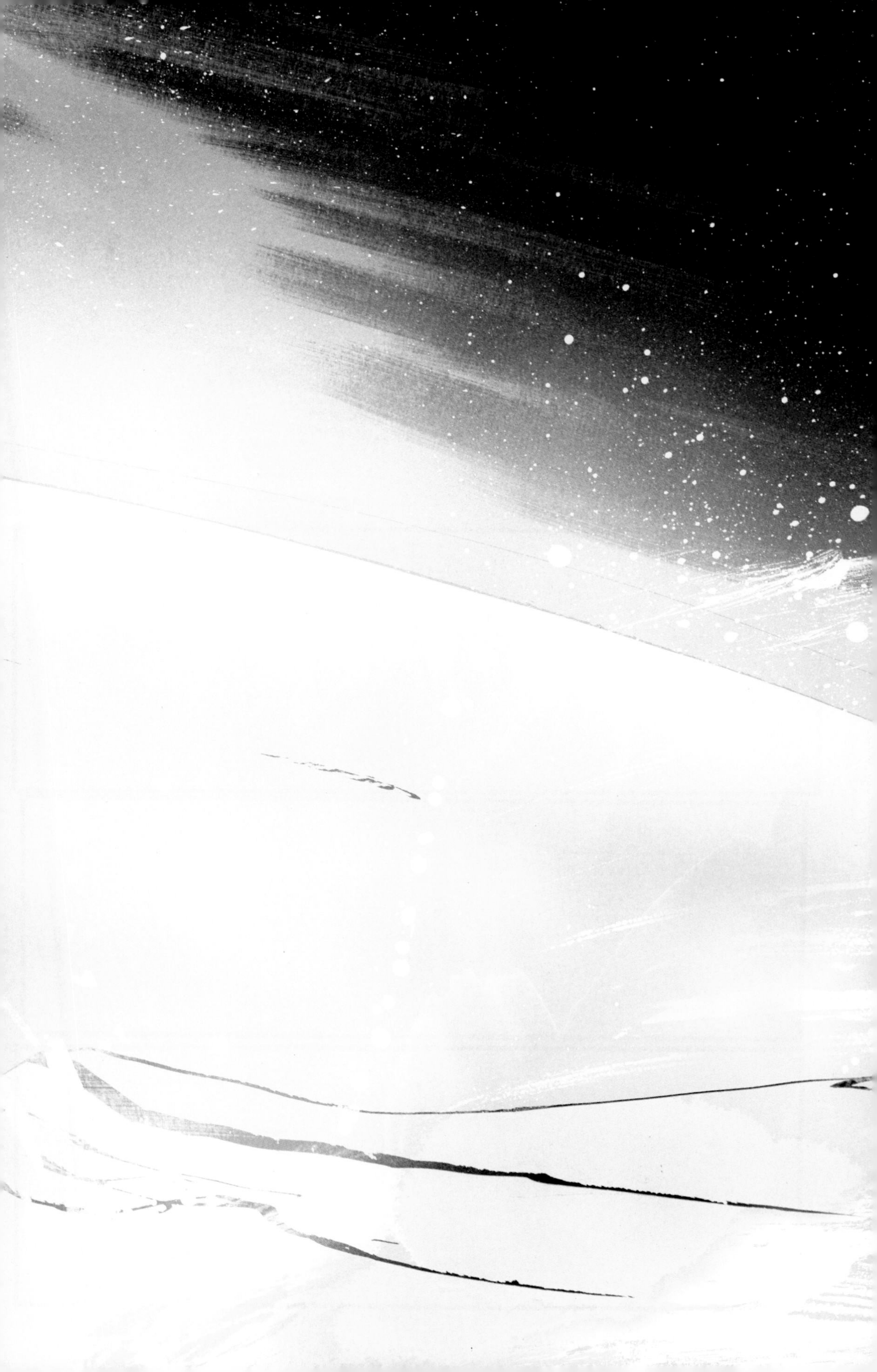

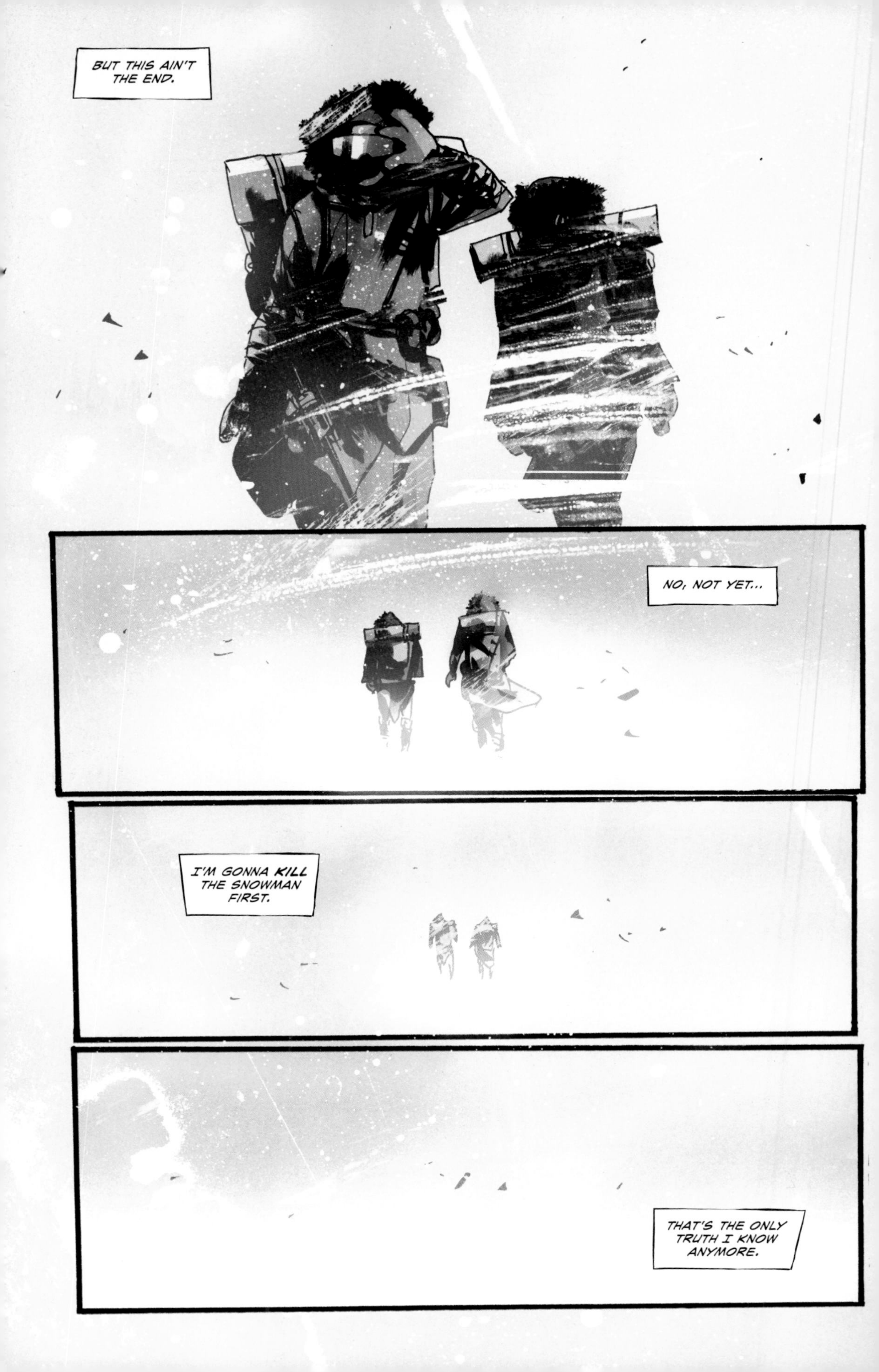
BUT THIS AIN'T THE END.
NO, NOT YET...
I'M GONNA KILL THE SNOWMAN FIRST.
THAT'S THE ONLY TRUTH I KNOW ANYMORE.

SNOW ANGELS™

SKETCHBOOK — NOTES BY JOCK

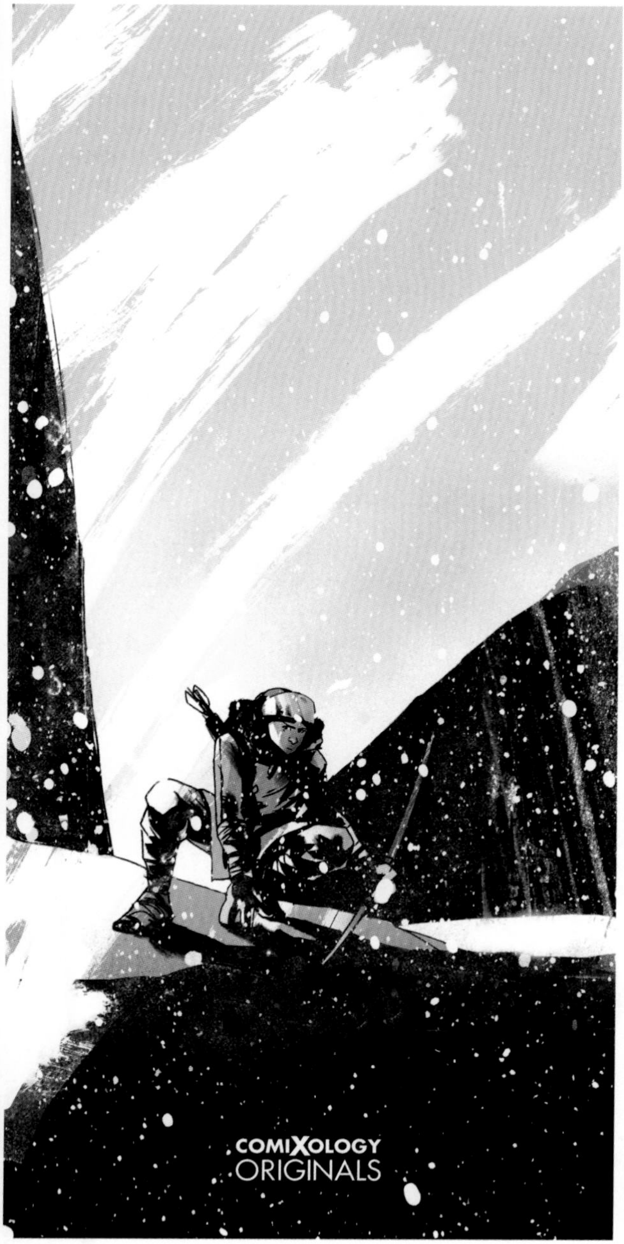
comiXology
ORIGINALS

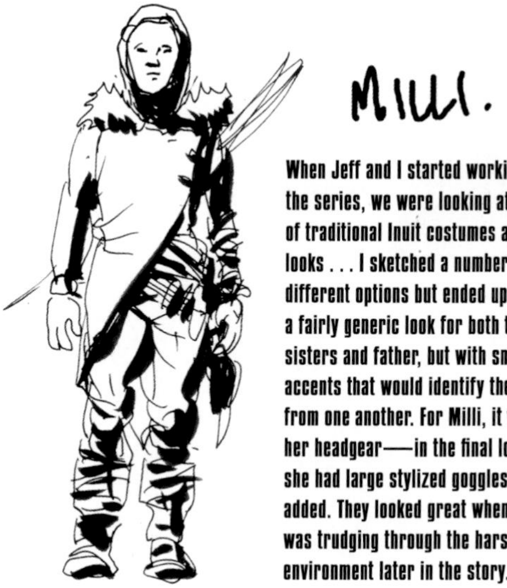
MILLI.

When Jeff and I started working on the series, we were looking at a lot of traditional Inuit costumes and looks . . . I sketched a number of different options but ended up with a fairly generic look for both the sisters and father, but with small accents that would identify them from one another. For Milli, it was her headgear—in the final look she had large stylized goggles added. They looked great when she was trudging through the harsh environment later in the story.

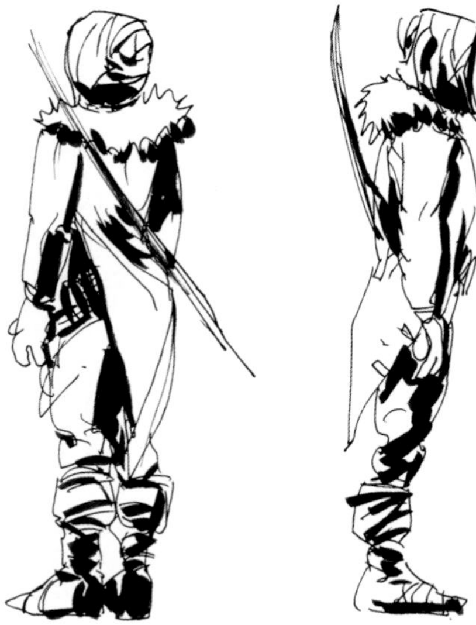

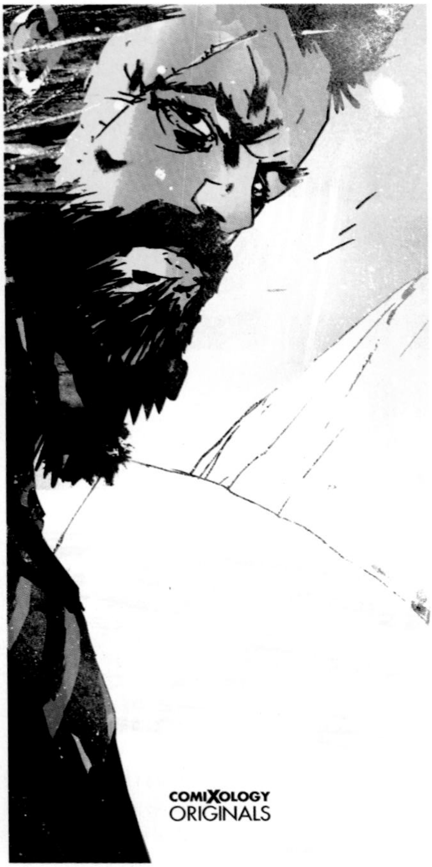
comiXology
ORIGINALS

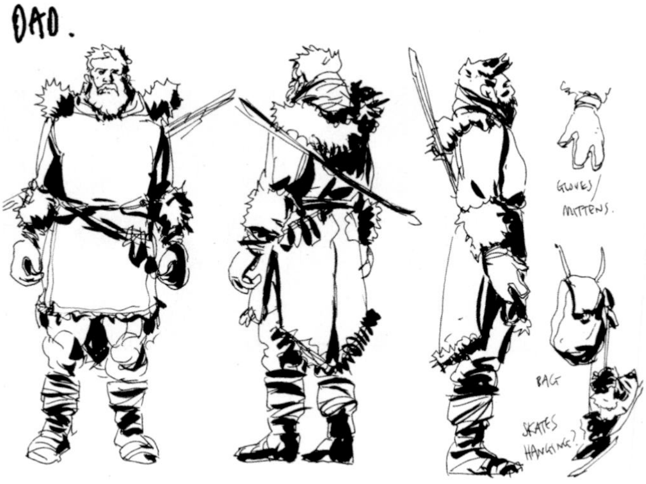
DAD.
GLOVES/
MITTENS.
BAG
SKATES
HANGING?

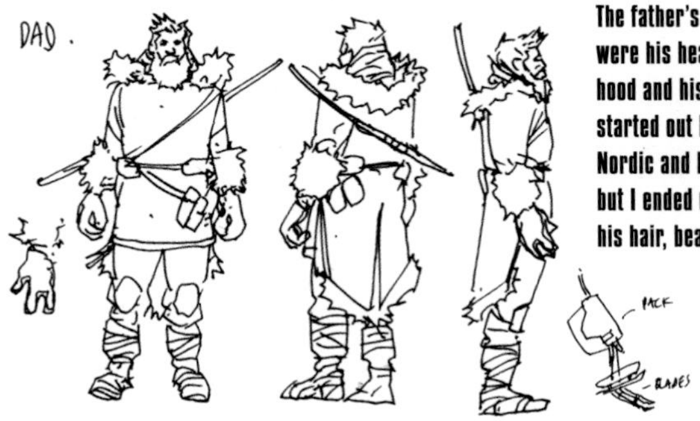
DAD.
PACK
BLADES

The father's visual accents were his heavy fur-lined hood and his beard. He started out looking more Nordic and blond (*below*) but I ended up darkening his hair, beard, and fur.

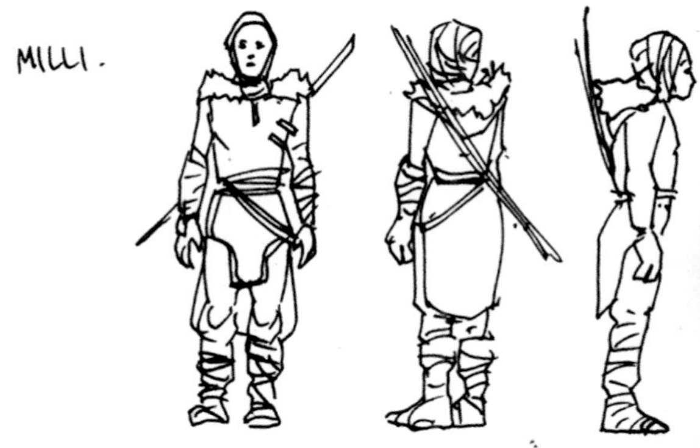
MILLI.

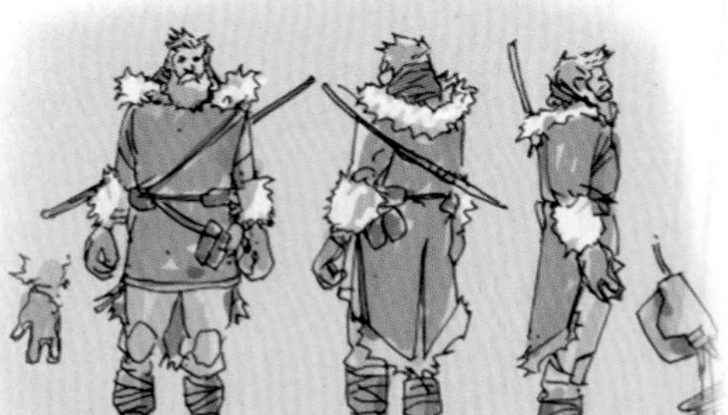

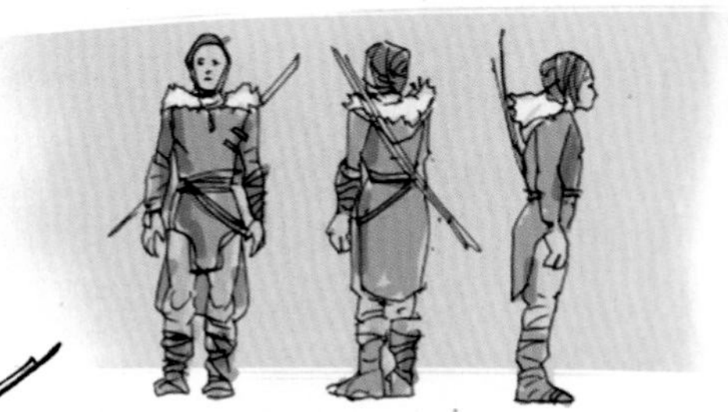

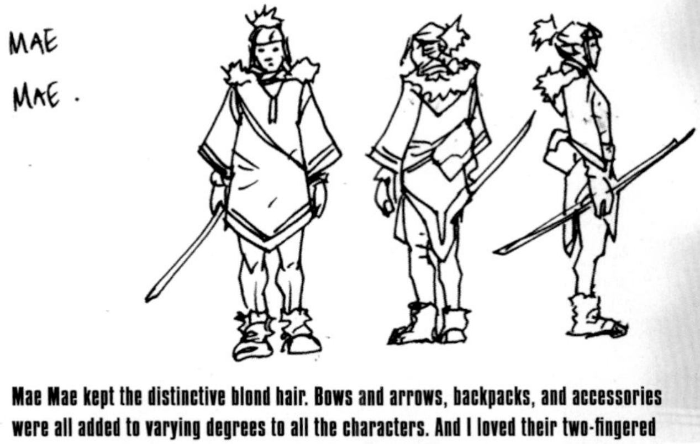
MAE
MAE.

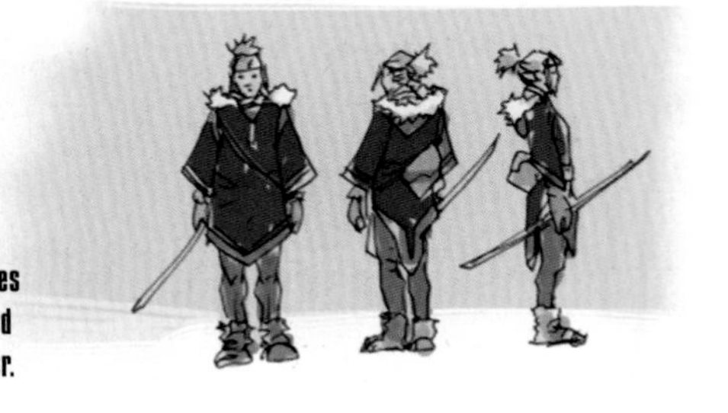

Mae Mae kept the distinctive blond hair. Bows and arrows, backpacks, and accessories were all added to varying degrees to all the characters. And I loved their two-fingered mittens! I didn't design them this way, but they made drawing their hands a LOT easier.

The Snowman—is he 100 percent mech? Is he a guy in a suit? We wanted to skirt that question when we first introduced him to heighten the mystery of the character, so I went for a heavily mechanized look. The lights that form his face can subtly change depending on his mood.

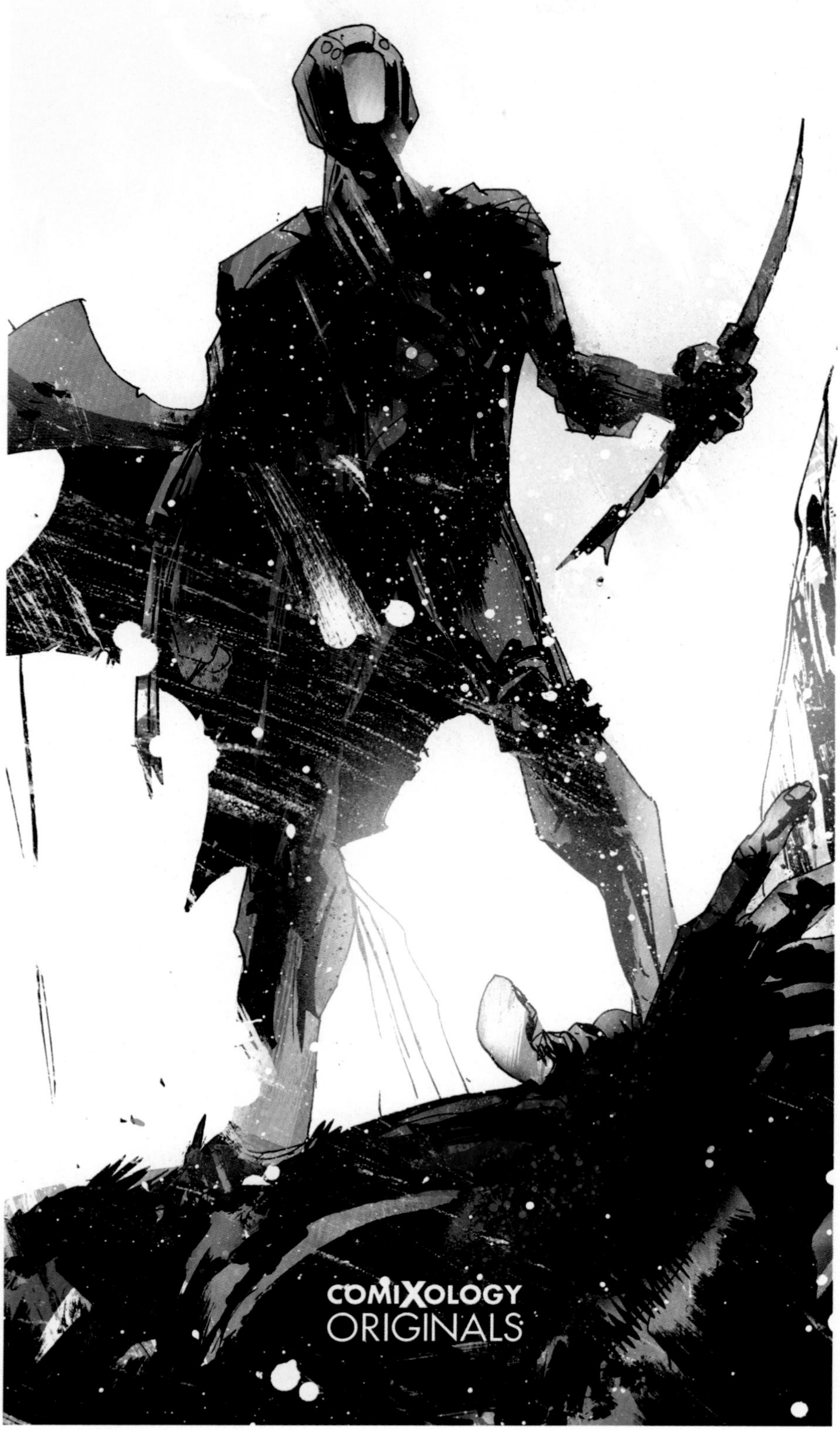
comiXology
ORIGINALS

SNOW ANGELS

I work on breakdowns very quickly to try and get the rhythm of the storytelling working well. These were my first pass from Jeff's initial script, and the layout of the pages stayed almost identical through to the final art. I found Jeff's scripts clear and concise and very easy to work from. It came together very quickly once we were moving on the series.

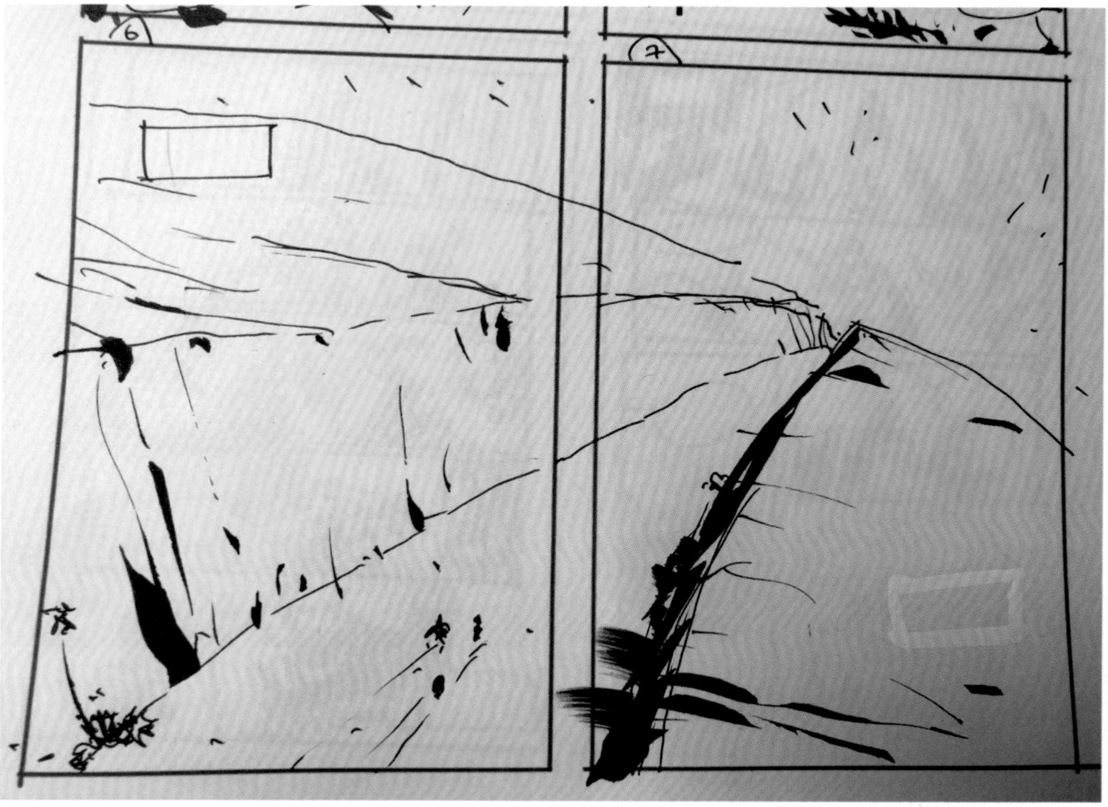

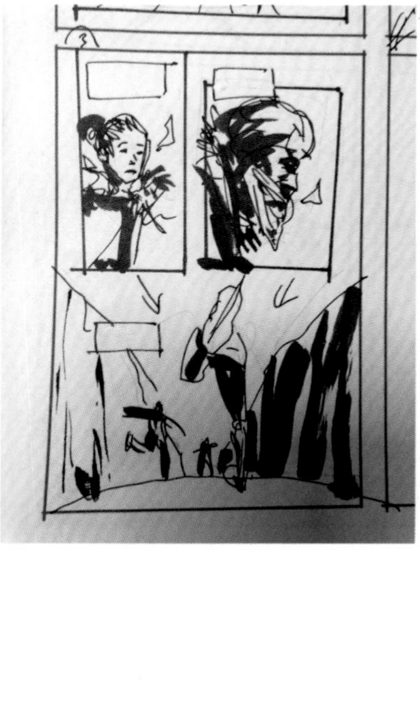

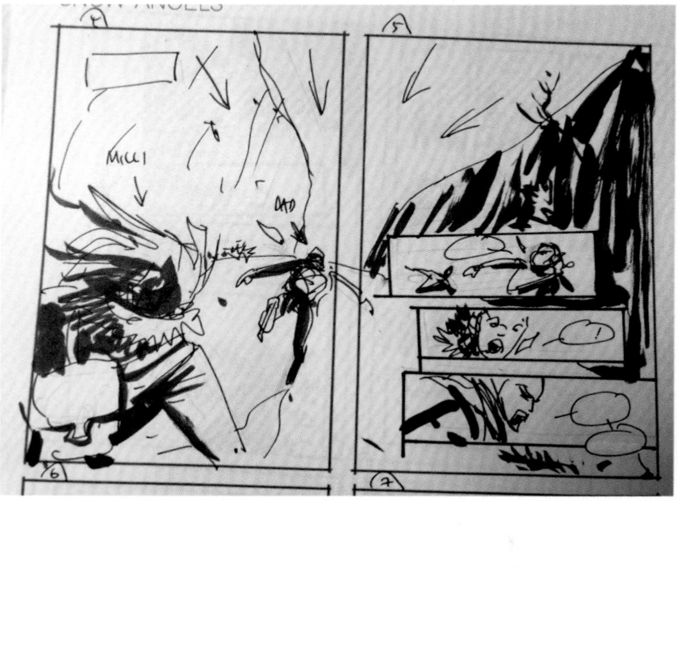
MILLI
DAD

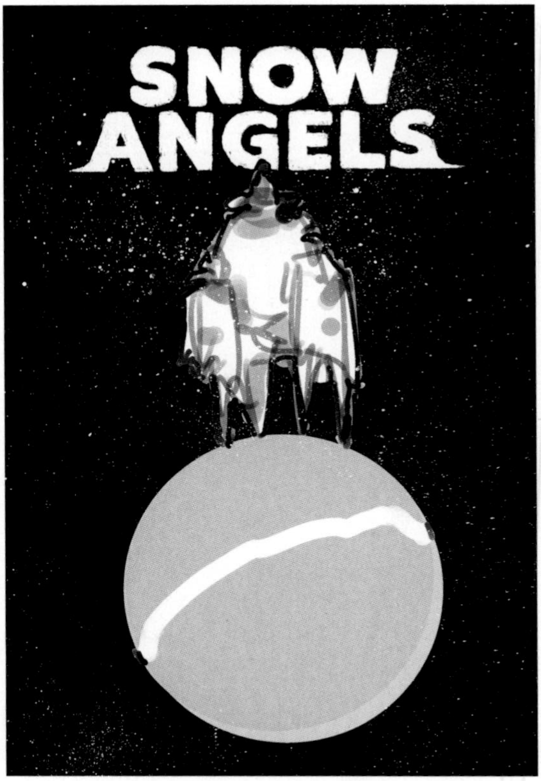
SNOW
ANGELS

Very early cover ideas——I think they're a little too fantastical for the tone of the series, but when I pulled it back to feature The Trench itself, stuff started to stick. The single figure of Milli in the deep canyon was developed for the cover of a short prose story released with the series, but it worked so well I added the entire family unit and that ended up as our final series-launch cover for issue #1.

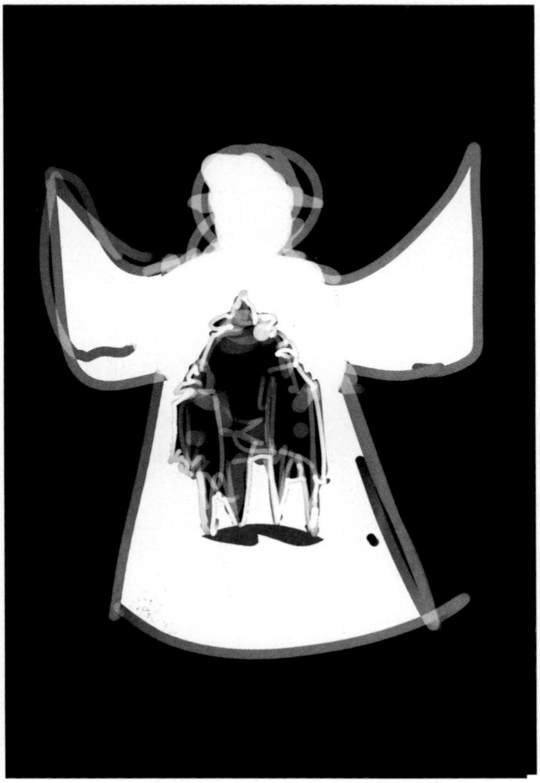

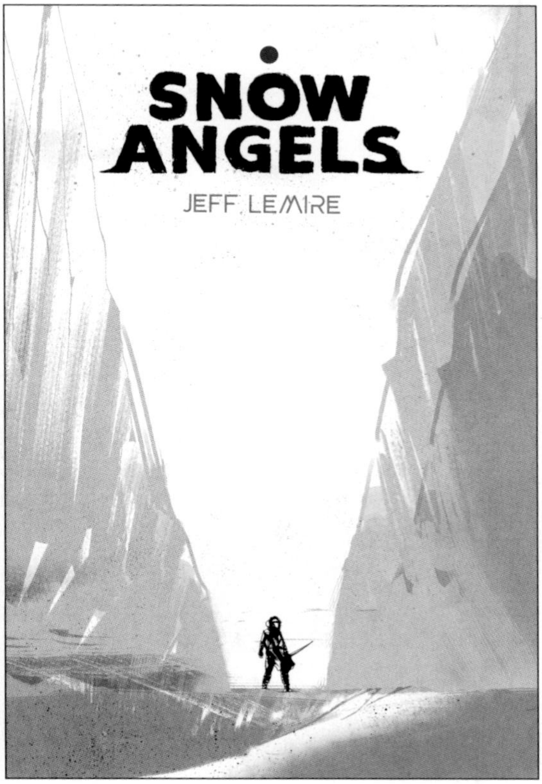
SNOW
ANGELS
JEFF LEMIRE

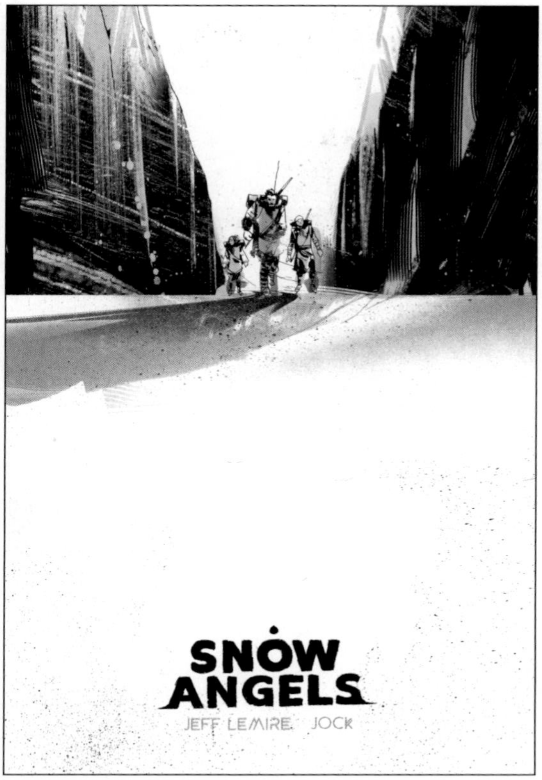
SNOW
ANGELS
JEFF LEMIRE JOCK

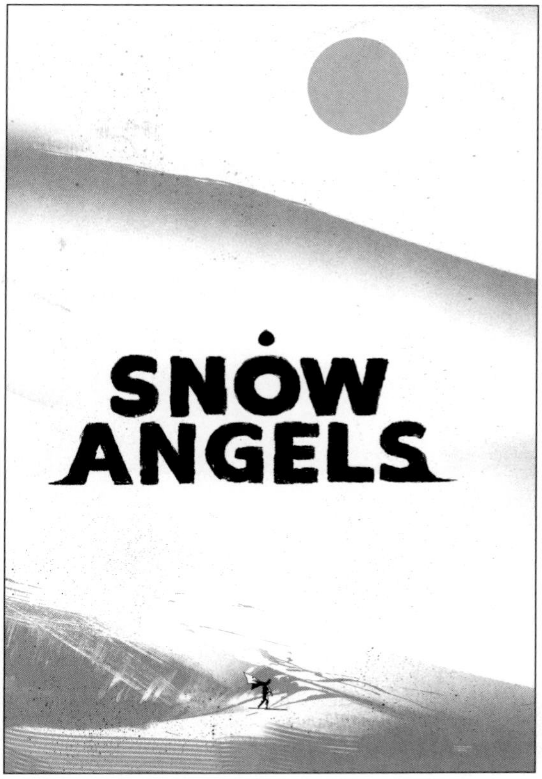
SNOW
ANGELS

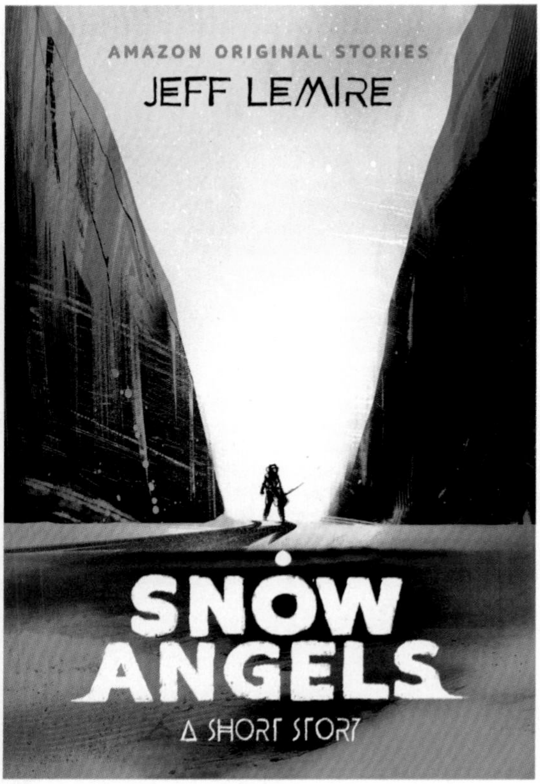
AMAZON ORIGINAL STORIES
JEFF LEMIRE
SNOW
ANGELS
A SHORT STORY

COMIXOLOGY COMES TO DARK HORSE BOOKS!

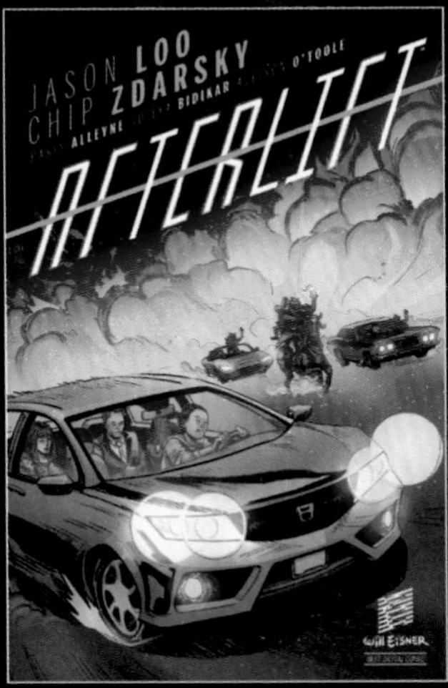
JASON LOO
CHIP ZDARSKY
AFTERLIFT

ISBN 978-1-50672-440-9 / $19.99

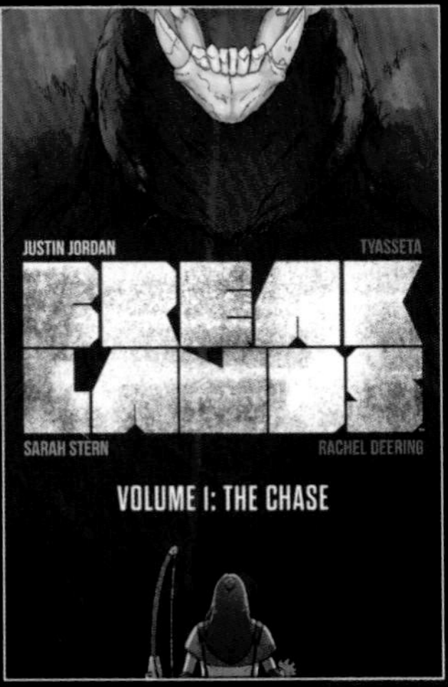
JUSTIN JORDAN
TYASSETA
BREAKLANDS
SARAH STERN
RACHEL DEERING
VOLUME I: THE CHASE

ISBN 978-1-50672-441-6 / $19.99

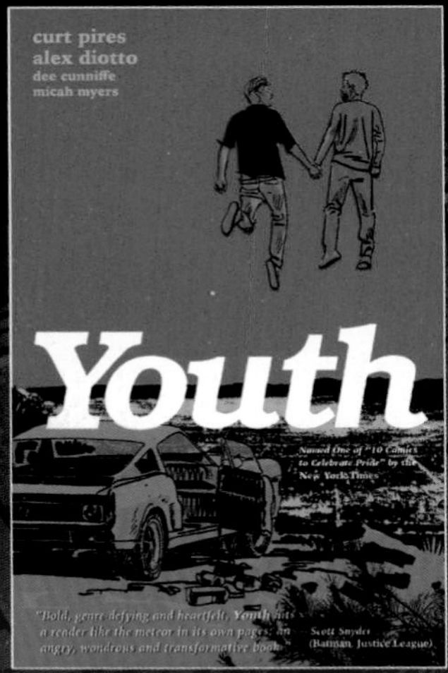
curt pires
alex diotto
dee cunniffe
micah myers
Youth

ISBN 978-1-50672-461-4 / $19.99

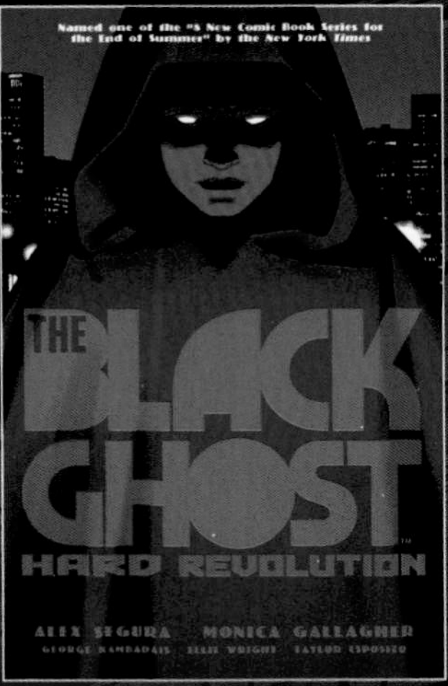
THE BLACK GHOST
HARD REVOLUTION
ALEX SEGURA MONICA GALLAGHER

ISBN 978-1-50672-446-1 / $19.99

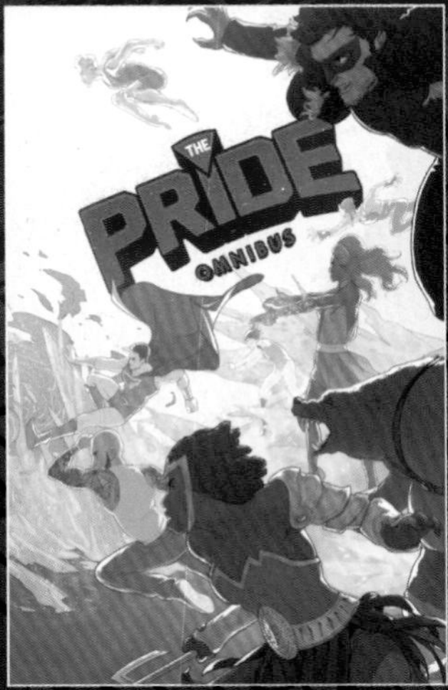
THE PRIDE
OMNIBUS

ISBN 978-1-50672-447-8 / $29.99

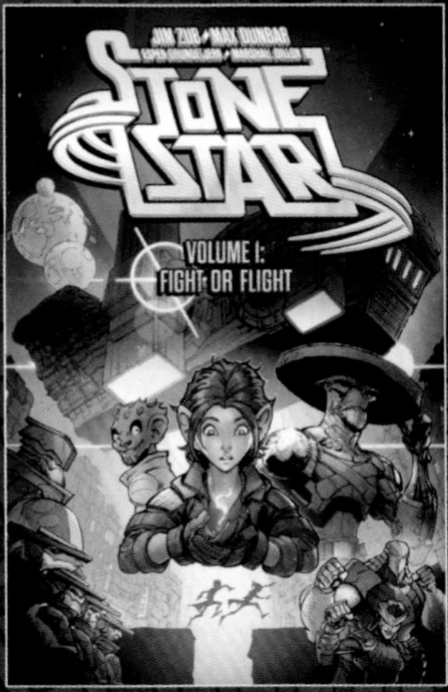
JIM ZUB • MAX DUNBAR
STONE STAR
VOLUME I:
FIGHT OR FLIGHT

ISBN 978-1-50672-458-4 / $19.99

AFTERLIFT

Written by Chip Zdarsky, art by Jason Loo

This Eisner Award–winning series from Chip Zdarsky (*Sex Criminals*, Daredevil) and Jason Loo (*The Pitiful Human-Lizard*) features car chases, demon bounty hunters, and figuring out your place in this world and the next.

BREAKLANDS

Written by Justin Jordan, art by Tyasseta and Sarah Stern

Generations after the end of the civilization, everyone has powers; you need them just to survive in the new age. Everyone except Kasa Fain. Unfortunately, her little brother, who has the potential to reshape the world, is kidnapped by people who intend to do just that. *Mad Max* meets *Akira* in a genre-mashing, expectation-smashing new hit series from Justin Jordan, creator of *Luther Strode*, *Spread*, and *Reaver*!

YOUTH

Written by Curt Pires, art by Alex Diotto and Dee Cunniffe

A coming of age story of two queer teenagers who run away from their lives in a bigoted small town, and attempt to make their way to California. Along the way their car breaks down and they join a group of fellow misfits on the road. travelling the country together in a van, they party and attempt to find themselves. And then . . . something happens. The story combines the violence of coming of age with the violence of the superhero narrative—as well as the beauty.

THE BLACK GHOST SEASON ONE: HARD REVOLUTION

Written by Alex Segura and Monica Gallagher, art by George Kamabdais

Meet Lara Dominguez—a troubled Creighton cops reporter obsessed with the city's debonair vigilante the Black Ghost. With the help of a mysterious cyberinformant named LONE, Lara's inched closer to uncovering the Ghost's identity. But as she searches for the breakthrough story she desperately needs, Lara will have to navigate the corruption of her city, the uncertainties of virtues, and her own personal demons. Will she have the strength to be part of the solution—or will she become the problem?

THE PRIDE OMNIBUS

Joseph Glass, Gavin Mitchell and Cem Iroz

FabMan is sick of being seen as a joke. Tired of the LGBTQ+ community being seen as inferior to straight heroes, he thinks it's about damn time he did something about it. Bringing together some of the world's greatest LGBTQ+ superheroes, the Pride is born to protect the world and fight prejudice, misrepresentation and injustice—not to mention a pesky supervillain or two.

STONE STAR

Jim Zub and Max Zunbar

The brand-new space-fantasy saga that takes flight on comiXology Originals from fan-favorite creators Jim Zub (*Avengers*, *Samurai Jack*) and Max Dunbar (*Champions*, *Dungeons & Dragons*)! The nomadic space station called Stone Star brings gladiatorial entertainment to ports across the galaxy. Inside this gargantuan vessel of tournaments and temptations, foragers and fighters struggle to survive. A young thief named Dail discovers a dark secret in the depths of Stone Star and must decide his destiny—staying hidden in the shadows or standing tall in the searing spotlight of the arena. Either way, his life, and the cosmos itself, will never be the same!

AVAILABLE AT YOUR LOCAL COMICS SHOP OR BOOKSTORE / To find a comics shop near you, visit comicshoplocator.com / For more information or to order direct, visit darkhorse.com

DARK HORSE BOOKS

COMIXOLOGY ORIGINALS